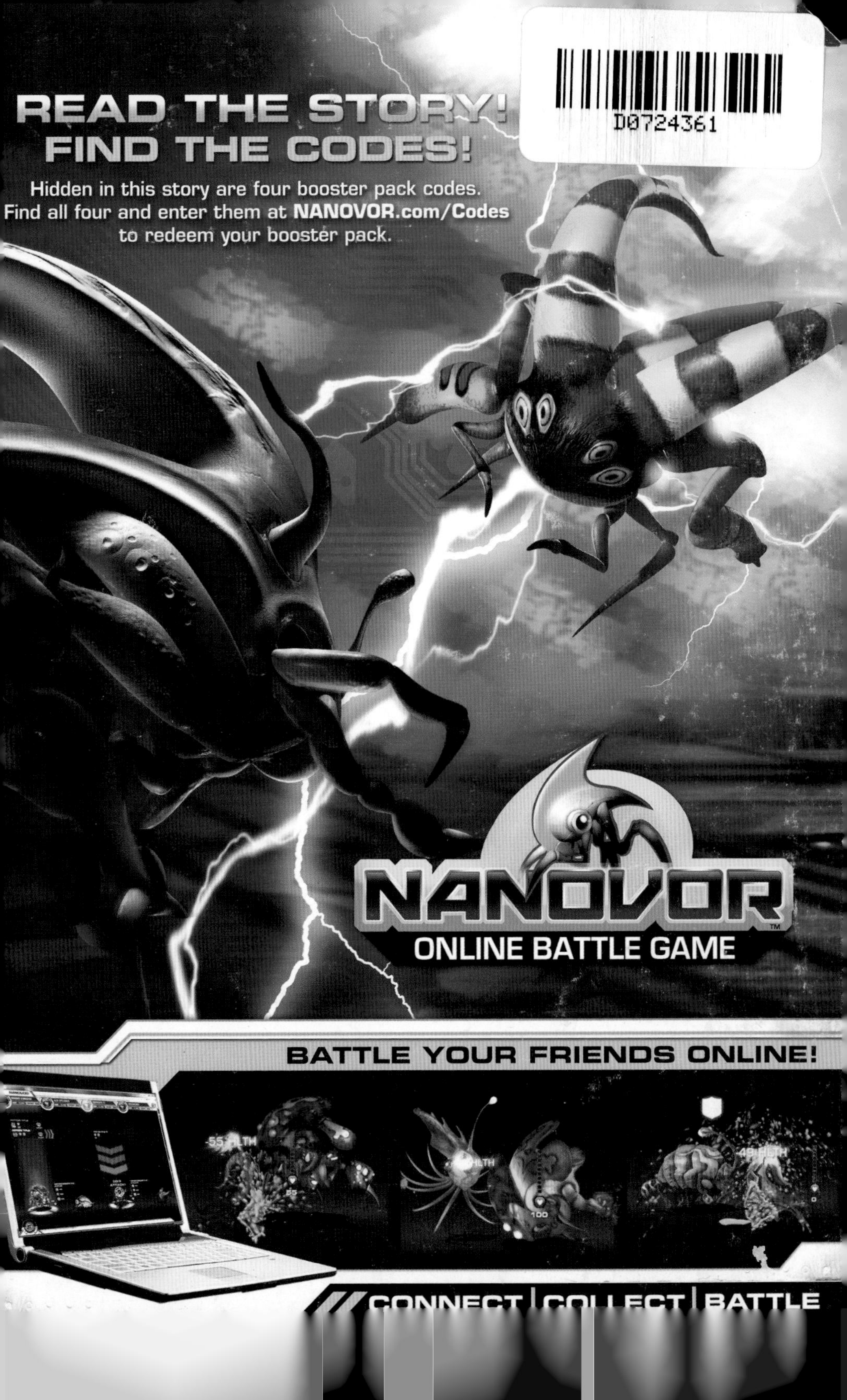
READ THE STORY!
FIND THE CODES!
Hidden in this story are four booster pack codes.
Find all four and enter them at NANOVOR.com/Codes
to redeem your booster pack.
NANOVOR™
ONLINE BATTLE GAME
BATTLE YOUR FRIENDS ONLINE!
-55 HLTH
55
100
48 HLTH
CONNECT | COLLECT | BATTLE

NANOVOR
—GAME DAY—

Written by : ERIK BURNHAM

Art by : FELIPE TORRENT

Color by : JON ALDERINK

Letters by : NEIL UYETAKE & ROBBIE ROBBINS

Original Series Edits by : TOM WALTZ

Collection Edits by : JUSTIN EISINGER & MARIAH HUEHNER

Collection Design by : NEIL UYETAKE

Front Cover Art by : ANTON BOGATY

Back Cover Art by : MARTHEUS WADE

IDW Publishing
Operations:
Ted Adams, Chief Executive Officer
Greg Goldstein, Chief Operating Officer
Matthew Ruzicka, CPA, Chief Financial Officer
Alan Payne, VP of Sales
Lorelei Bunjes, Dir. of Digital Services
AnnaMaria White, Marketing & PR Manager
Marci Hubbard, Executive Assistant
Alonzo Simon, Shipping Manager
Angela Loggins, Staff Accountant

Editorial:
Chris Ryall, Publisher/Editor-in-Chief
Scott Dunbier, Editor, Special Projects
Andy Schmidt, Senior Editor
Bob Schreck, Senior Editor
Justin Eisinger, Editor
Kris Oprisko, Editor/Foreign Lic.
Denton J. Tipton, Editor
Tom Waltz, Editor
Mariah Huehner, Associate Editor
Carlos Guzman, Editorial Assistant

Design:
Robbie Robbins, EVP/Sr. Graphic Artist

www.IDWpublishing.com   ISBN: 978-1-60010-602-6   13 12 11 10   1 2 3 4

Special thanks to Sharon Turner Mulvihill, Shane Small, Jessica Price, Javier Gravito, and Eduardo Alpuente for their invaluable assistance.

NANOVOR: GAME DAY. FEBRUARY 2010. FIRST PRINTING. NANOVOR: GAME DAY © 2010 Smith & Tinker, Inc. All Rights Reserved. NANOVOR, NANOSCOPE, NANOSCANNER, SMITH & TINKER and associated logos are trademarks and/or registered trademarks of Smith & Tinker, Inc. in the U.S. and other countries. © 2010 Idea and Design Works, LLC. IDW Publishing, a division of Idea and Design Works, LLC. Editorial offices: 5080 Santa Fe St., San Diego, CA 92109. The IDW logo is registered in the U.S. Patent and Trademark Office. All Rights Reserved. Any similarities to persons living or dead are purely coincidental. With the exception of artwork used for review purposes, none of the contents of this publication may be reprinted without the permission of Idea and Design Works, LLC. Printed in Korea.

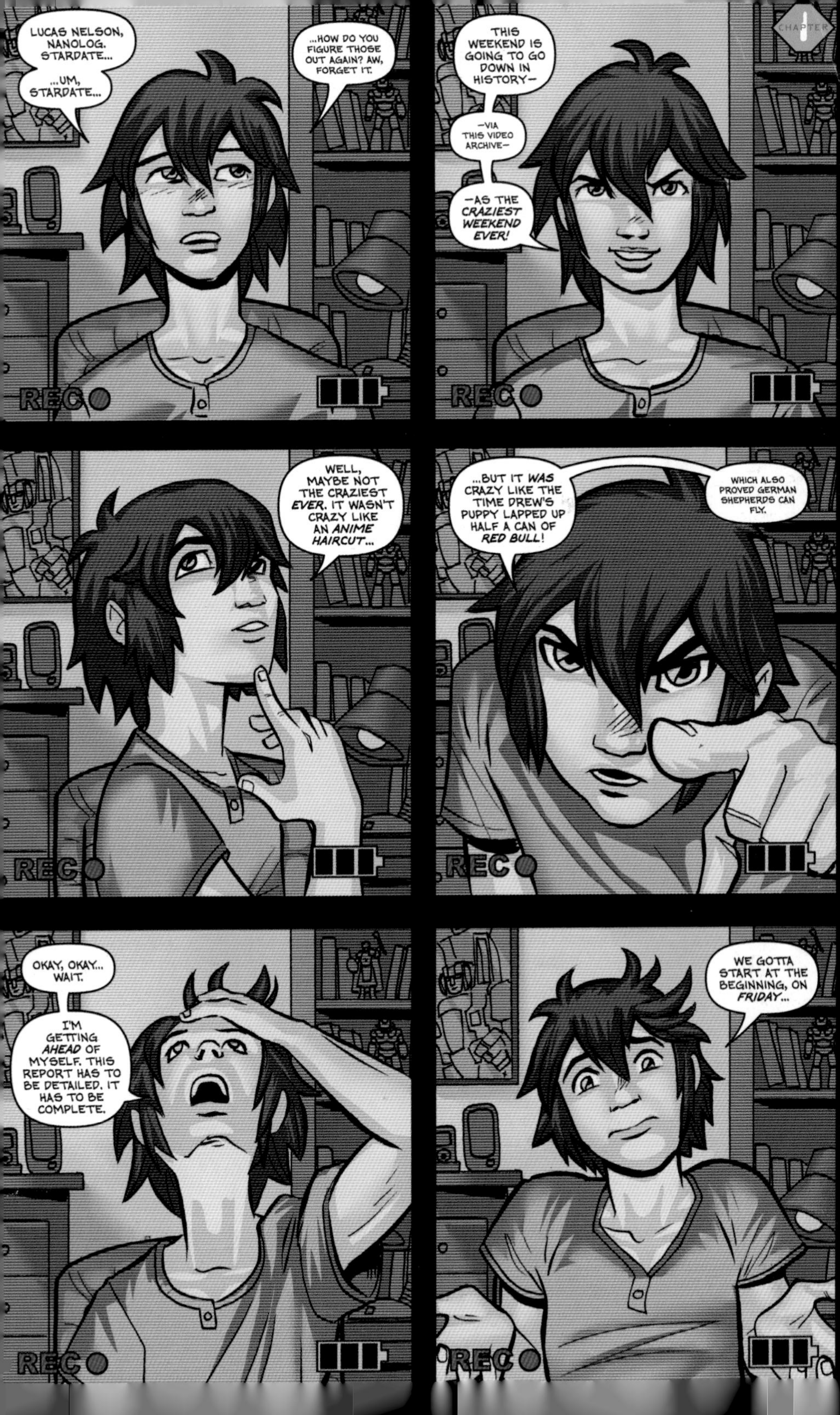
CHAPTER 1
LUCAS NELSON, NANOLOG. STARDATE...
...UM, STARDATE...
...HOW DO YOU FIGURE THOSE OUT AGAIN? AW, FORGET IT.
REC
THIS WEEKEND IS GOING TO GO DOWN IN HISTORY—
—VIA THIS VIDEO ARCHIVE—
—AS THE CRAZIEST WEEKEND EVER!
REC
WELL, MAYBE NOT THE CRAZIEST EVER. IT WASN'T CRAZY LIKE AN ANIME HAIRCUT...
REC
...BUT IT WAS CRAZY LIKE THE TIME DREW'S PUPPY LAPPED UP HALF A CAN OF RED BULL!
WHICH ALSO PROVED GERMAN SHEPHERDS CAN FLY.
REC
OKAY, OKAY... WAIT.
I'M GETTING AHEAD OF MYSELF. THIS REPORT HAS TO BE DETAILED. IT HAS TO BE COMPLETE.
REC
WE GOTTA START AT THE BEGINNING, ON FRIDAY...
REC

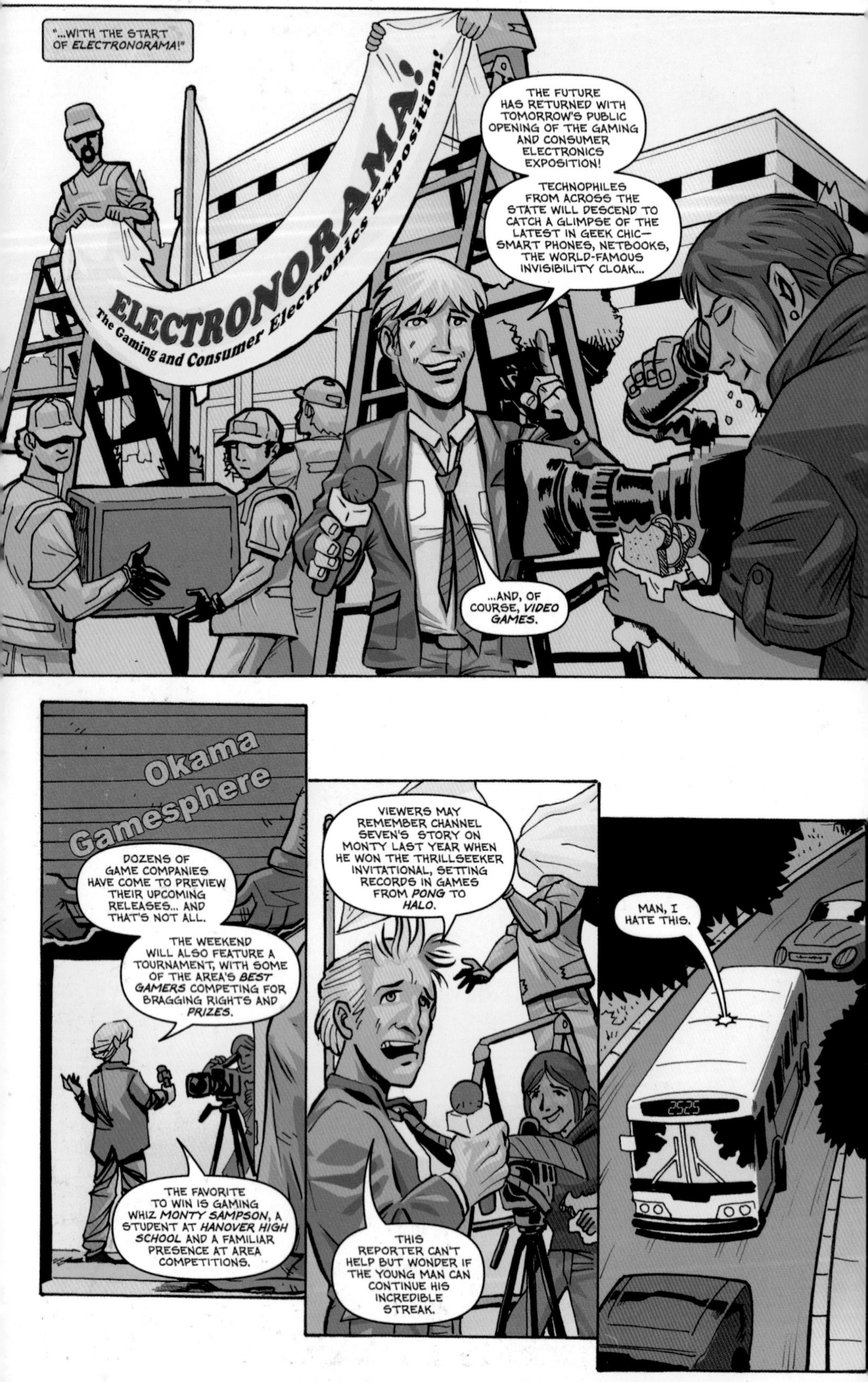
"...WITH THE START OF *ELECTRONORAMA!*"
ELECTRONORAMA!
The Gaming and Consumer Electronics Exposition!
THE FUTURE HAS RETURNED WITH TOMORROW'S PUBLIC OPENING OF THE GAMING AND CONSUMER ELECTRONICS EXPOSITION!
TECHNOPHILES FROM ACROSS THE STATE WILL DESCEND TO CATCH A GLIMPSE OF THE LATEST IN GEEK CHIC— SMART PHONES, NETBOOKS, THE WORLD-FAMOUS INVISIBILITY CLOAK...
...AND, OF COURSE, *VIDEO GAMES*.
Okama Gamesphere
DOZENS OF GAME COMPANIES HAVE COME TO PREVIEW THEIR UPCOMING RELEASES... AND THAT'S NOT ALL.
THE WEEKEND WILL ALSO FEATURE A TOURNAMENT, WITH SOME OF THE AREA'S *BEST GAMERS* COMPETING FOR BRAGGING RIGHTS AND *PRIZES*.
THE FAVORITE TO WIN IS GAMING WHIZ *MONTY SAMPSON*, A STUDENT AT *HANOVER HIGH SCHOOL* AND A FAMILIAR PRESENCE AT AREA COMPETITIONS.
VIEWERS MAY REMEMBER CHANNEL SEVEN'S STORY ON MONTY LAST YEAR WHEN HE WON THE THRILLSEEKER INVITATIONAL, SETTING RECORDS IN GAMES FROM *PONG* TO *HALO*.
THIS REPORTER CAN'T HELP BUT WONDER IF THE YOUNG MAN CAN CONTINUE HIS INCREDIBLE STREAK.
MAN, I HATE THIS.
2525

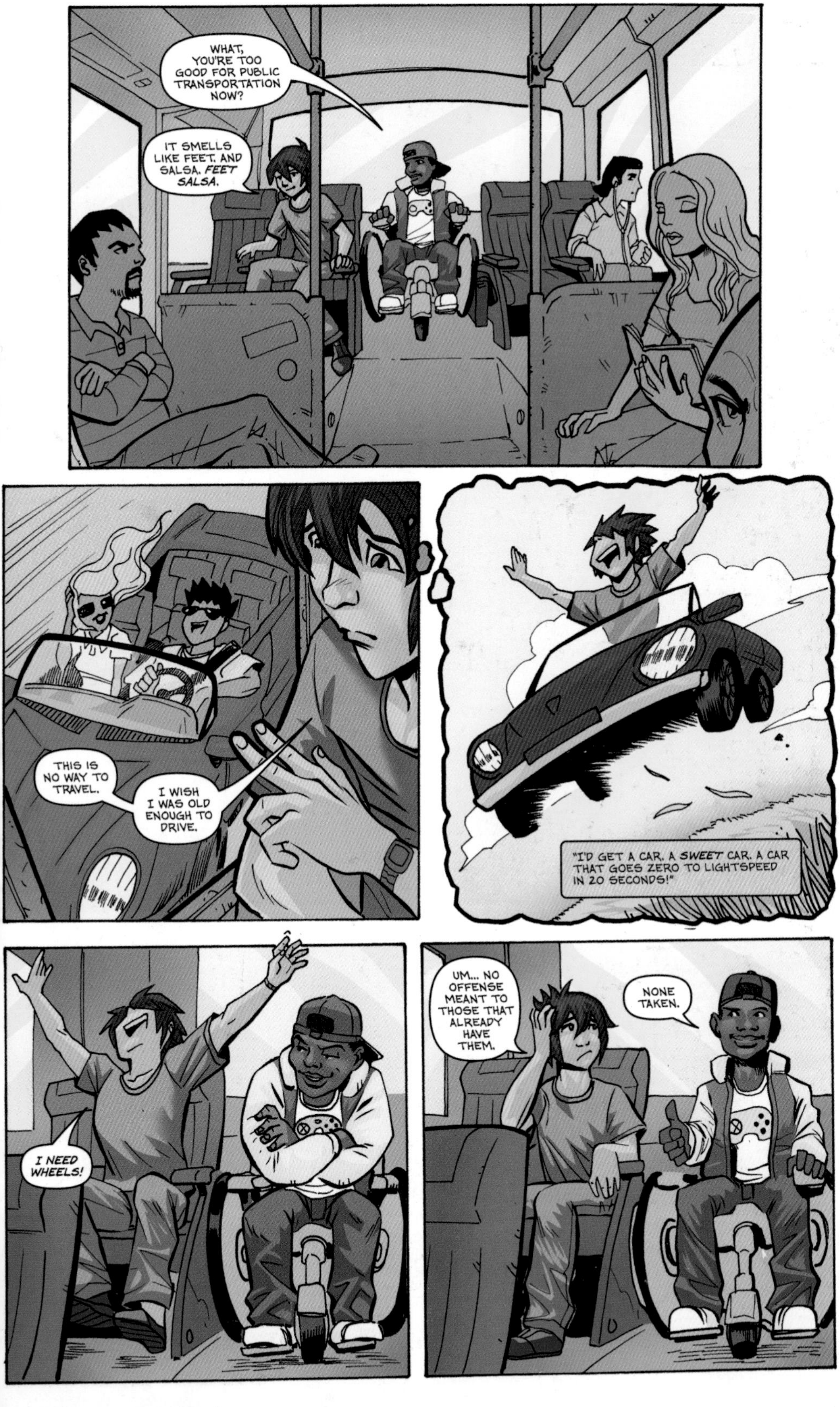
WHAT, YOU'RE TOO GOOD FOR PUBLIC TRANSPORTATION NOW?
IT SMELLS LIKE FEET. AND SALSA. *FEET SALSA.*
THIS IS NO WAY TO TRAVEL.
I WISH I WAS OLD ENOUGH TO DRIVE.
"I'D GET A CAR. A *SWEET* CAR. A CAR THAT GOES ZERO TO LIGHTSPEED IN 20 SECONDS!"
I NEED WHEELS!
UM... NO OFFENSE MEANT TO THOSE THAT ALREADY HAVE THEM.
NONE TAKEN.

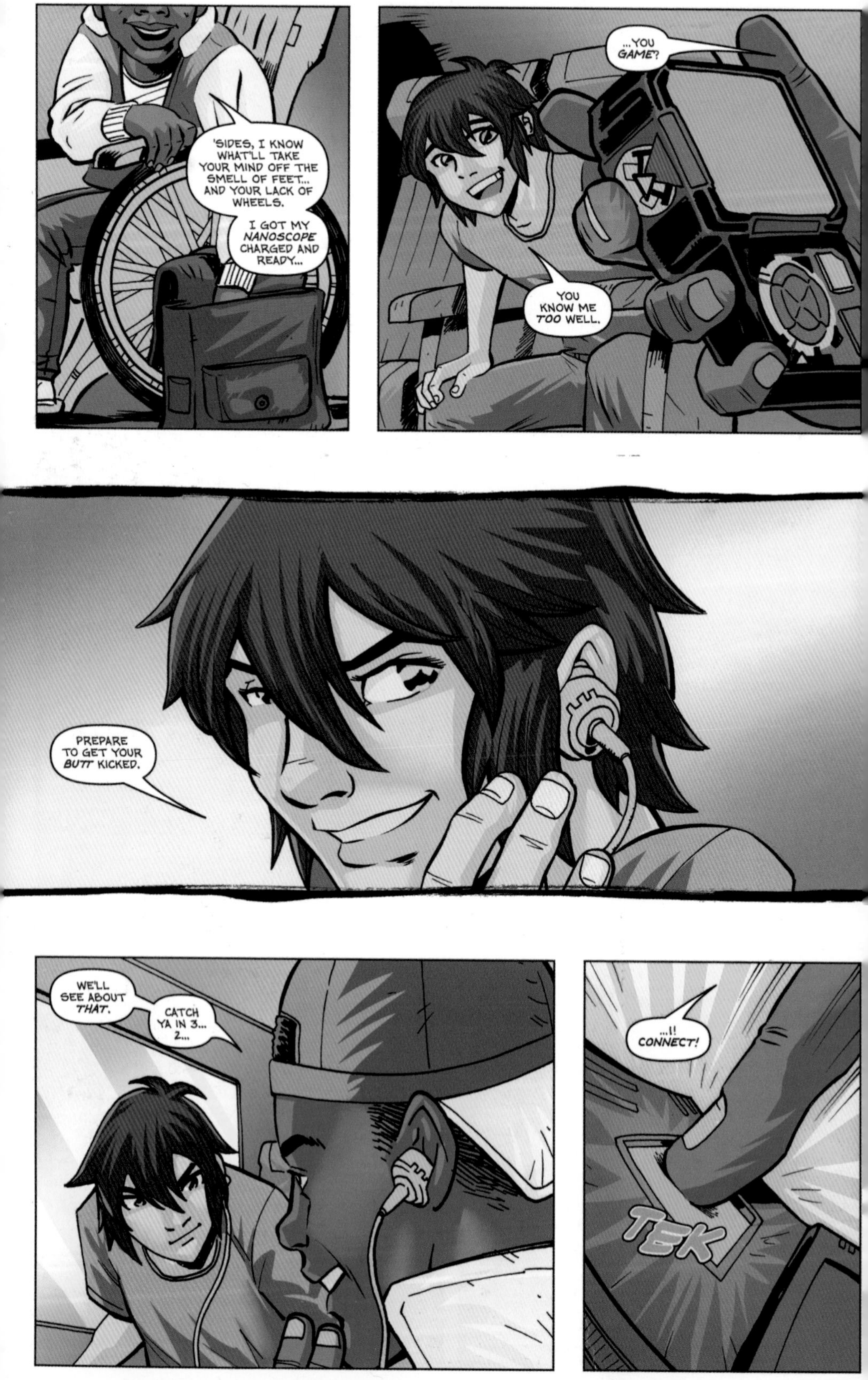
'SIDES, I KNOW WHAT'LL TAKE YOUR MIND OFF THE SMELL OF FEET... AND YOUR LACK OF WHEELS.
I GOT MY *NANOSCOPE* CHARGED AND READY...
...YOU *GAME*?
YOU KNOW ME *TOO* WELL.
PREPARE TO GET YOUR *BUTT* KICKED.
WE'LL SEE ABOUT *THAT*.
CATCH YA IN 3... 2...
...1! CONNECT!
TEK

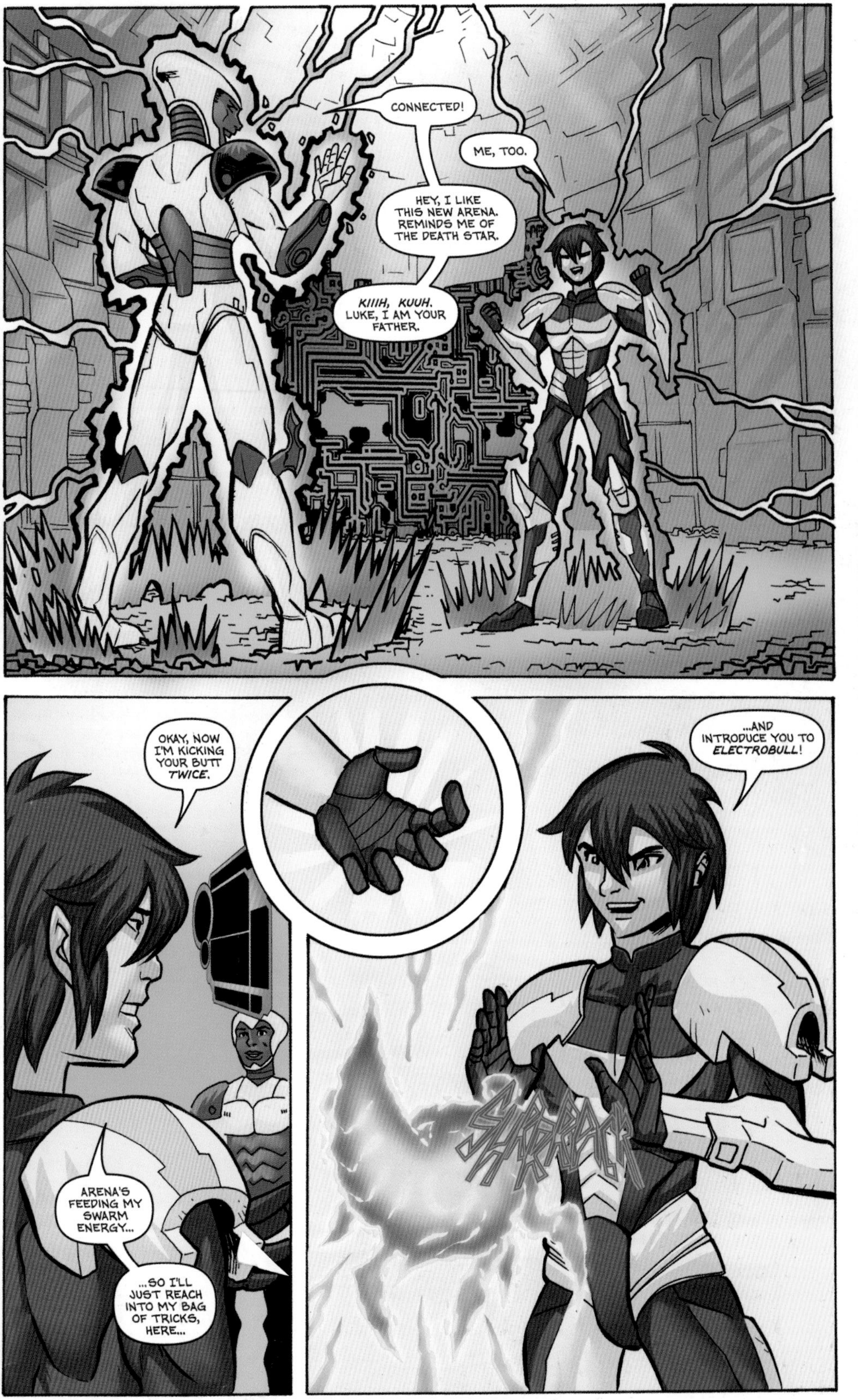
CONNECTED!
ME, TOO.
HEY, I LIKE THIS NEW ARENA. REMINDS ME OF THE DEATH STAR.
KIIIH, KUUH. LUKE, I AM YOUR FATHER.
OKAY, NOW I'M KICKING YOUR BUTT *TWICE*.
ARENA'S FEEDING MY SWARM ENERGY...
...SO I'LL JUST REACH INTO MY BAG OF TRICKS, HERE...
...AND INTRODUCE YOU TO *ELECTROBULL*!
SHRRAAK

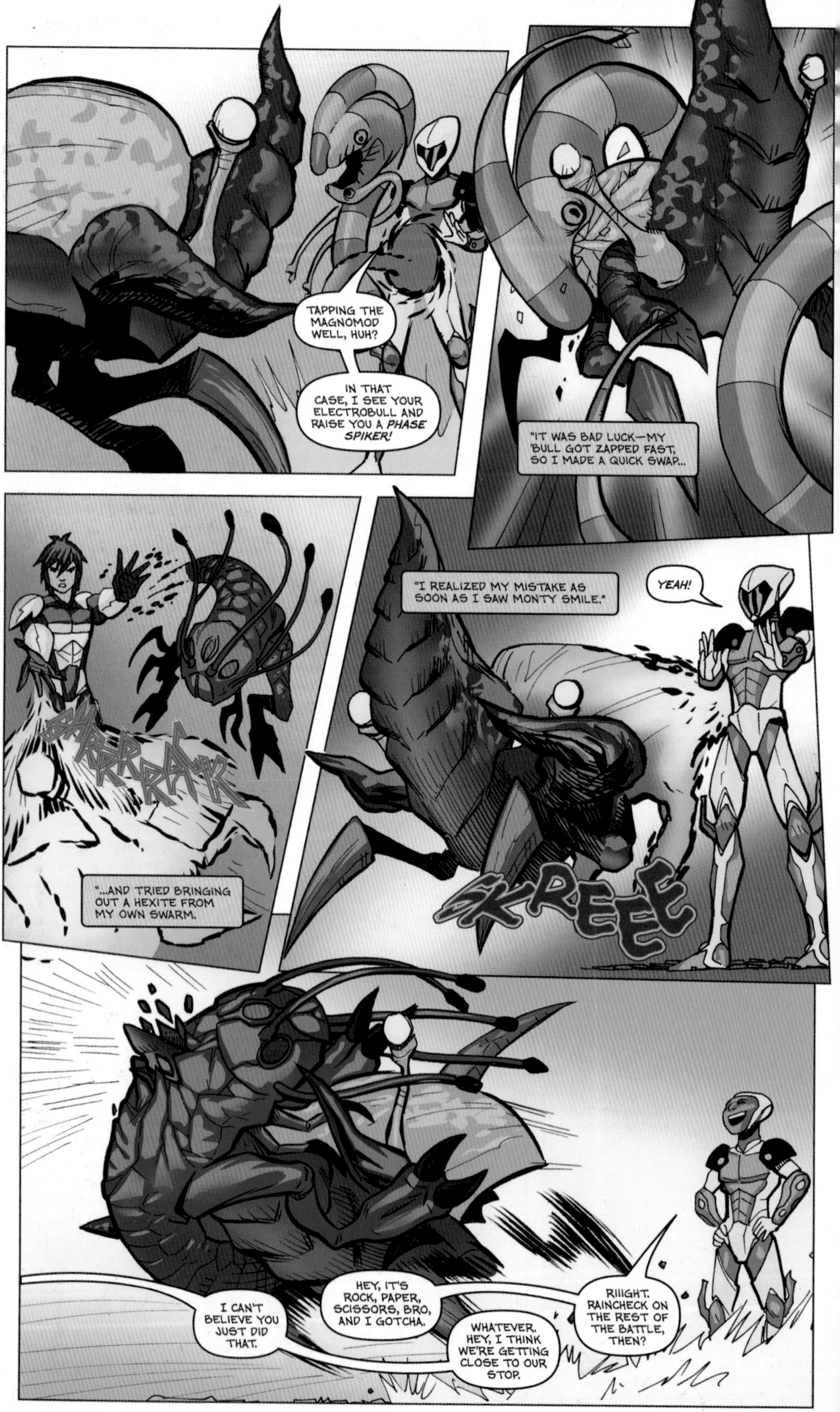

TAPPING THE MAGNOMOD WELL, HUH?
IN THAT CASE, I SEE YOUR ELECTROBULL AND RAISE YOU A *PHASE SPIKER!*
"IT WAS BAD LUCK—MY 'BULL GOT ZAPPED FAST, SO I MADE A QUICK SWAP...
SHRRRRACK
"...AND TRIED BRINGING OUT A HEXITE FROM MY OWN SWARM.
"I REALIZED MY MISTAKE AS SOON AS I SAW MONTY SMILE."
YEAH!
SKREEE
I CAN'T BELIEVE YOU JUST DID THAT.
HEY, IT'S ROCK, PAPER, SCISSORS, BRO, AND I GOTCHA.
WHATEVER. HEY, I THINK WE'RE GETTING CLOSE TO OUR STOP.
RIIIGHT. RAINCHECK ON THE REST OF THE BATTLE, THEN?

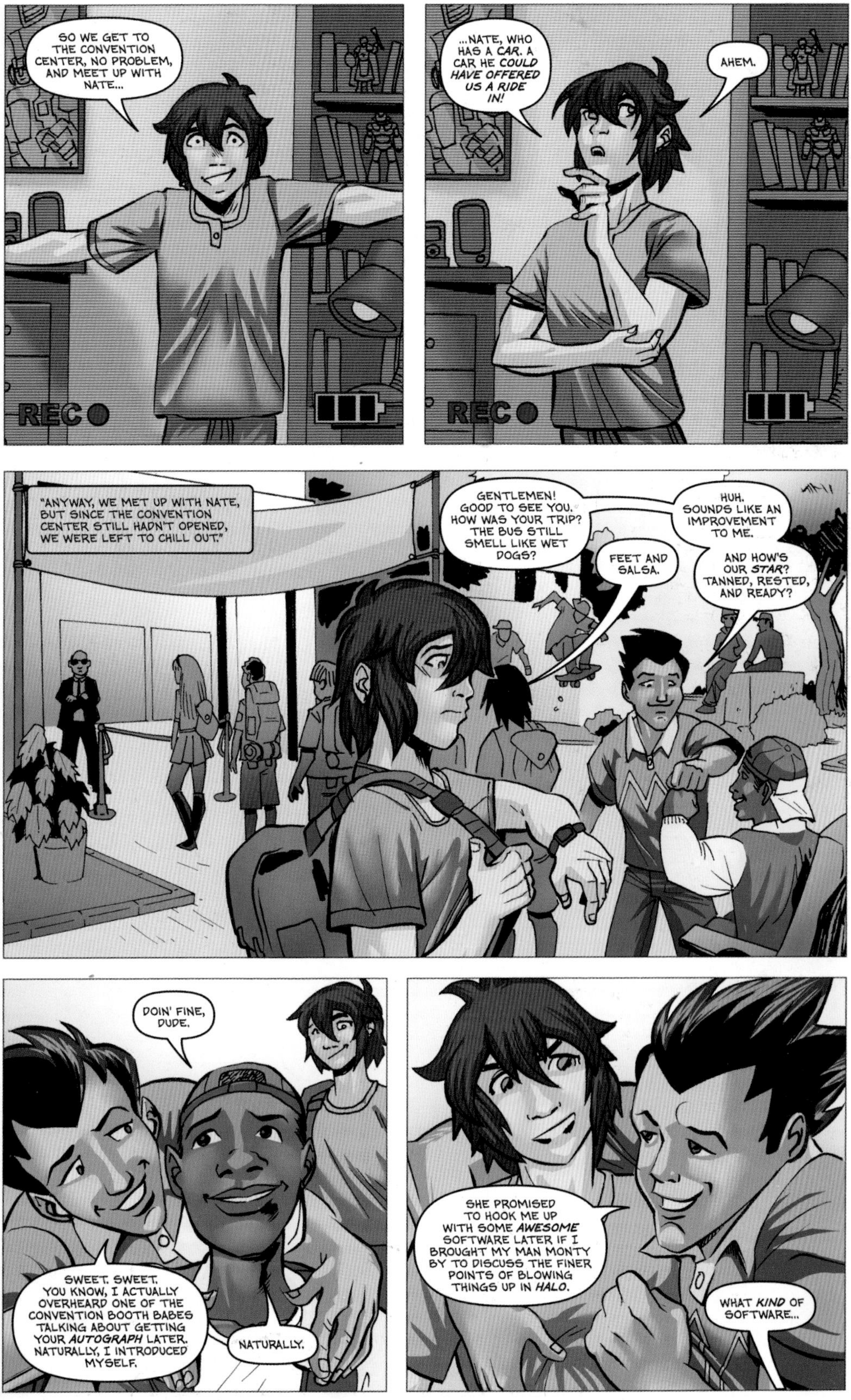

SO WE GET TO THE CONVENTION CENTER, NO PROBLEM, AND MEET UP WITH NATE...
REC
...NATE, WHO HAS A *CAR*. A CAR HE *COULD HAVE OFFERED US A RIDE IN!*
AHEM.
REC
"ANYWAY, WE MET UP WITH NATE, BUT SINCE THE CONVENTION CENTER STILL HADN'T OPENED, WE WERE LEFT TO CHILL OUT."
GENTLEMEN! GOOD TO SEE YOU. HOW WAS YOUR TRIP? THE BUS STILL SMELL LIKE WET DOGS?
FEET AND SALSA.
HUH. SOUNDS LIKE AN IMPROVEMENT TO ME.
AND HOW'S OUR *STAR*? TANNED, RESTED, AND READY?
DOIN' FINE, DUDE.
SWEET. SWEET. YOU KNOW, I ACTUALLY OVERHEARD ONE OF THE CONVENTION BOOTH BABES TALKING ABOUT GETTING YOUR *AUTOGRAPH* LATER. NATURALLY, I INTRODUCED MYSELF.
NATURALLY.
SHE PROMISED TO HOOK ME UP WITH SOME *AWESOME* SOFTWARE LATER IF I BROUGHT MY MAN MONTY BY TO DISCUSS THE FINER POINTS OF BLOWING THINGS UP IN *HALO*.
WHAT *KIND* OF SOFTWARE...

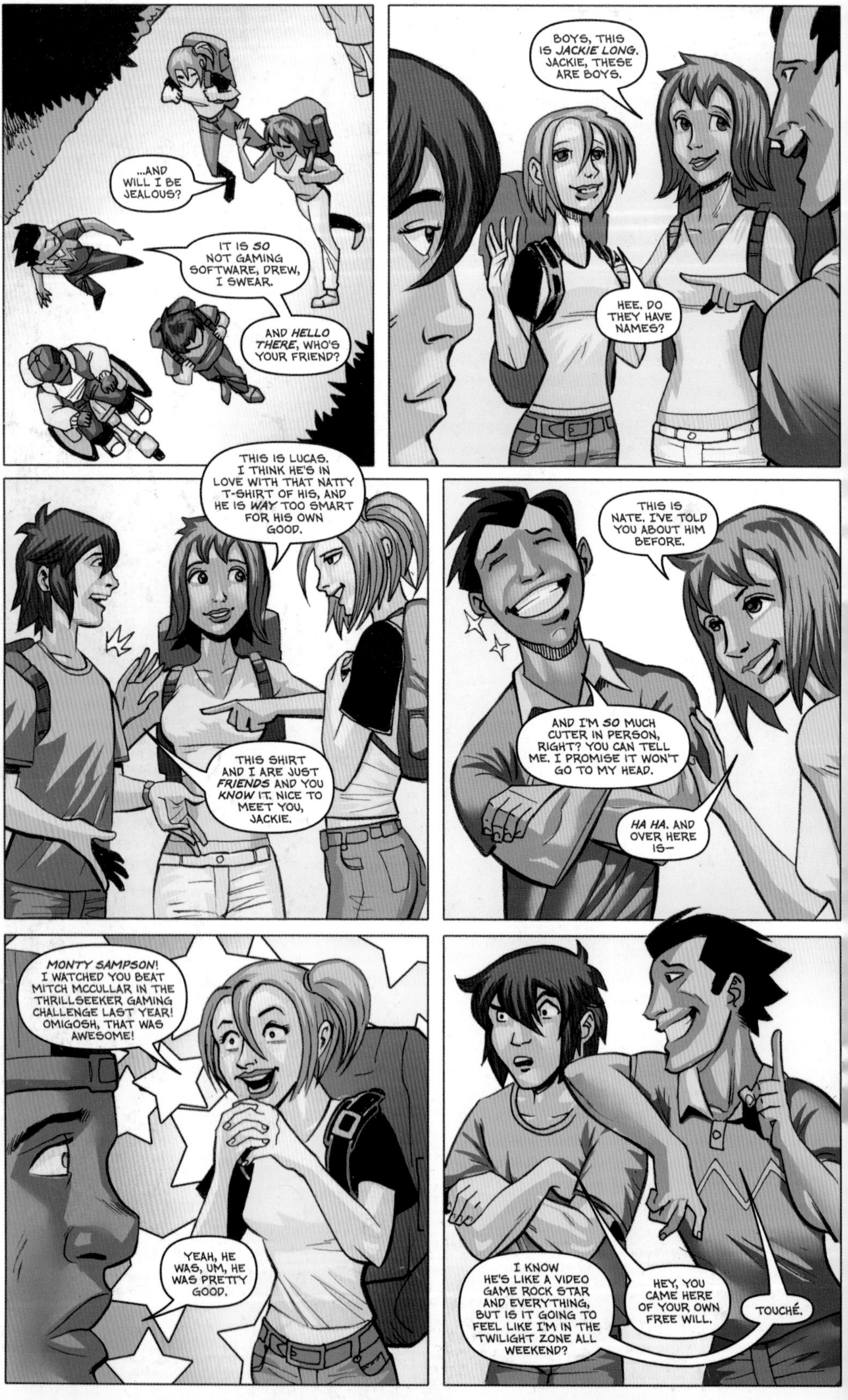
...AND WILL I BE JEALOUS?
IT IS SO NOT GAMING SOFTWARE, DREW, I SWEAR.
AND HELLO THERE, WHO'S YOUR FRIEND?
BOYS, THIS IS JACKIE LONG. JACKIE, THESE ARE BOYS.
HEE. DO THEY HAVE NAMES?
THIS IS LUCAS. I THINK HE'S IN LOVE WITH THAT NATTY T-SHIRT OF HIS, AND HE IS WAY TOO SMART FOR HIS OWN GOOD.
THIS SHIRT AND I ARE JUST FRIENDS AND YOU KNOW IT. NICE TO MEET YOU, JACKIE.
THIS IS NATE. I'VE TOLD YOU ABOUT HIM BEFORE.
AND I'M SO MUCH CUTER IN PERSON, RIGHT? YOU CAN TELL ME. I PROMISE IT WON'T GO TO MY HEAD.
HA HA. AND OVER HERE IS—
MONTY SAMPSON! I WATCHED YOU BEAT MITCH MCCULLAR IN THE THRILLSEEKER GAMING CHALLENGE LAST YEAR! OMIGOSH, THAT WAS AWESOME!
YEAH, HE WAS, UM, HE WAS PRETTY GOOD.
I KNOW HE'S LIKE A VIDEO GAME ROCK STAR AND EVERYTHING, BUT IS IT GOING TO FEEL LIKE I'M IN THE TWILIGHT ZONE ALL WEEKEND?
HEY, YOU CAME HERE OF YOUR OWN FREE WILL.
TOUCHÉ.

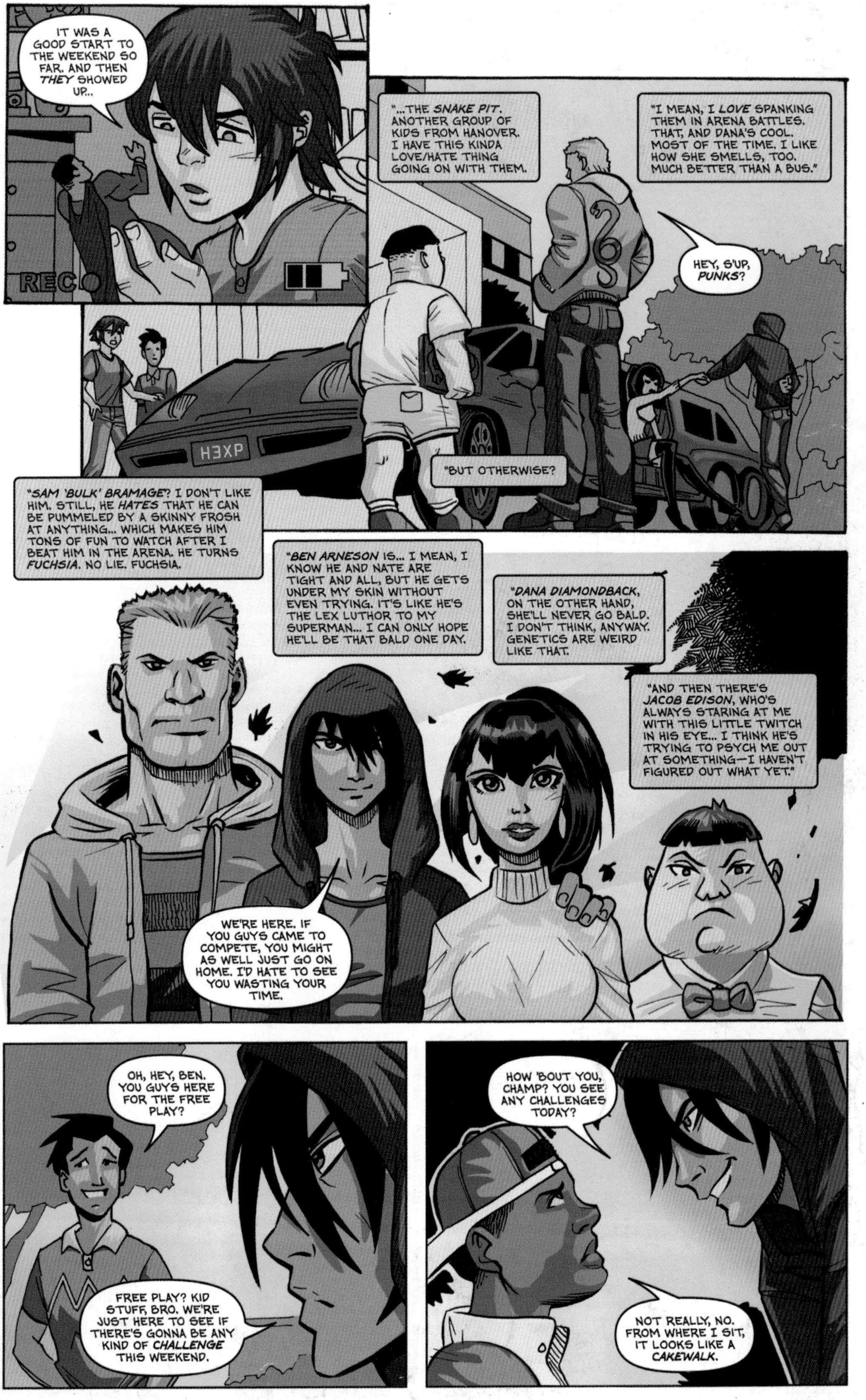

IT WAS A GOOD START TO THE WEEKEND SO FAR. AND THEN *THEY* SHOWED UP...
REC
"...THE *SNAKE PIT*. ANOTHER GROUP OF KIDS FROM HANOVER. I HAVE THIS KINDA LOVE/HATE THING GOING ON WITH THEM.
"I MEAN, I *LOVE* SPANKING THEM IN ARENA BATTLES. THAT, AND DANA'S COOL. MOST OF THE TIME. I LIKE HOW SHE SMELLS, TOO. MUCH BETTER THAN A BUS."
HEY, S'UP, *PUNKS*?
H3XP
"BUT OTHERWISE?
"*SAM 'BULK' BRAMAGE*? I DON'T LIKE HIM. STILL, HE *HATES* THAT HE CAN BE PUMMELED BY A SKINNY FROSH AT ANYTHING... WHICH MAKES HIM TONS OF FUN TO WATCH AFTER I BEAT HIM IN THE ARENA. HE TURNS *FUCHSIA*. NO LIE. FUCHSIA.
"*BEN ARNESON* IS... I MEAN, I KNOW HE AND NATE ARE TIGHT AND ALL, BUT HE GETS UNDER MY SKIN WITHOUT EVEN TRYING. IT'S LIKE HE'S THE LEX LUTHOR TO MY SUPERMAN... I CAN ONLY HOPE HE'LL BE THAT BALD ONE DAY.
"*DANA DIAMONDBACK*, ON THE OTHER HAND, SHE'LL NEVER GO BALD. I DON'T THINK, ANYWAY. GENETICS ARE WEIRD LIKE THAT.
"AND THEN THERE'S *JACOB EDISON*, WHO'S ALWAYS STARING AT ME WITH THIS LITTLE TWITCH IN HIS EYE... I THINK HE'S TRYING TO PSYCH ME OUT AT SOMETHING—I HAVEN'T FIGURED OUT WHAT YET."
WE'RE HERE. IF YOU GUYS CAME TO COMPETE, YOU MIGHT AS WELL JUST GO ON HOME. I'D HATE TO SEE YOU WASTING YOUR TIME.
OH, HEY, BEN. YOU GUYS HERE FOR THE FREE PLAY?
FREE PLAY? KID STUFF, BRO. WE'RE JUST HERE TO SEE IF THERE'S GONNA BE ANY KIND OF *CHALLENGE* THIS WEEKEND.
HOW 'BOUT YOU, CHAMP? YOU SEE ANY CHALLENGES TODAY?
NOT REALLY, NO. FROM WHERE I SIT, IT LOOKS LIKE A *CAKEWALK*.

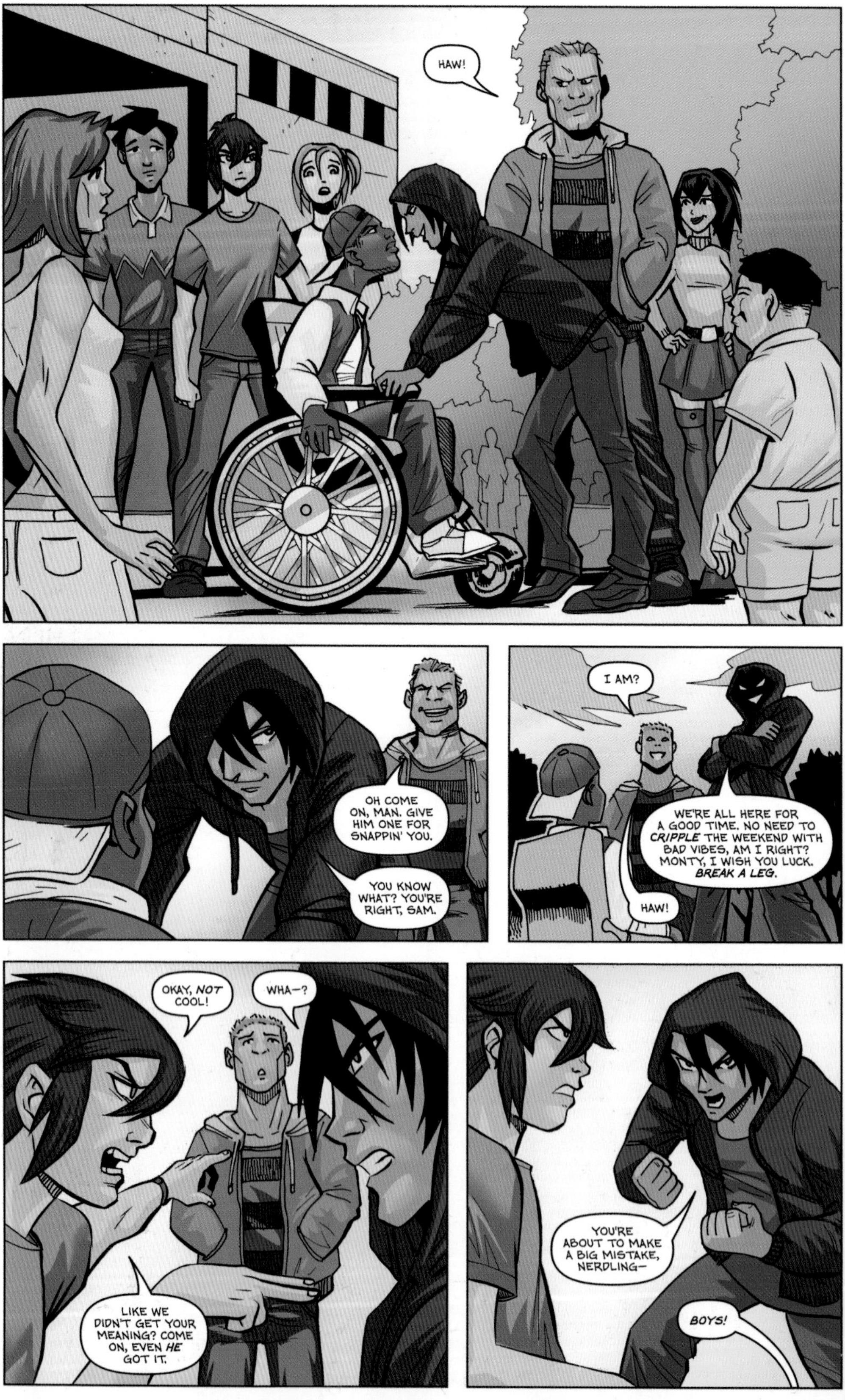
HAW!
OH COME ON, MAN. GIVE HIM ONE FOR SNAPPIN' YOU.
YOU KNOW WHAT? YOU'RE RIGHT, SAM.
I AM?
WE'RE ALL HERE FOR A GOOD TIME. NO NEED TO CRIPPLE THE WEEKEND WITH BAD VIBES, AM I RIGHT? MONTY, I WISH YOU LUCK. BREAK A LEG.
HAW!
OKAY, NOT COOL!
WHA—?
LIKE WE DIDN'T GET YOUR MEANING? COME ON, EVEN HE GOT IT.
YOU'RE ABOUT TO MAKE A BIG MISTAKE, NERDLING—
BOYS!

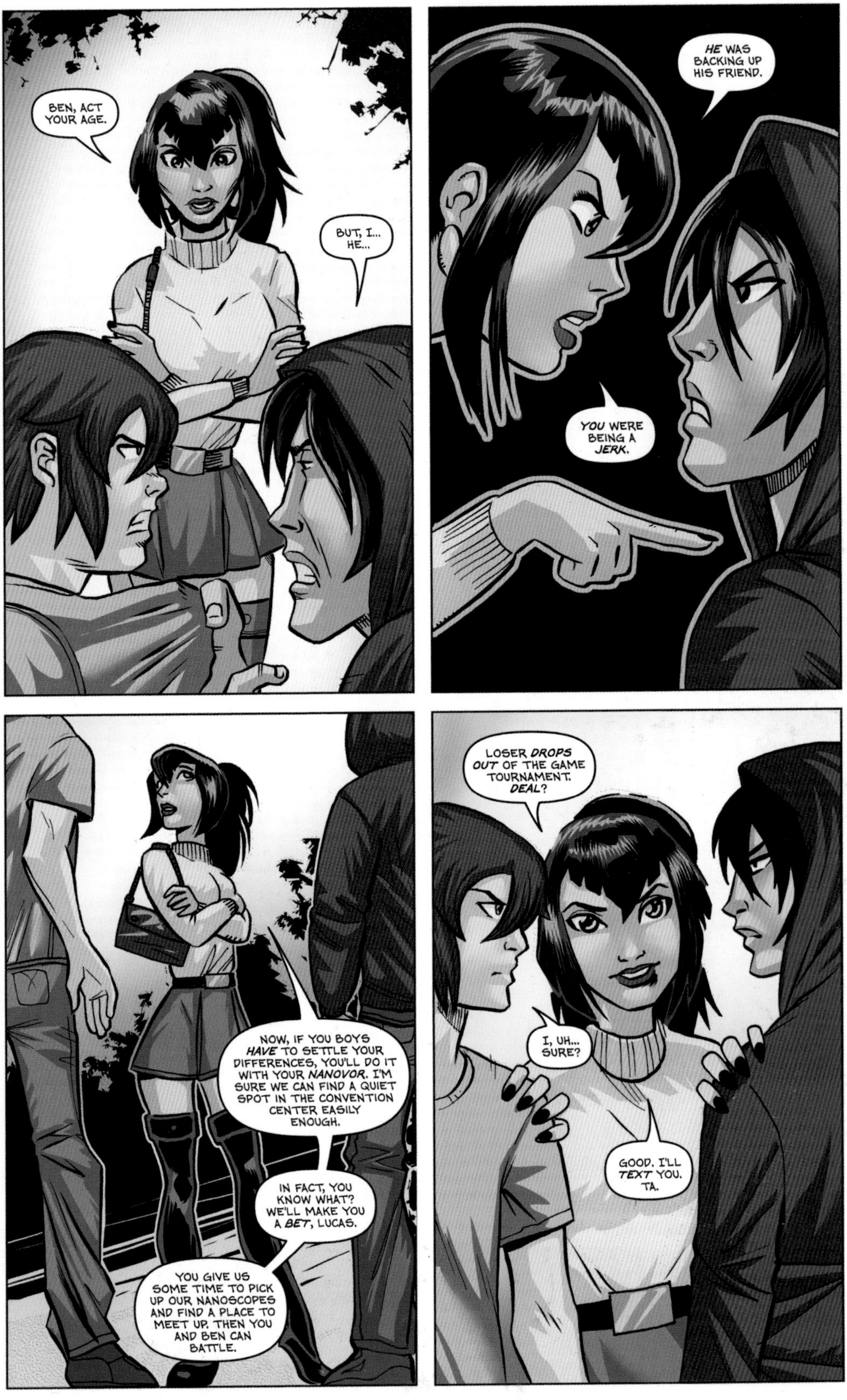
BEN, ACT YOUR AGE.
BUT, I... HE...
HE WAS BACKING UP HIS FRIEND.
YOU WERE BEING A JERK.
NOW, IF YOU BOYS HAVE TO SETTLE YOUR DIFFERENCES, YOU'LL DO IT WITH YOUR NANOVOR. I'M SURE WE CAN FIND A QUIET SPOT IN THE CONVENTION CENTER EASILY ENOUGH.
IN FACT, YOU KNOW WHAT? WE'LL MAKE YOU A BET, LUCAS.
YOU GIVE US SOME TIME TO PICK UP OUR NANOSCOPES AND FIND A PLACE TO MEET UP. THEN YOU AND BEN CAN BATTLE.
LOSER DROPS OUT OF THE GAME TOURNAMENT. DEAL?
I, UH... SURE?
GOOD. I'LL TEXT YOU. TA.

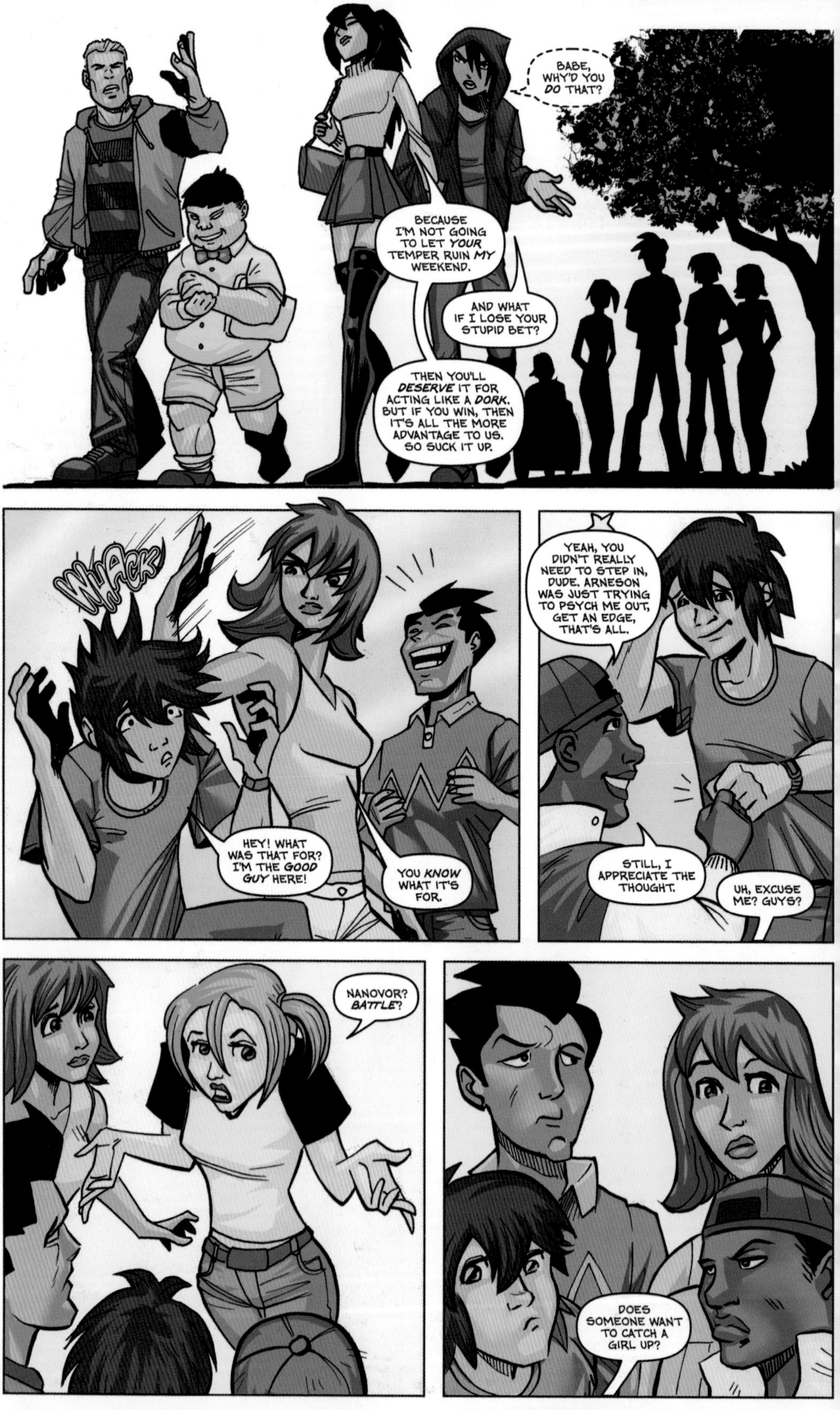
BABE, WHY'D YOU *DO* THAT?
BECAUSE I'M NOT GOING TO LET *YOUR* TEMPER RUIN *MY* WEEKEND.
AND WHAT IF I LOSE YOUR STUPID BET?
THEN YOU'LL *DESERVE* IT FOR ACTING LIKE A *DORK*. BUT IF YOU WIN, THEN IT'S ALL THE MORE ADVANTAGE TO US. SO SUCK IT UP.
WHACK
HEY! WHAT WAS THAT FOR? I'M THE *GOOD GUY* HERE!
YOU *KNOW* WHAT IT'S FOR.
YEAH, YOU DIDN'T REALLY NEED TO STEP IN, DUDE. ARNESON WAS JUST TRYING TO PSYCH ME OUT, GET AN EDGE, THAT'S ALL.
STILL, I APPRECIATE THE THOUGHT.
UH, EXCUSE ME? GUYS?
NANOVOR? *BATTLE*?
DOES SOMEONE WANT TO CATCH A GIRL UP?

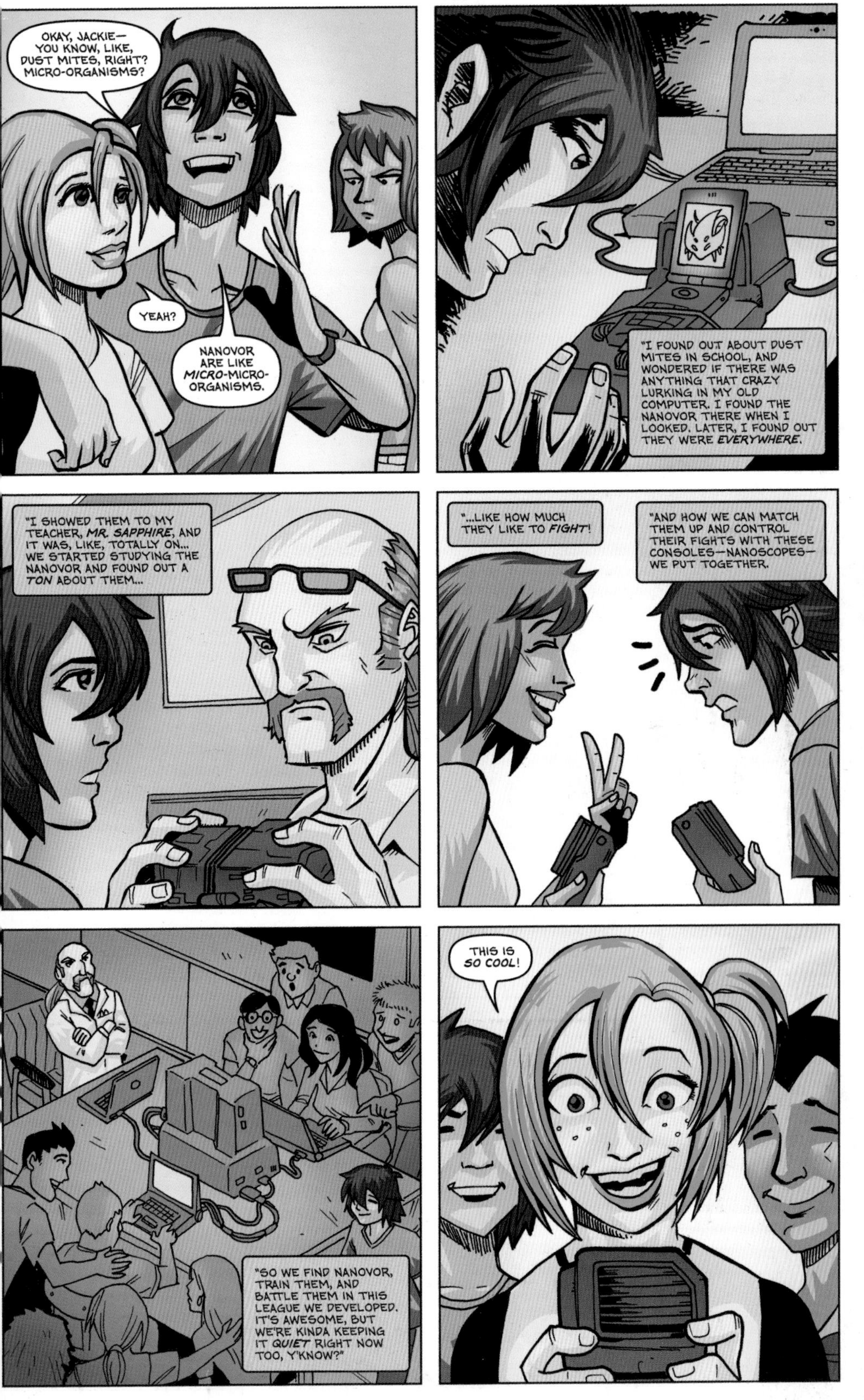
OKAY, JACKIE—
YOU KNOW, LIKE, DUST MITES, RIGHT? MICRO-ORGANISMS?
YEAH?
NANOVOR ARE LIKE *MICRO*-MICRO-ORGANISMS.
"I FOUND OUT ABOUT DUST MITES IN SCHOOL, AND WONDERED IF THERE WAS ANYTHING THAT CRAZY LURKING IN MY OLD COMPUTER. I FOUND THE NANOVOR THERE WHEN I LOOKED. LATER, I FOUND OUT THEY WERE *EVERYWHERE*.
"I SHOWED THEM TO MY TEACHER, *MR. SAPPHIRE*, AND IT WAS, LIKE, TOTALLY ON... WE STARTED STUDYING THE NANOVOR AND FOUND OUT A *TON* ABOUT THEM...
"...LIKE HOW MUCH THEY LIKE TO *FIGHT*!
"AND HOW WE CAN MATCH THEM UP AND CONTROL THEIR FIGHTS WITH THESE CONSOLES—NANOSCOPES—WE PUT TOGETHER.
"SO WE FIND NANOVOR, TRAIN THEM, AND BATTLE THEM IN THIS LEAGUE WE DEVELOPED. IT'S AWESOME, BUT WE'RE KINDA KEEPING IT *QUIET* RIGHT NOW TOO, Y'KNOW?"
THIS IS *SO COOL*!

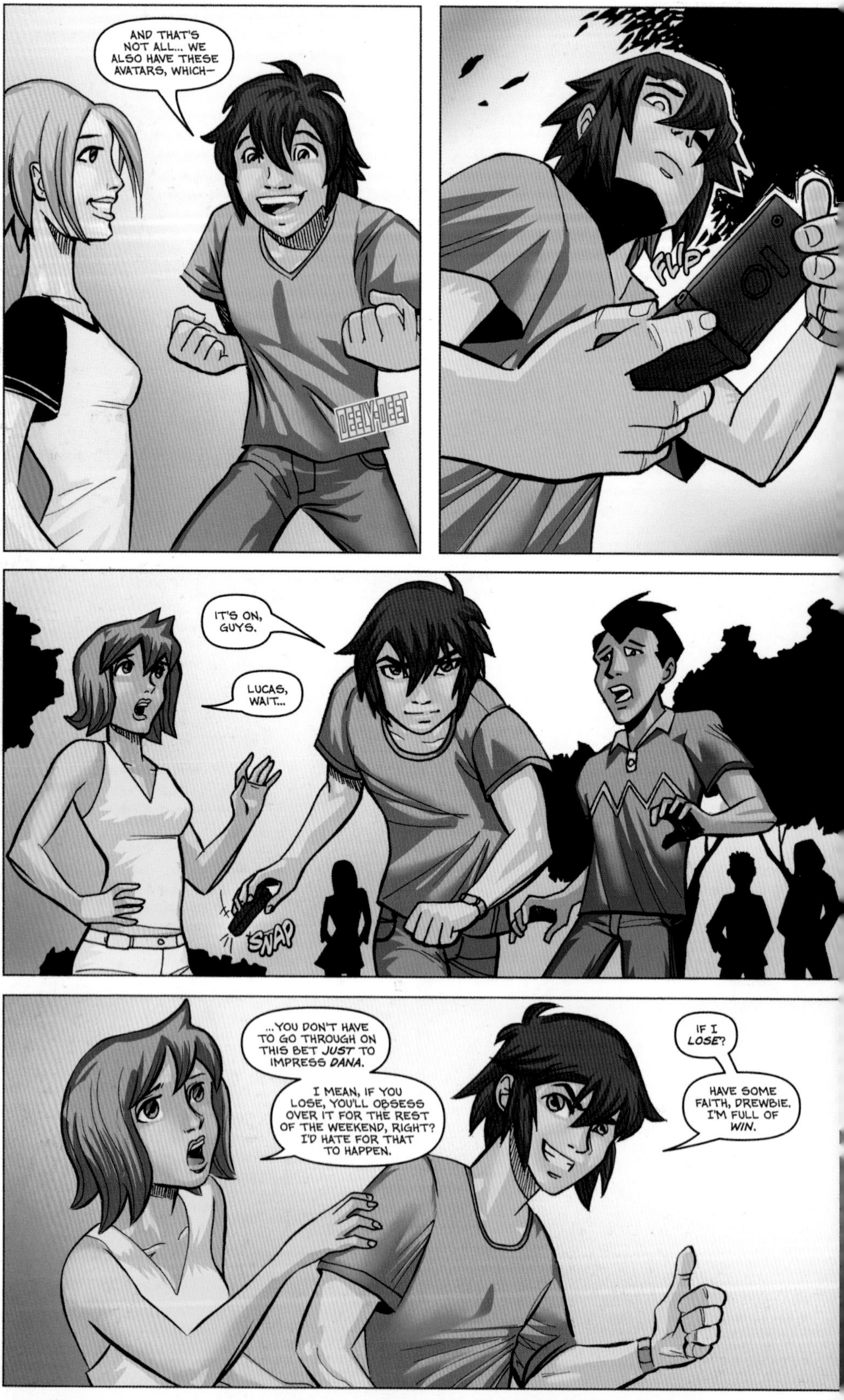
AND THAT'S NOT ALL... WE ALSO HAVE THESE AVATARS, WHICH—
DEELY-DEET
FLIP
IT'S ON, GUYS.
LUCAS, WAIT...
SNAP
...YOU DON'T HAVE TO GO THROUGH ON THIS BET JUST TO IMPRESS DANA.
I MEAN, IF YOU LOSE, YOU'LL OBSESS OVER IT FOR THE REST OF THE WEEKEND, RIGHT? I'D HATE FOR THAT TO HAPPEN.
IF I LOSE?
HAVE SOME FAITH, DREWBIE. I'M FULL OF WIN.

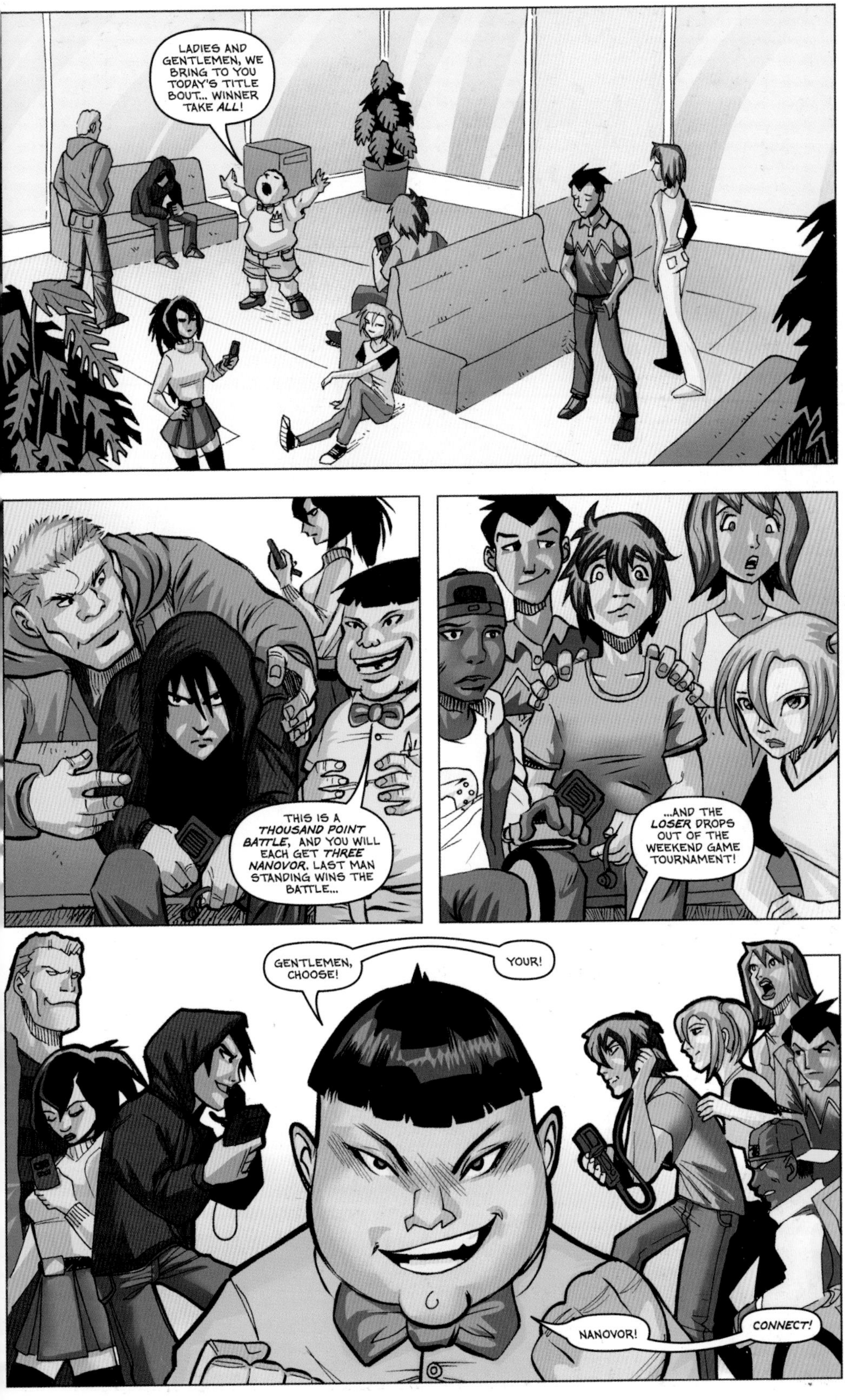
LADIES AND GENTLEMEN, WE BRING TO YOU TODAY'S TITLE BOUT... WINNER TAKE ALL!
THIS IS A THOUSAND POINT BATTLE, AND YOU WILL EACH GET THREE NANOVOR. LAST MAN STANDING WINS THE BATTLE...
...AND THE LOSER DROPS OUT OF THE WEEKEND GAME TOURNAMENT!
GENTLEMEN, CHOOSE!
YOUR!
NANOVOR!
CONNECT!

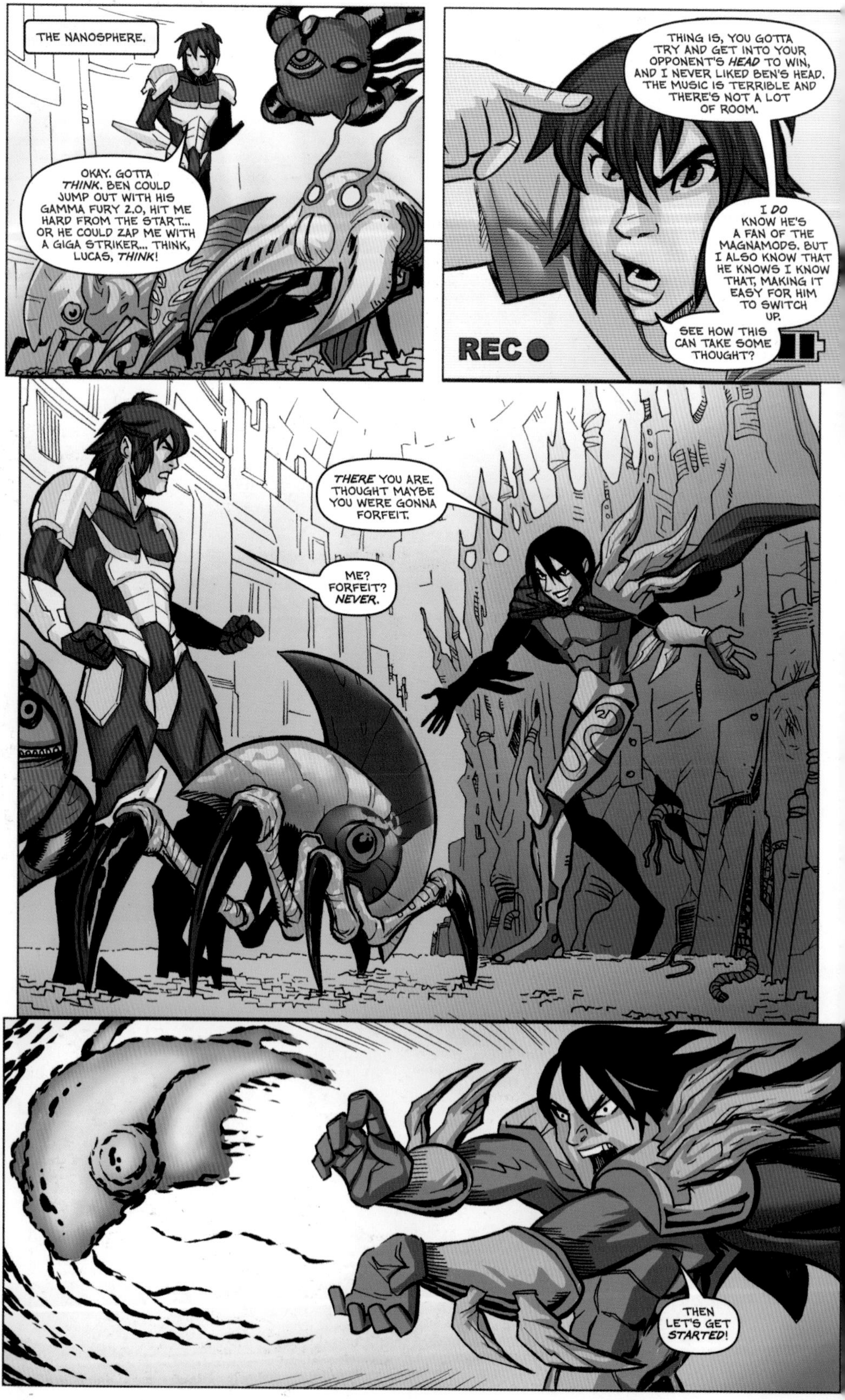
THE NANOSPHERE.
OKAY. GOTTA THINK. BEN COULD JUMP OUT WITH HIS GAMMA FURY 2.0, HIT ME HARD FROM THE START... OR HE COULD ZAP ME WITH A GIGA STRIKER... THINK, LUCAS, THINK!
THING IS, YOU GOTTA TRY AND GET INTO YOUR OPPONENT'S HEAD TO WIN, AND I NEVER LIKED BEN'S HEAD. THE MUSIC IS TERRIBLE AND THERE'S NOT A LOT OF ROOM.
I DO KNOW HE'S A FAN OF THE MAGNAMODS. BUT I ALSO KNOW THAT HE KNOWS I KNOW THAT, MAKING IT EASY FOR HIM TO SWITCH UP.
SEE HOW THIS CAN TAKE SOME THOUGHT?
REC
THERE YOU ARE. THOUGHT MAYBE YOU WERE GONNA FORFEIT.
ME? FORFEIT? NEVER.
THEN LET'S GET STARTED!

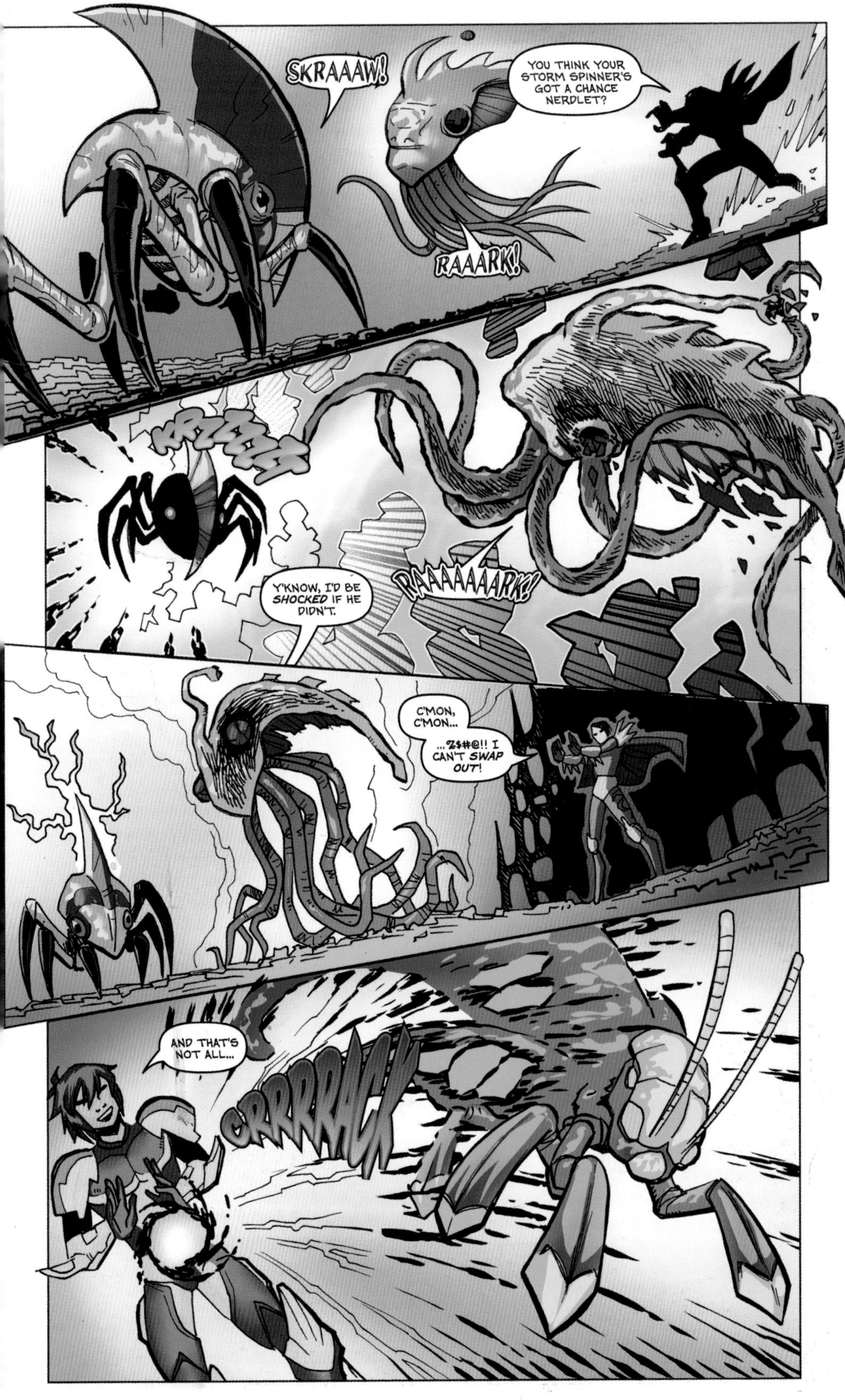
SKRAAAW!
YOU THINK YOUR STORM SPINNER'S GOT A CHANCE NERDLET?
RAAARK!
Y'KNOW, I'D BE *SHOCKED* IF HE DIDN'T.
RAAAAAAARK!
C'MON, C'MON...
...%$#@!! I CAN'T *SWAP OUT*!
AND THAT'S NOT ALL...
CRRRRACK!

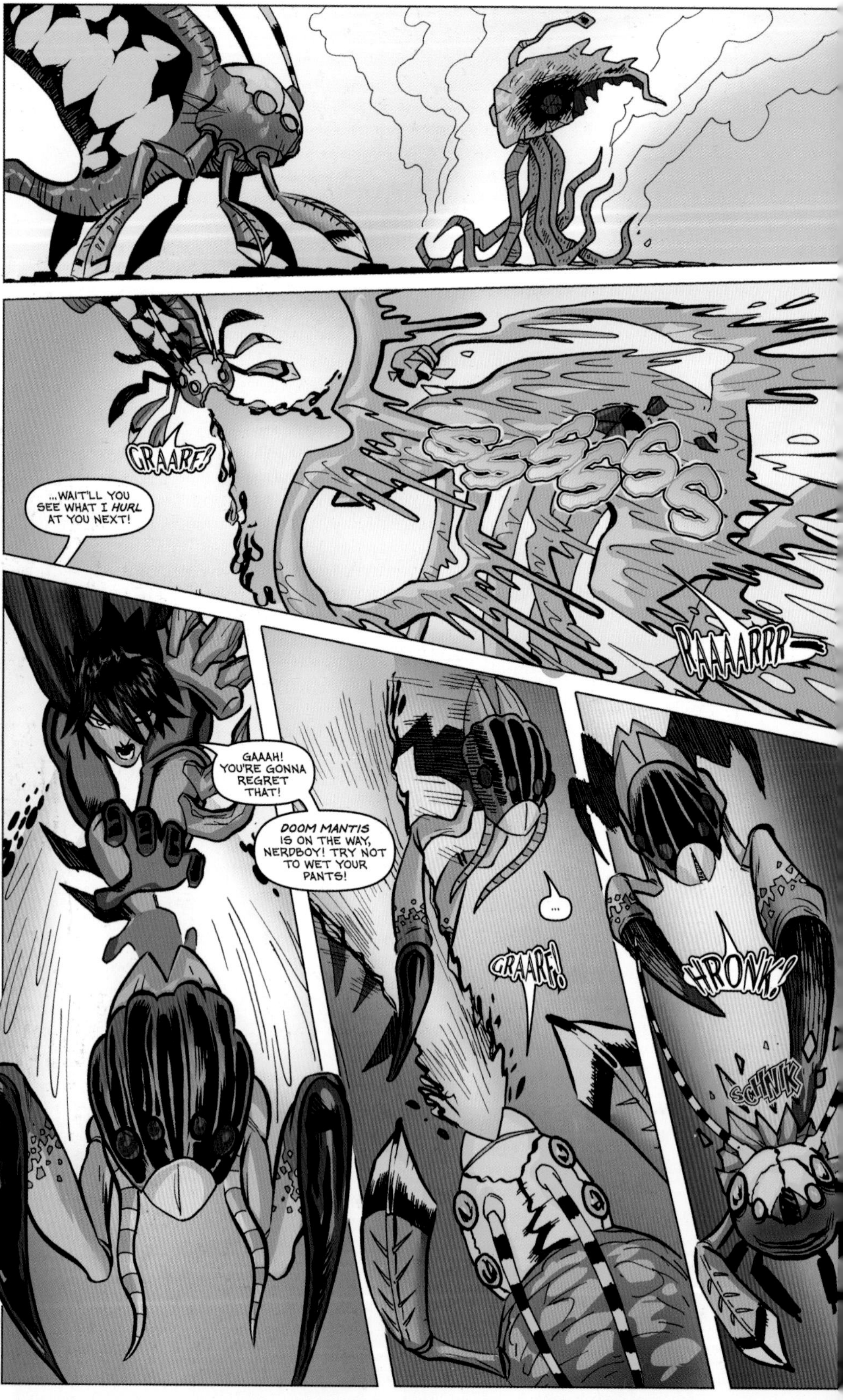
GRAARF!
...WAIT'LL YOU SEE WHAT I HURL AT YOU NEXT!
SSSSSS
RAAAARRR
GAAAH! YOU'RE GONNA REGRET THAT!
DOOM MANTIS IS ON THE WAY, NERDBOY! TRY NOT TO WET YOUR PANTS!
...
GRAARF!
HRONK!
SCHNIK

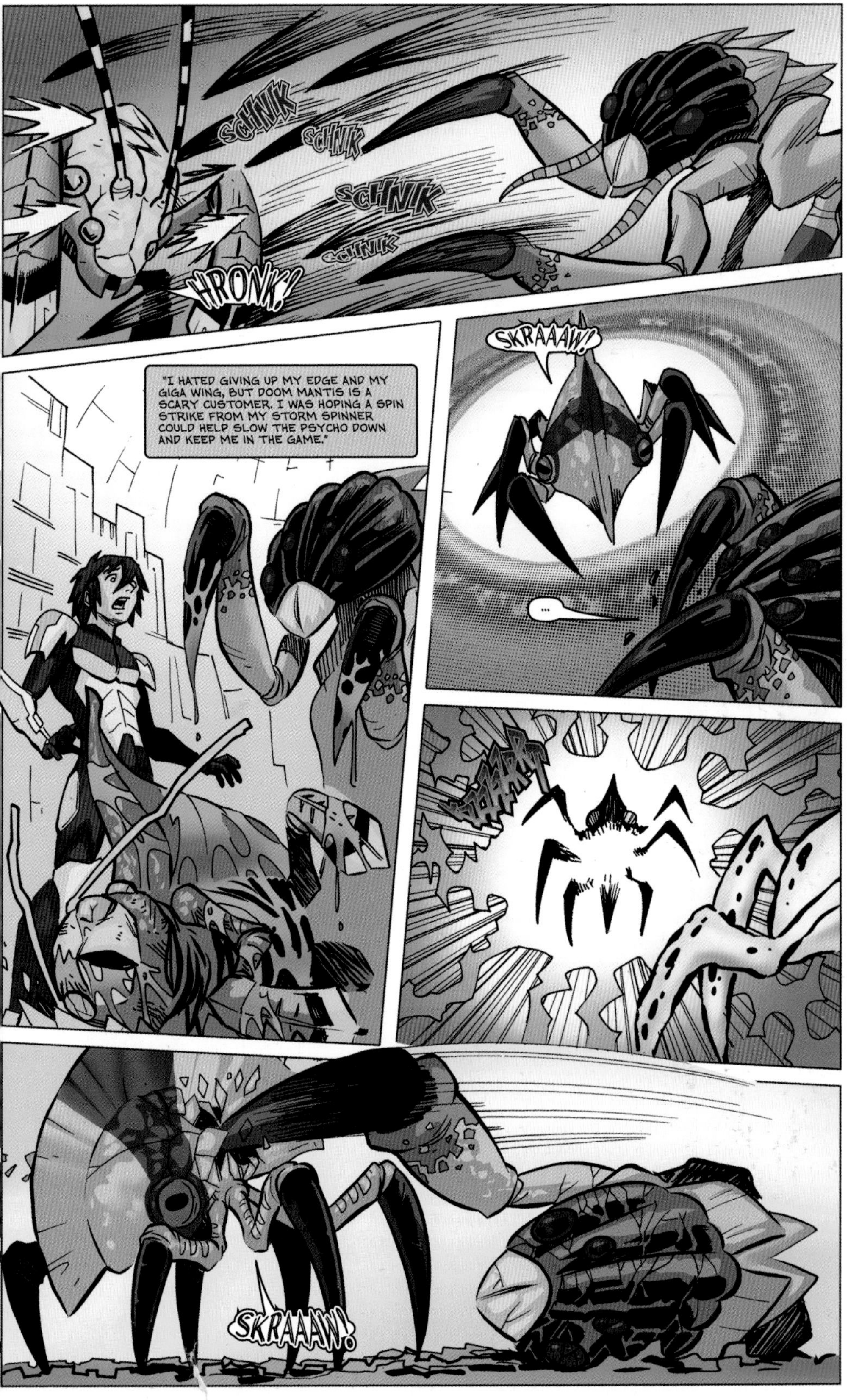
SCHNIK
SCHNIK
SCHNIK
SCHNIK
HRONK!
"I HATED GIVING UP MY EDGE AND MY GIGA WING, BUT DOOM MANTIS IS A SCARY CUSTOMER. I WAS HOPING A SPIN STRIKE FROM MY STORM SPINNER COULD HELP SLOW THE PSYCHO DOWN AND KEEP ME IN THE GAME."
SKRAAAW!
...
SKRAAAW!

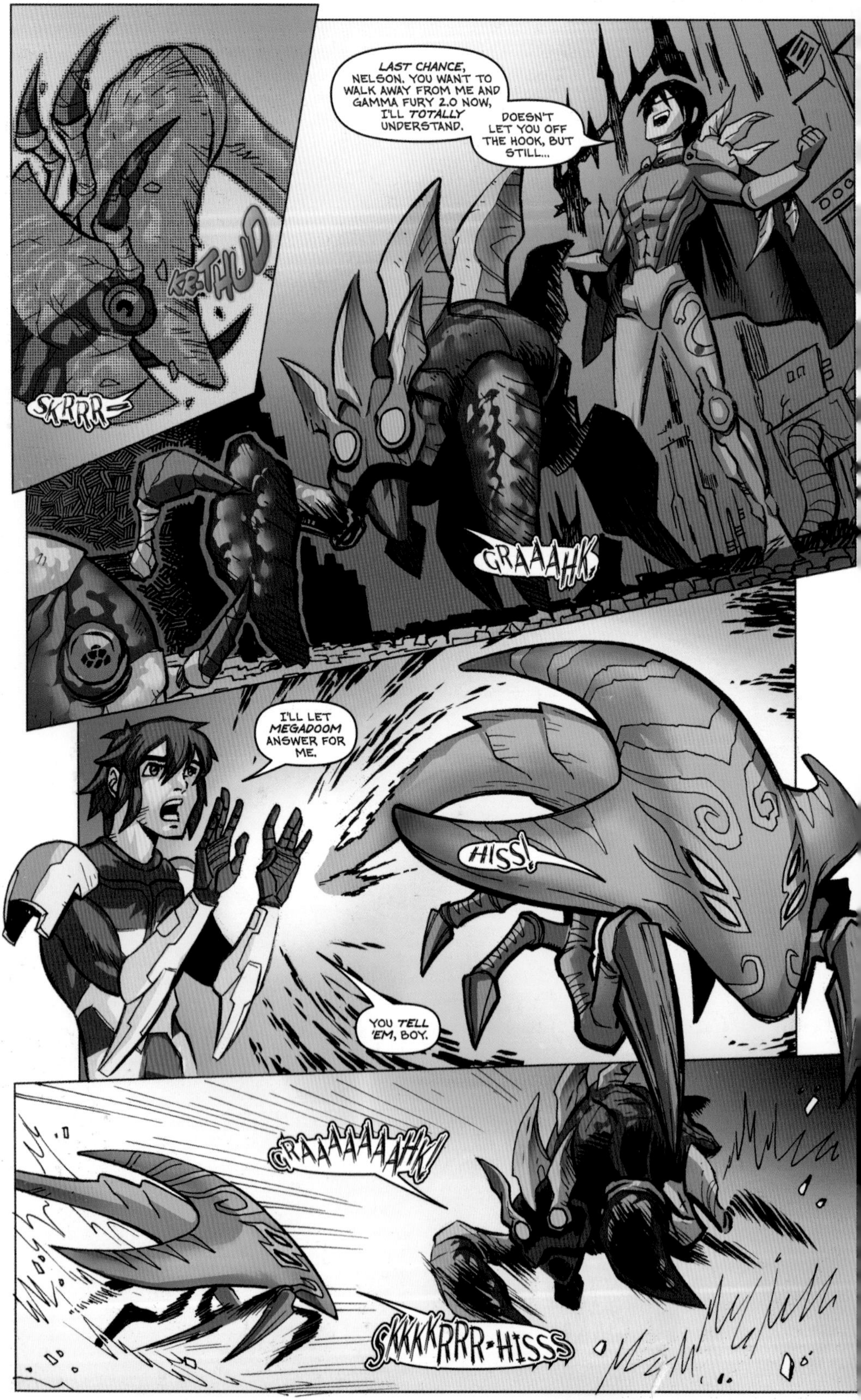
SKRRR—
KR-THUD
LAST CHANCE, NELSON. YOU WANT TO WALK AWAY FROM ME AND GAMMA FURY 2.0 NOW, I'LL TOTALLY UNDERSTAND.
DOESN'T LET YOU OFF THE HOOK, BUT STILL...
GRAAAHK
I'LL LET MEGADOOM ANSWER FOR ME.
HISS!
YOU TELL 'EM, BOY.
GRAAAAAAAHK!
SKKKRRR-HISSS

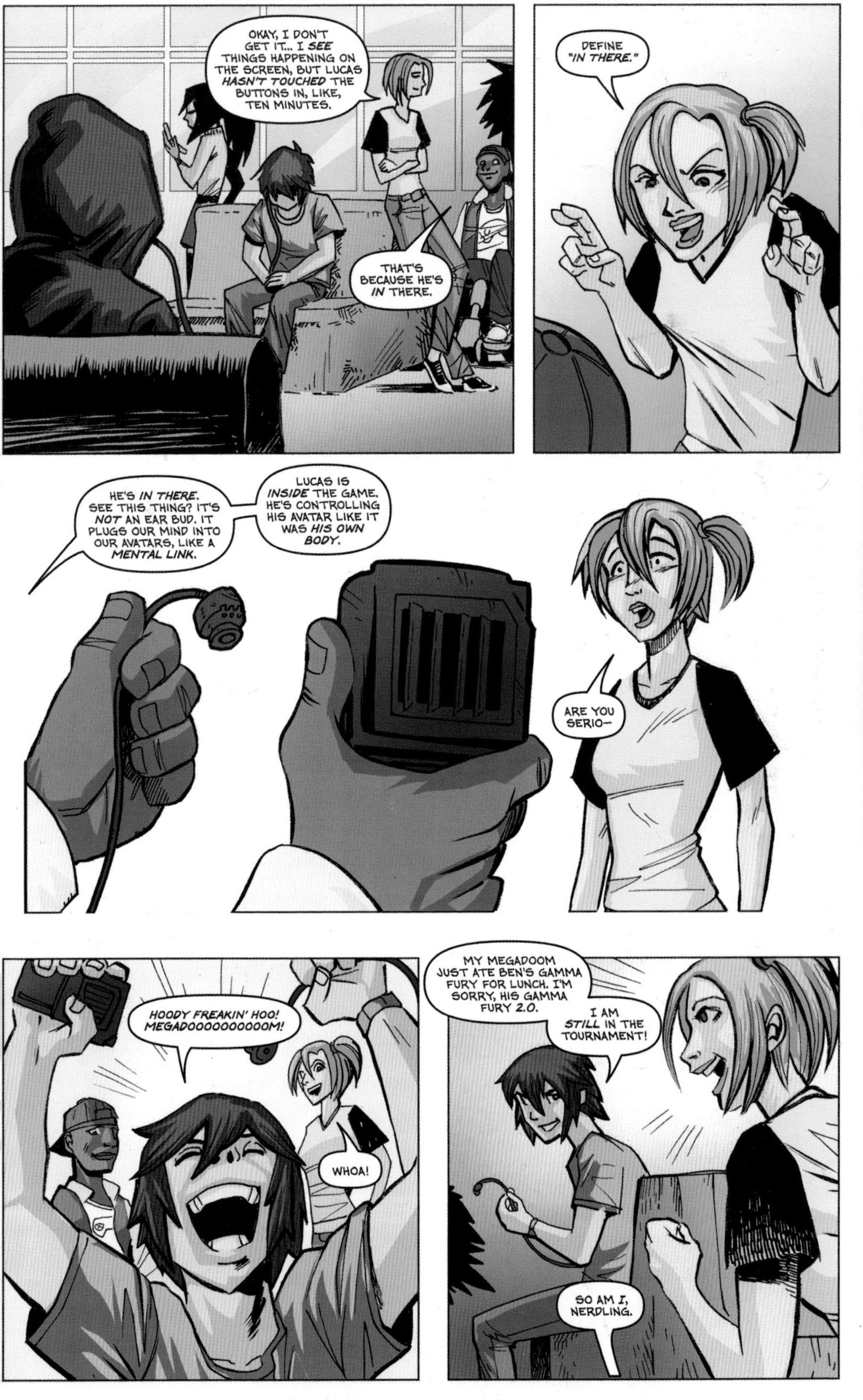

OKAY, I DON'T GET IT... I SEE THINGS HAPPENING ON THE SCREEN, BUT LUCAS HASN'T TOUCHED THE BUTTONS IN, LIKE, TEN MINUTES.
THAT'S BECAUSE HE'S IN THERE.
DEFINE "IN THERE."
HE'S IN THERE. SEE THIS THING? IT'S NOT AN EAR BUD. IT PLUGS OUR MIND INTO OUR AVATARS, LIKE A MENTAL LINK.
LUCAS IS INSIDE THE GAME. HE'S CONTROLLING HIS AVATAR LIKE IT WAS HIS OWN BODY.
ARE YOU SERIO—
HOODY FREAKIN' HOO! MEGADOOOOOOOOOOM!
WHOA!
MY MEGADOOM JUST ATE BEN'S GAMMA FURY FOR LUNCH. I'M SORRY, HIS GAMMA FURY 2.0.
I AM STILL IN THE TOURNAMENT!
SO AM I, NERDLING.

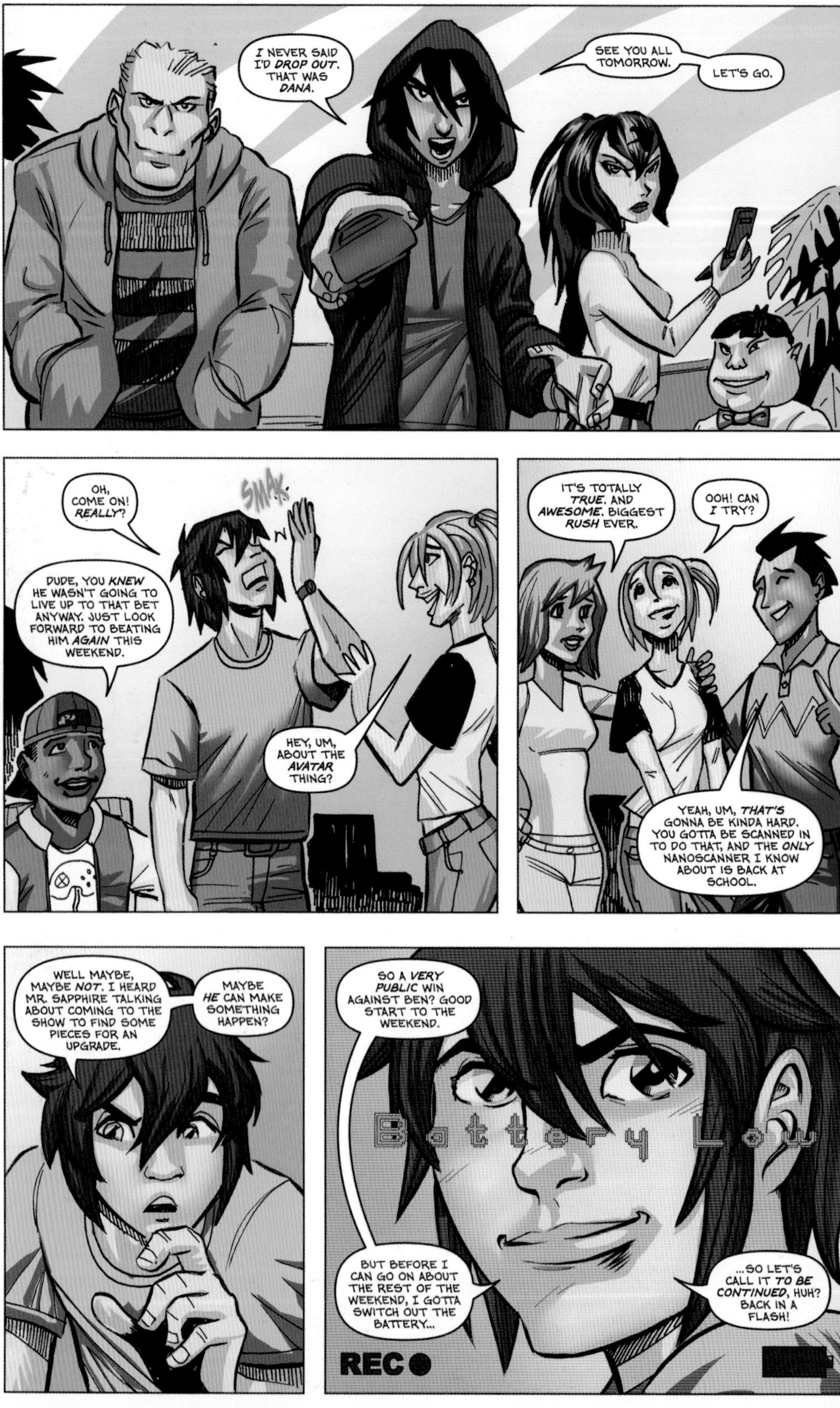

I NEVER SAID I'D DROP OUT. THAT WAS DANA.
SEE YOU ALL TOMORROW.
LET'S GO.
OH, COME ON! REALLY?
SMAK
DUDE, YOU KNEW HE WASN'T GOING TO LIVE UP TO THAT BET ANYWAY. JUST LOOK FORWARD TO BEATING HIM AGAIN THIS WEEKEND.
HEY, UM, ABOUT THE AVATAR THING?
IT'S TOTALLY TRUE. AND AWESOME. BIGGEST RUSH EVER.
OOH! CAN I TRY?
YEAH, UM, THAT'S GONNA BE KINDA HARD. YOU GOTTA BE SCANNED IN TO DO THAT, AND THE ONLY NANOSCANNER I KNOW ABOUT IS BACK AT SCHOOL.
WELL MAYBE, MAYBE NOT. I HEARD MR. SAPPHIRE TALKING ABOUT COMING TO THE SHOW TO FIND SOME PIECES FOR AN UPGRADE.
MAYBE HE CAN MAKE SOMETHING HAPPEN?
SO A VERY PUBLIC WIN AGAINST BEN? GOOD START TO THE WEEKEND.
Battery Low
BUT BEFORE I CAN GO ON ABOUT THE REST OF THE WEEKEND, I GOTTA SWITCH OUT THE BATTERY...
...SO LET'S CALL IT TO BE CONTINUED, HUH? BACK IN A FLASH!
REC

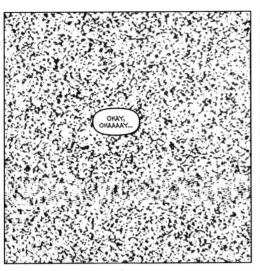

OKAY, OKAAAAY...

CHAPTER 2

...AND WE'RE BACK!

CHARGING

REC

OKEEDOKE, SO I HAD SOME FOOD—TACOS, WHICH WERE AWESOME—AND FOUND THE AC ADAPTER FOR THIS CAMERA, SO I CAN KEEP UP ON MY WEEKEND REPORT UNINTERRUPTED.

REC

SO FAR, MEGADOOM AND I SPANKED BEN ARNESON IN A BATTLE WHERE THE LOSER WAS SUPPOSED TO WALK FROM THE GAME TOURNEY.

I WON, BUT HE DIDN'T WALK. SHOCKER.

REC

ALSO, WE ALL MET DREW'S FRIEND JACKIE, WHO GOT SUPER-PSYCHED ABOUT THE NANOSPHERE.

REC

PROBLEM IS, SHE COULDN'T EXPLORE IT WITHOUT GETTING SCANNED IN, AND NANOSCANNERS AREN'T LIKE MCDONALD'S. THERE'S ONLY ONE.

REC

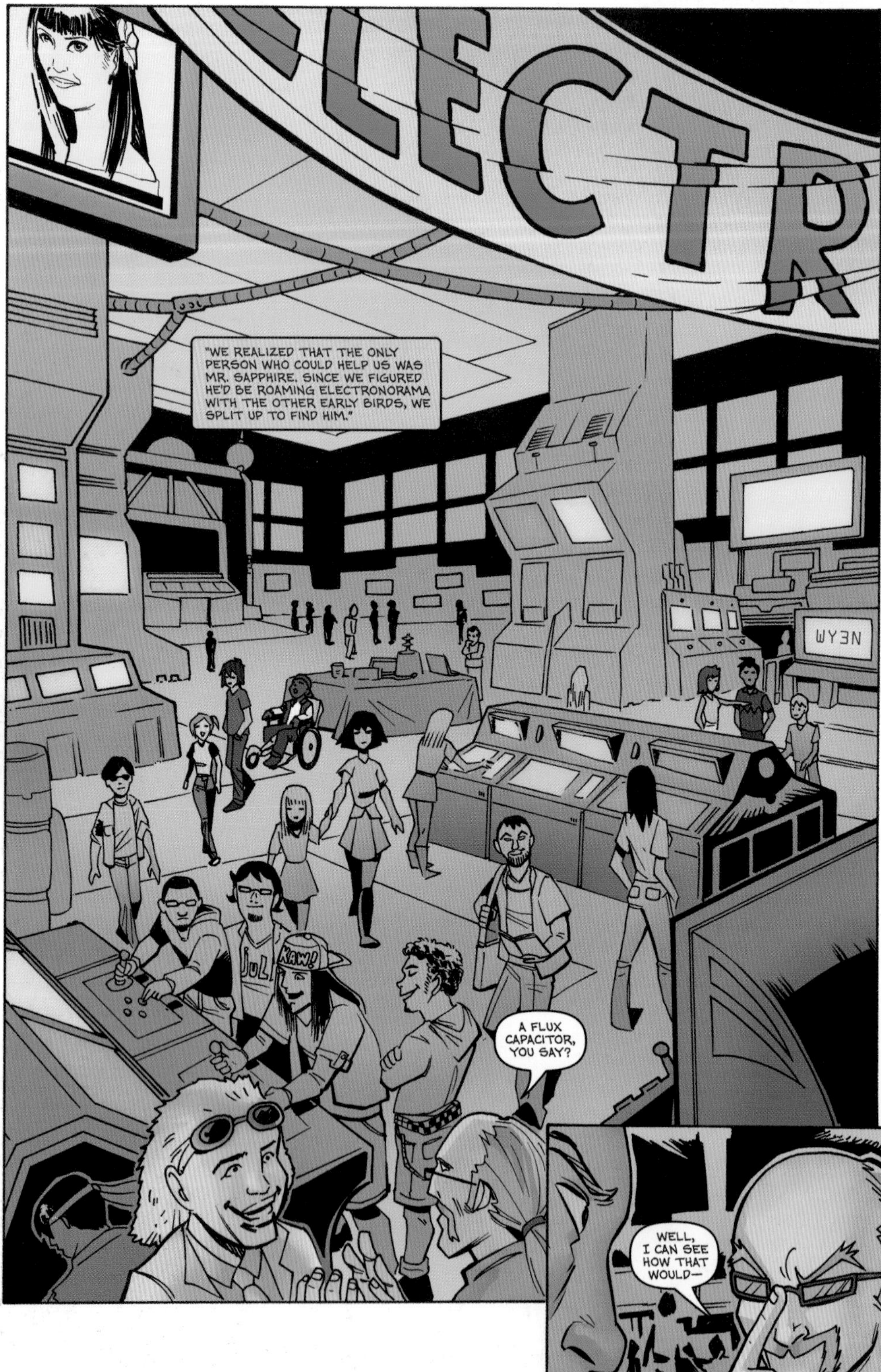
ELECTR
"WE REALIZED THAT THE ONLY PERSON WHO COULD HELP US WAS MR. SAPPHIRE. SINCE WE FIGURED HE'D BE ROAMING ELECTRONORAMA WITH THE OTHER EARLY BIRDS, WE SPLIT UP TO FIND HIM."
WY3N
JUL
KAW!
A FLUX CAPACITOR, YOU SAY?
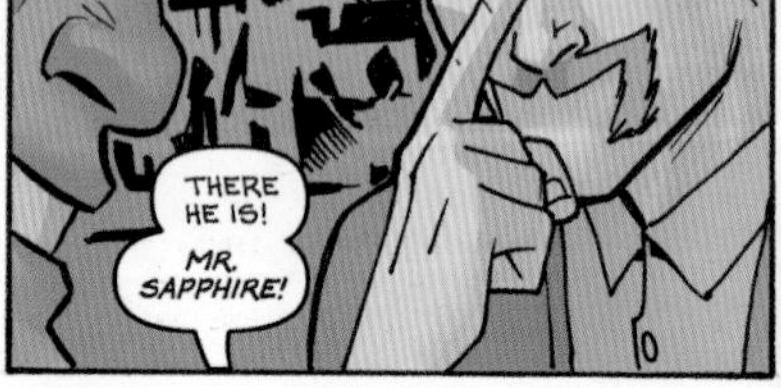
WELL, I CAN SEE HOW THAT WOULD—
THERE HE IS! MR. SAPPHIRE!

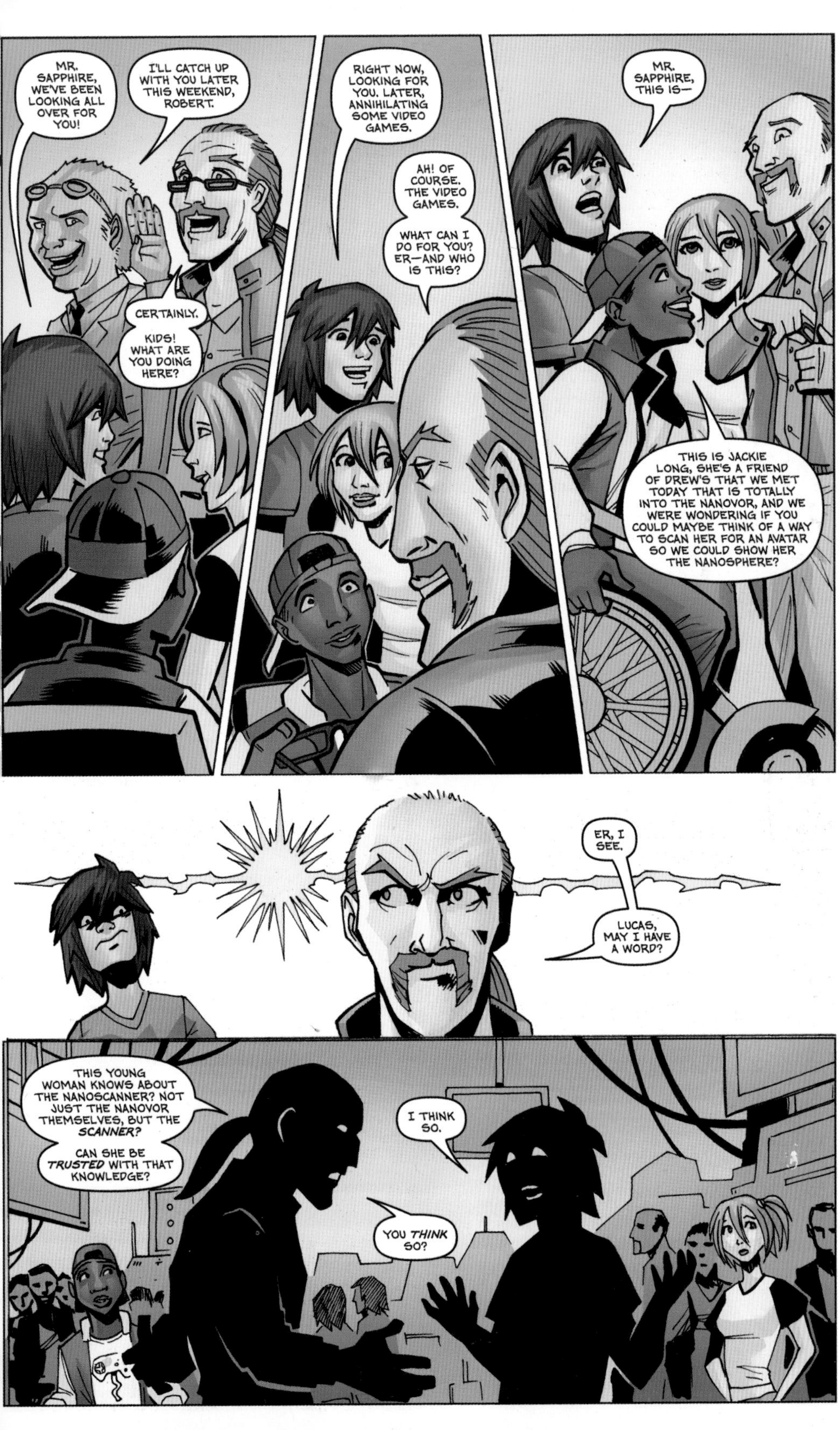
MR. SAPPHIRE, WE'VE BEEN LOOKING ALL OVER FOR YOU!
I'LL CATCH UP WITH YOU LATER THIS WEEKEND, ROBERT.
CERTAINLY.
KIDS! WHAT ARE YOU DOING HERE?
RIGHT NOW, LOOKING FOR YOU. LATER, ANNIHILATING SOME VIDEO GAMES.
AH! OF COURSE. THE VIDEO GAMES.
WHAT CAN I DO FOR YOU? ER—AND WHO IS THIS?
MR. SAPPHIRE, THIS IS—
THIS IS JACKIE LONG, SHE'S A FRIEND OF DREW'S THAT WE MET TODAY THAT IS TOTALLY INTO THE NANOVOR, AND WE WERE WONDERING IF YOU COULD MAYBE THINK OF A WAY TO SCAN HER FOR AN AVATAR SO WE COULD SHOW HER THE NANOSPHERE?
ER, I SEE.
LUCAS, MAY I HAVE A WORD?
THIS YOUNG WOMAN KNOWS ABOUT THE NANOSCANNER? NOT JUST THE NANOVOR THEMSELVES, BUT THE *SCANNER?*
CAN SHE BE *TRUSTED* WITH THAT KNOWLEDGE?
I THINK SO.
YOU *THINK* SO?

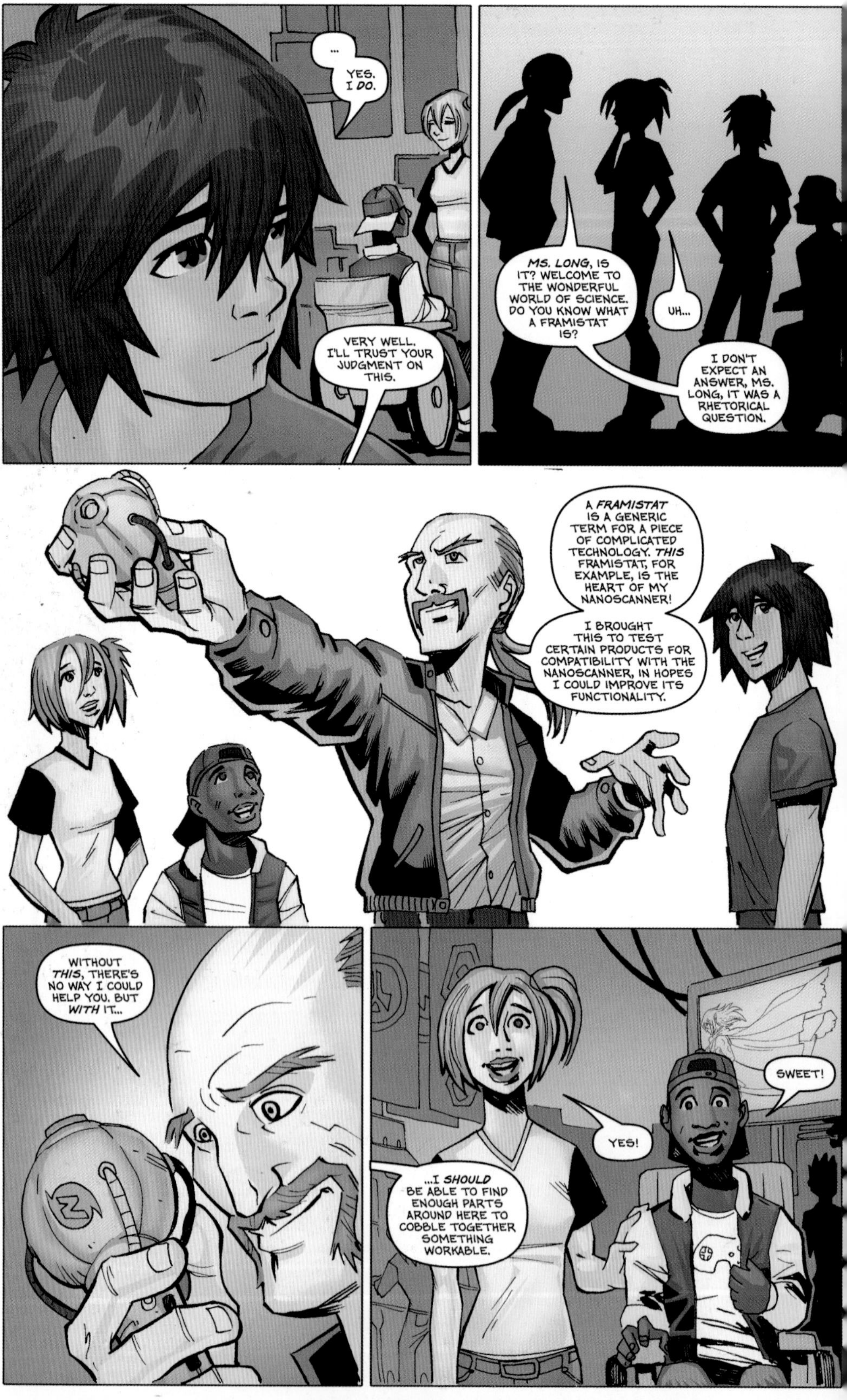
...
YES. I DO.
VERY WELL. I'LL TRUST YOUR JUDGMENT ON THIS.
MS. LONG, IS IT? WELCOME TO THE WONDERFUL WORLD OF SCIENCE. DO YOU KNOW WHAT A FRAMISTAT IS?
UH...
I DON'T EXPECT AN ANSWER, MS. LONG, IT WAS A RHETORICAL QUESTION.
A FRAMISTAT IS A GENERIC TERM FOR A PIECE OF COMPLICATED TECHNOLOGY. THIS FRAMISTAT, FOR EXAMPLE, IS THE HEART OF MY NANOSCANNER!
I BROUGHT THIS TO TEST CERTAIN PRODUCTS FOR COMPATIBILITY WITH THE NANOSCANNER, IN HOPES I COULD IMPROVE ITS FUNCTIONALITY.
WITHOUT THIS, THERE'S NO WAY I COULD HELP YOU. BUT WITH IT...
...I SHOULD BE ABLE TO FIND ENOUGH PARTS AROUND HERE TO COBBLE TOGETHER SOMETHING WORKABLE.
YES!
SWEET!

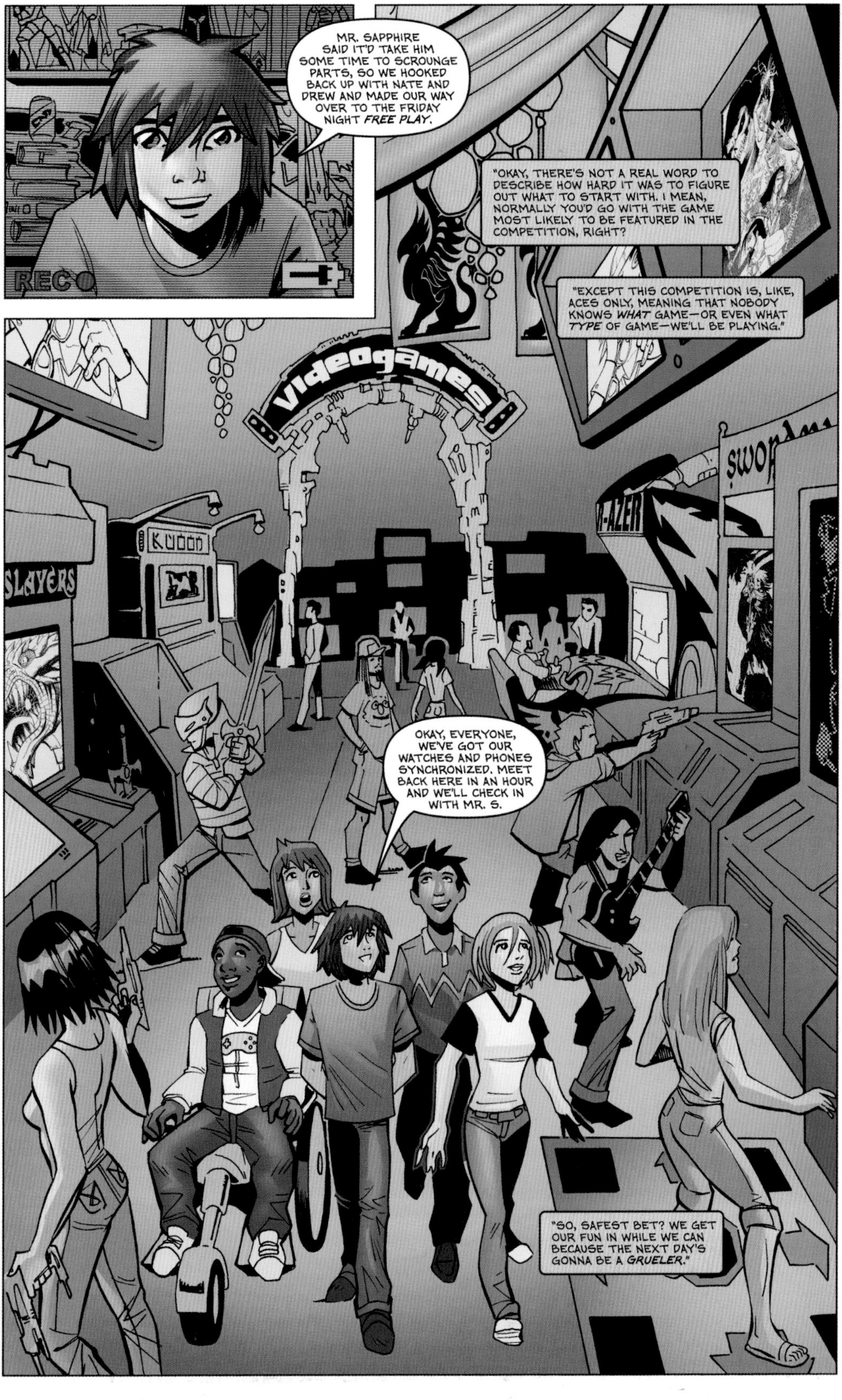
RECO
MR. SAPPHIRE SAID IT'D TAKE HIM SOME TIME TO SCROUNGE PARTS, SO WE HOOKED BACK UP WITH NATE AND DREW AND MADE OUR WAY OVER TO THE FRIDAY NIGHT *FREE PLAY*.
"OKAY, THERE'S NOT A REAL WORD TO DESCRIBE HOW HARD IT WAS TO FIGURE OUT WHAT TO START WITH. I MEAN, NORMALLY YOU'D GO WITH THE GAME MOST LIKELY TO BE FEATURED IN THE COMPETITION, RIGHT?
"EXCEPT THIS COMPETITION IS, LIKE, ACES ONLY, MEANING THAT NOBODY KNOWS *WHAT* GAME—OR EVEN WHAT *TYPE* OF GAME—WE'LL BE PLAYING."
Videogames
SLAYERS
OKAY, EVERYONE, WE'VE GOT OUR WATCHES AND PHONES SYNCHRONIZED. MEET BACK HERE IN AN HOUR AND WE'LL CHECK IN WITH MR. S.
"SO, SAFEST BET? WE GET OUR FUN IN WHILE WE CAN BECAUSE THE NEXT DAY'S GONNA BE A *GRUELER*."

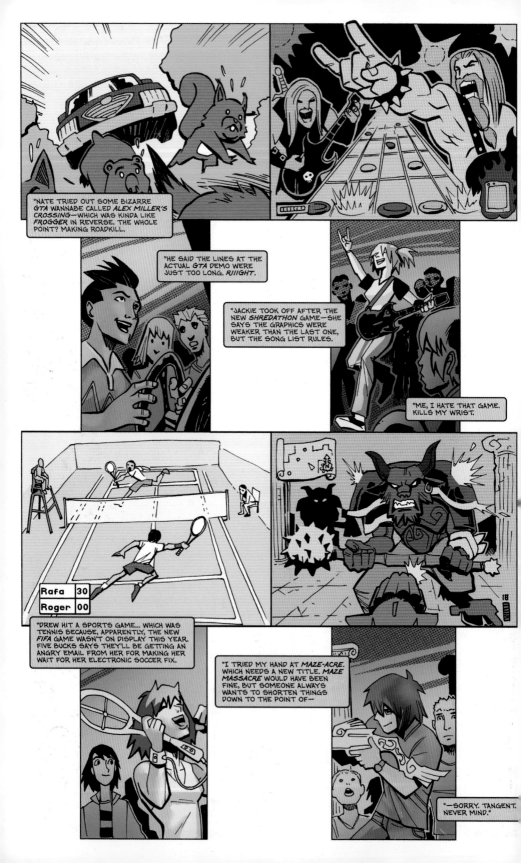

"NATE TRIED OUT SOME BIZARRE *GTA* WANNABE CALLED *ALEX MILLER'S CROSSING*—WHICH WAS KINDA LIKE *FROGGER* IN REVERSE. THE WHOLE POINT? MAKING ROADKILL.

"HE SAID THE LINES AT THE ACTUAL *GTA* DEMO WERE JUST TOO LONG. RIIIGHT.

"JACKIE TOOK OFF AFTER THE NEW *SHREDATHON* GAME—SHE SAYS THE GRAPHICS WERE WEAKER THAN THE LAST ONE, BUT THE SONG LIST RULES.

"ME, I HATE THAT GAME. KILLS MY WRIST.

Rafa | 30
Roger | 00

"DREW HIT A SPORTS GAME... WHICH WAS TENNIS BECAUSE, APPARENTLY, THE NEW *FIFA* GAME WASN'T ON DISPLAY THIS YEAR. FIVE BUCKS SAYS THEY'LL BE GETTING AN ANGRY EMAIL FROM HER FOR MAKING HER WAIT FOR HER ELECTRONIC SOCCER FIX.

"I TRIED MY HAND AT *MAZE-ACRE*. WHICH NEEDS A NEW TITLE. *MAZE MASSACRE* WOULD HAVE BEEN FINE, BUT SOMEONE ALWAYS WANTS TO SHORTEN THINGS DOWN TO THE POINT OF—

"—SORRY. TANGENT. NEVER MIND."

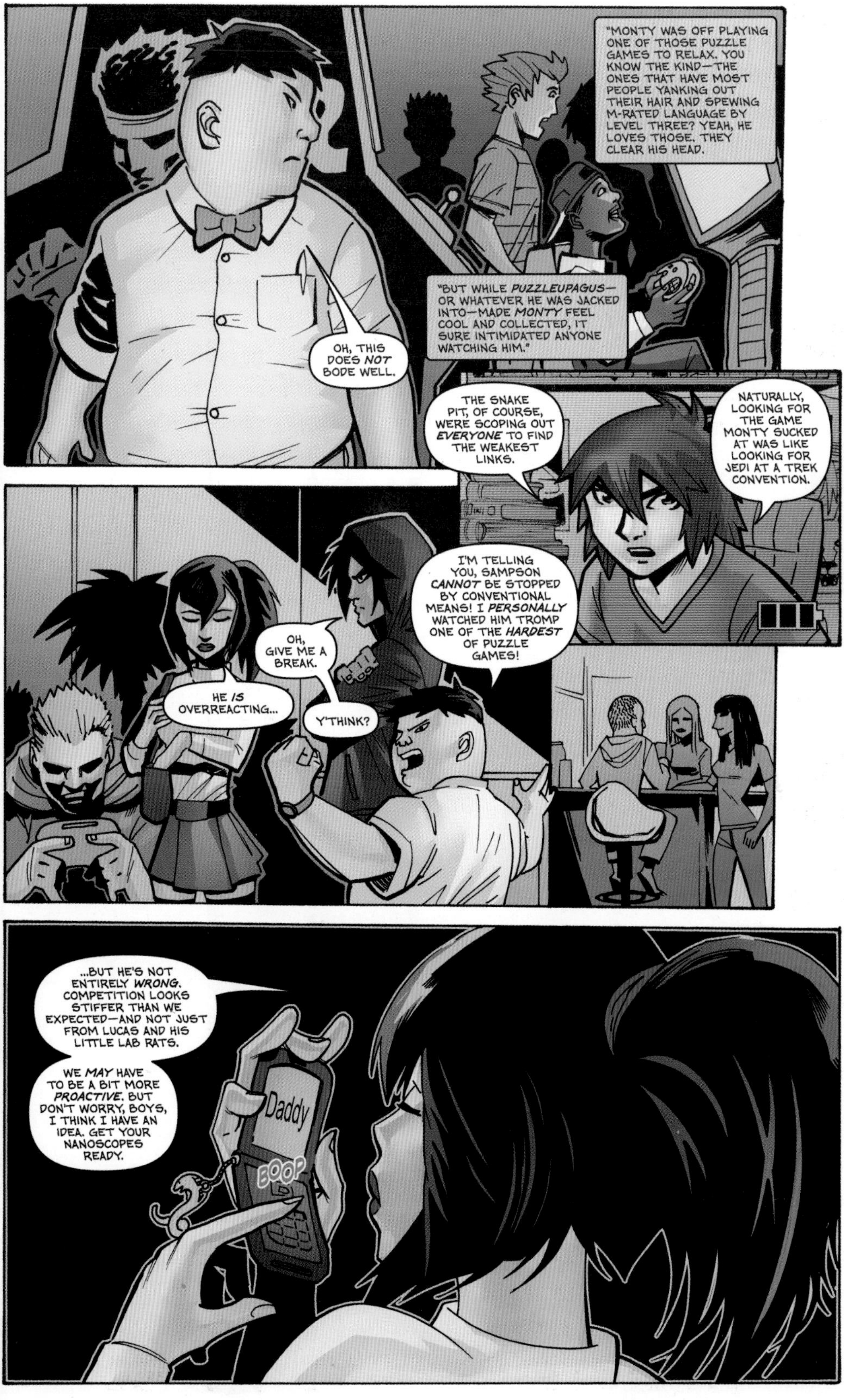
"MONTY WAS OFF PLAYING ONE OF THOSE PUZZLE GAMES TO RELAX. YOU KNOW THE KIND—THE ONES THAT HAVE MOST PEOPLE YANKING OUT THEIR HAIR AND SPEWING M-RATED LANGUAGE BY LEVEL THREE? YEAH, HE LOVES THOSE. THEY CLEAR HIS HEAD.
"BUT WHILE PUZZLEUPAGUS—OR WHATEVER HE WAS JACKED INTO—MADE MONTY FEEL COOL AND COLLECTED, IT SURE INTIMIDATED ANYONE WATCHING HIM."
OH, THIS DOES NOT BODE WELL.
THE SNAKE PIT, OF COURSE, WERE SCOPING OUT EVERYONE TO FIND THE WEAKEST LINKS.
NATURALLY, LOOKING FOR THE GAME MONTY SUCKED AT WAS LIKE LOOKING FOR JEDI AT A TREK CONVENTION.
I'M TELLING YOU, SAMPSON CANNOT BE STOPPED BY CONVENTIONAL MEANS! I PERSONALLY WATCHED HIM TROMP ONE OF THE HARDEST OF PUZZLE GAMES!
OH, GIVE ME A BREAK.
HE IS OVERREACTING...
Y'THINK?
...BUT HE'S NOT ENTIRELY WRONG. COMPETITION LOOKS STIFFER THAN WE EXPECTED—AND NOT JUST FROM LUCAS AND HIS LITTLE LAB RATS.
WE MAY HAVE TO BE A BIT MORE PROACTIVE. BUT DON'T WORRY, BOYS, I THINK I HAVE AN IDEA. GET YOUR NANOSCOPES READY.
Daddy
BOOP

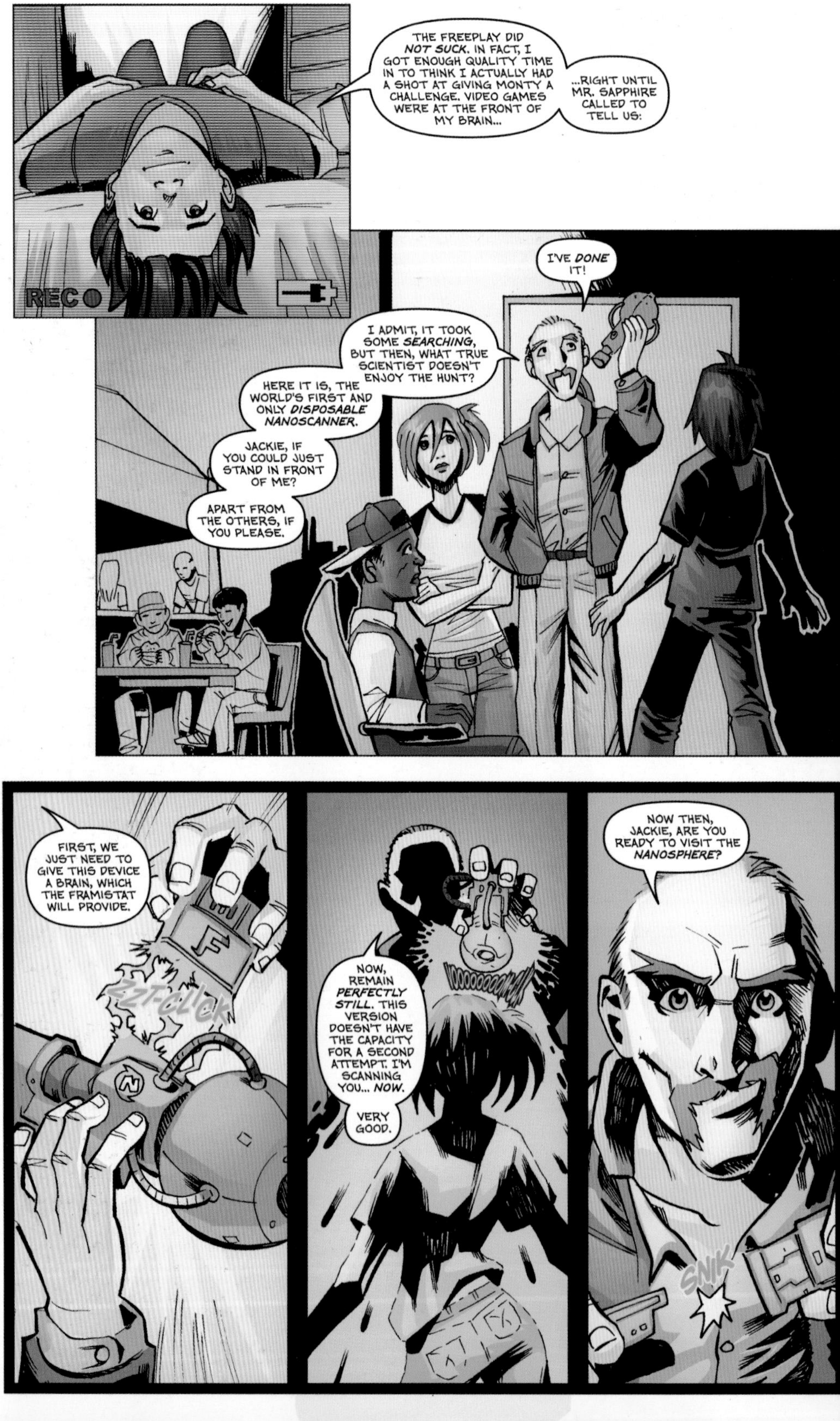

REC
THE FREEPLAY DID *NOT SUCK*. IN FACT, I GOT ENOUGH QUALITY TIME IN TO THINK I ACTUALLY HAD A SHOT AT GIVING MONTY A CHALLENGE. VIDEO GAMES WERE AT THE FRONT OF MY BRAIN...
...RIGHT UNTIL MR. SAPPHIRE CALLED TO TELL US:
I'VE *DONE* IT!
I ADMIT, IT TOOK SOME *SEARCHING*, BUT THEN, WHAT TRUE SCIENTIST DOESN'T ENJOY THE HUNT?
HERE IT IS, THE WORLD'S FIRST AND ONLY *DISPOSABLE NANOSCANNER*.
JACKIE, IF YOU COULD JUST STAND IN FRONT OF ME?
APART FROM THE OTHERS, IF YOU PLEASE.
FIRST, WE JUST NEED TO GIVE THIS DEVICE A BRAIN, WHICH THE FRAMISTAT WILL PROVIDE.
ZZT-CLICK
NOW, REMAIN *PERFECTLY STILL*. THIS VERSION DOESN'T HAVE THE CAPACITY FOR A SECOND ATTEMPT. I'M SCANNING YOU... *NOW*.
VERY GOOD.
NOW THEN, JACKIE, ARE YOU READY TO VISIT THE *NANOSPHERE*?
SNIK

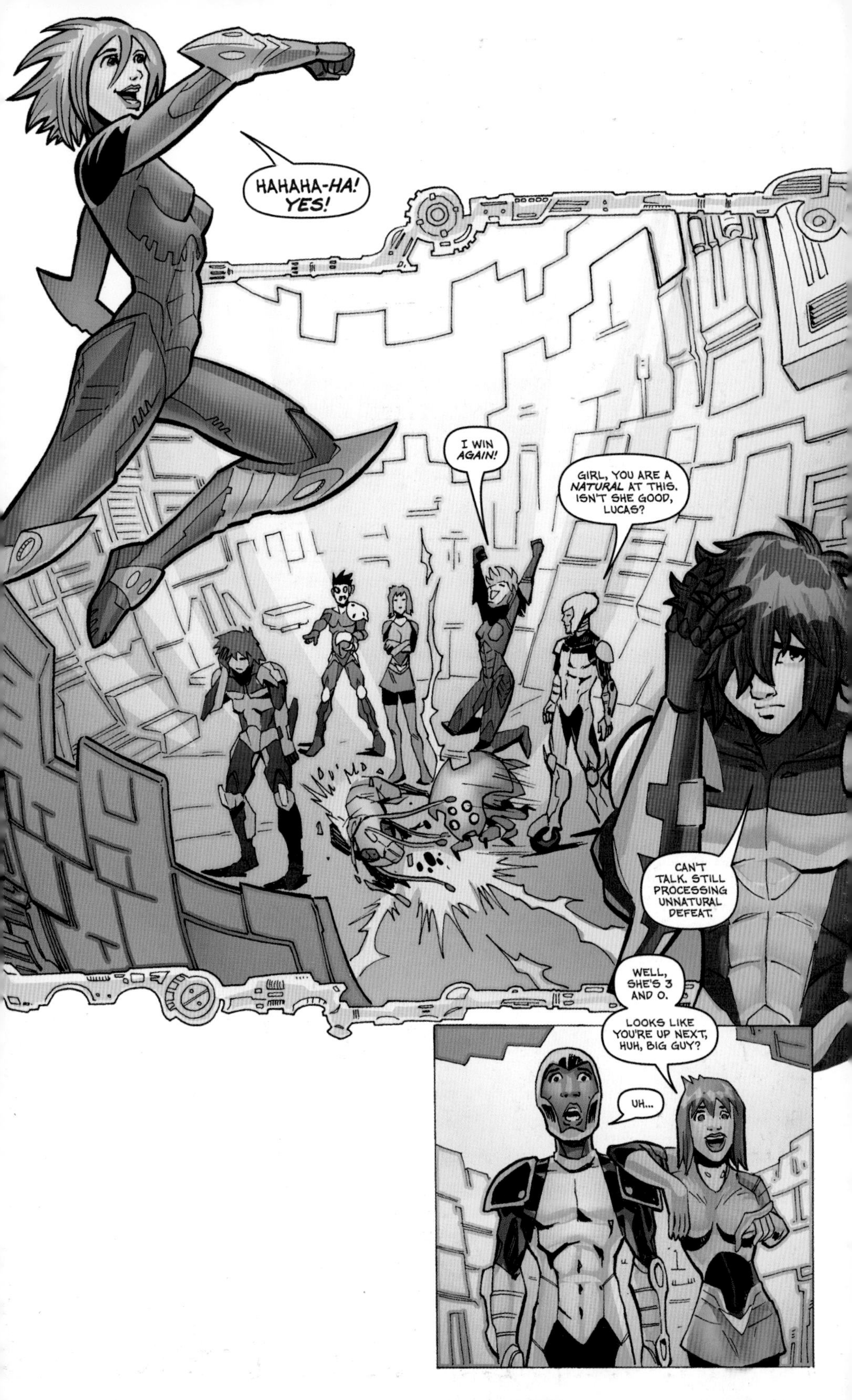
HAHAHA-HA! YES!
I WIN AGAIN!
GIRL, YOU ARE A NATURAL AT THIS. ISN'T SHE GOOD, LUCAS?
CAN'T TALK. STILL PROCESSING UNNATURAL DEFEAT.
WELL, SHE'S 3 AND 0.
LOOKS LIKE YOU'RE UP NEXT, HUH, BIG GUY?
UH...

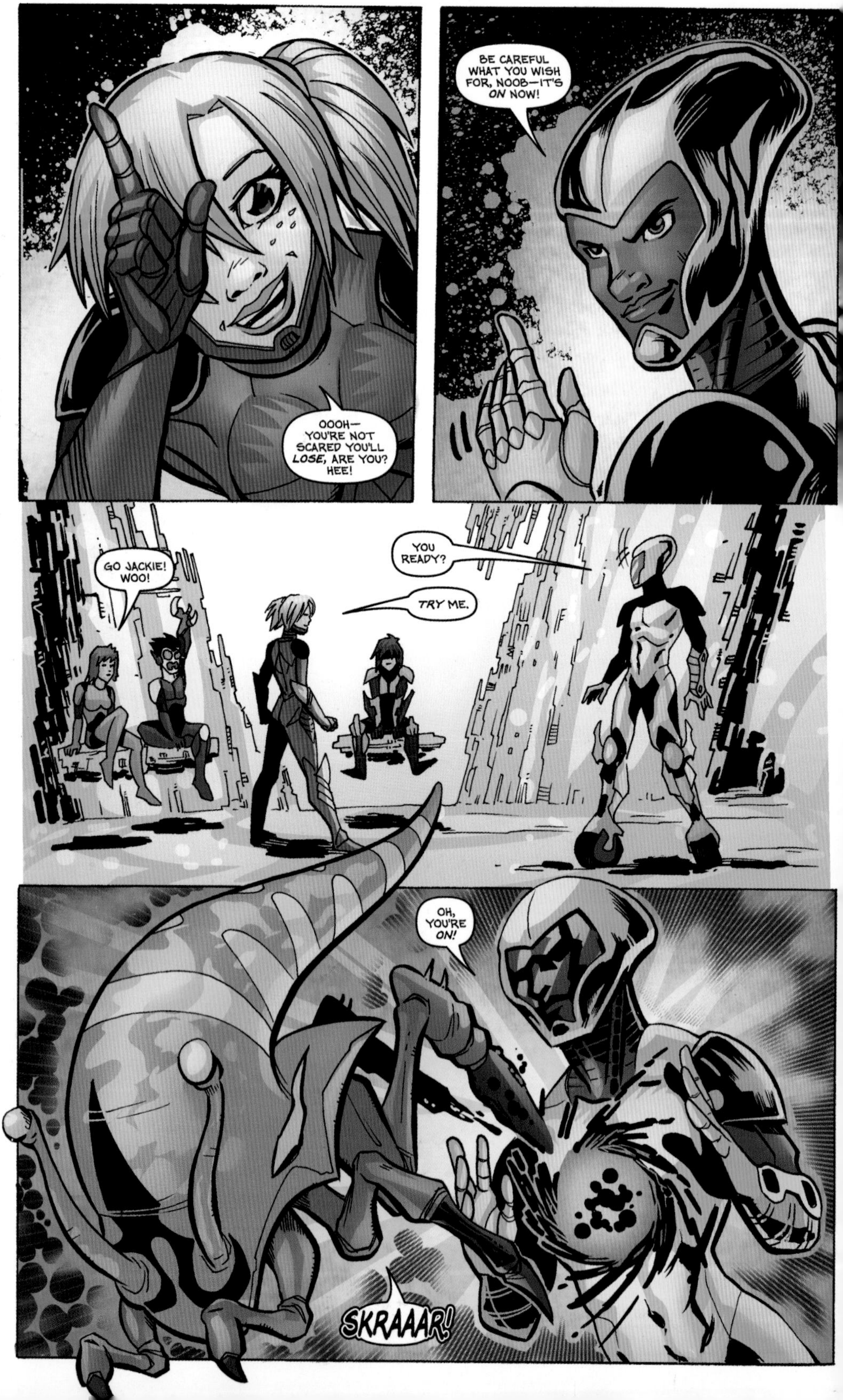
OOOH— YOU'RE NOT SCARED YOU'LL LOSE, ARE YOU? HEE!
BE CAREFUL WHAT YOU WISH FOR, NOOB—IT'S ON NOW!
GO JACKIE! WOO!
YOU READY?
TRY ME.
OH, YOU'RE ON!
SKRAAAR!

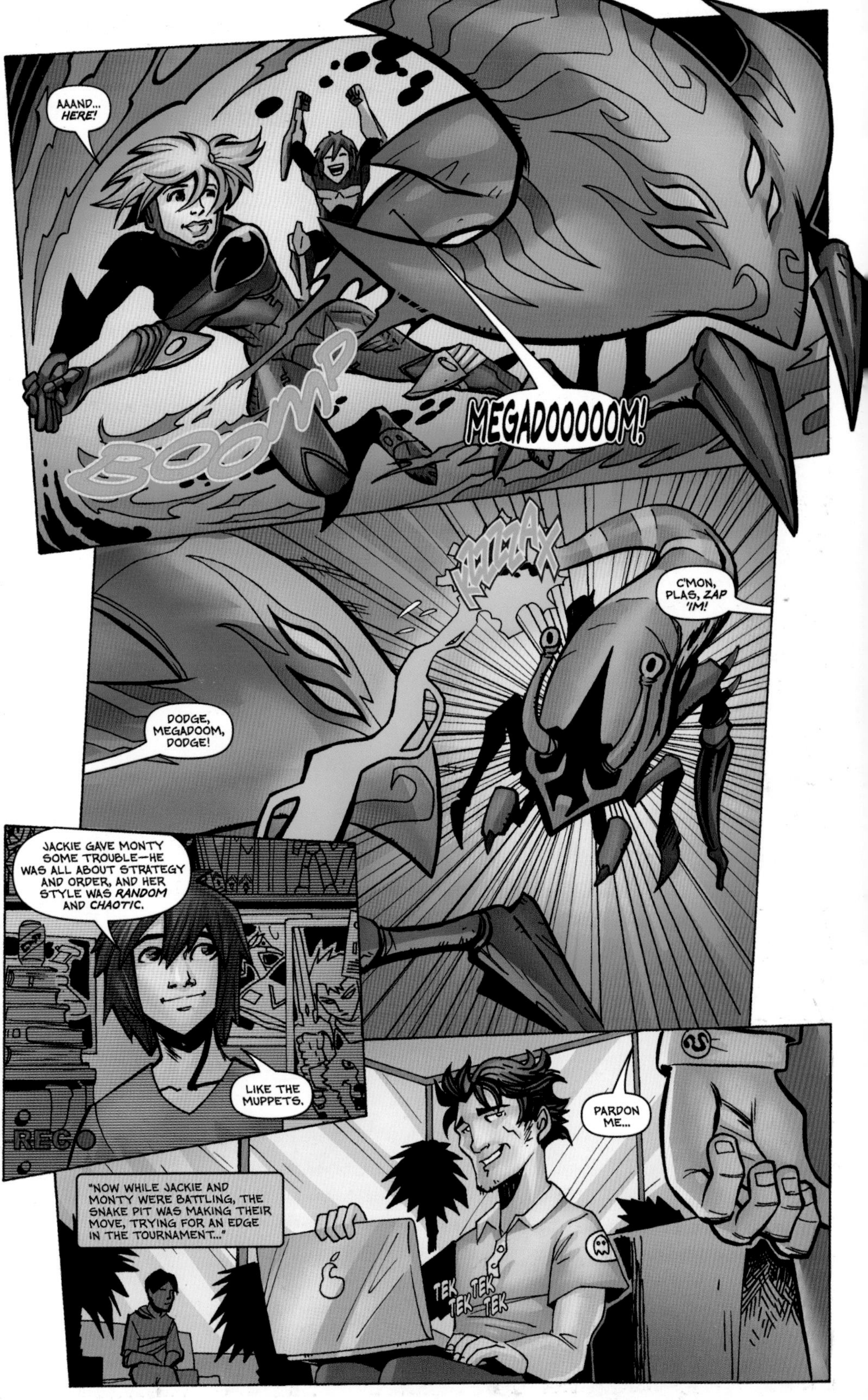
AAAND... HERE!
BOOMP
MEGADOOOOOM!
ZZZZAX
C'MON, PLAS, ZAP 'IM!
DODGE, MEGADOOM, DODGE!
JACKIE GAVE MONTY SOME TROUBLE—HE WAS ALL ABOUT STRATEGY AND ORDER, AND HER STYLE WAS RANDOM AND CHAOTIC.
LIKE THE MUPPETS.
REC
PARDON ME...
"NOW WHILE JACKIE AND MONTY WERE BATTLING, THE SNAKE PIT WAS MAKING THEIR MOVE, TRYING FOR AN EDGE IN THE TOURNAMENT..."
TEK TEK TEK TEK

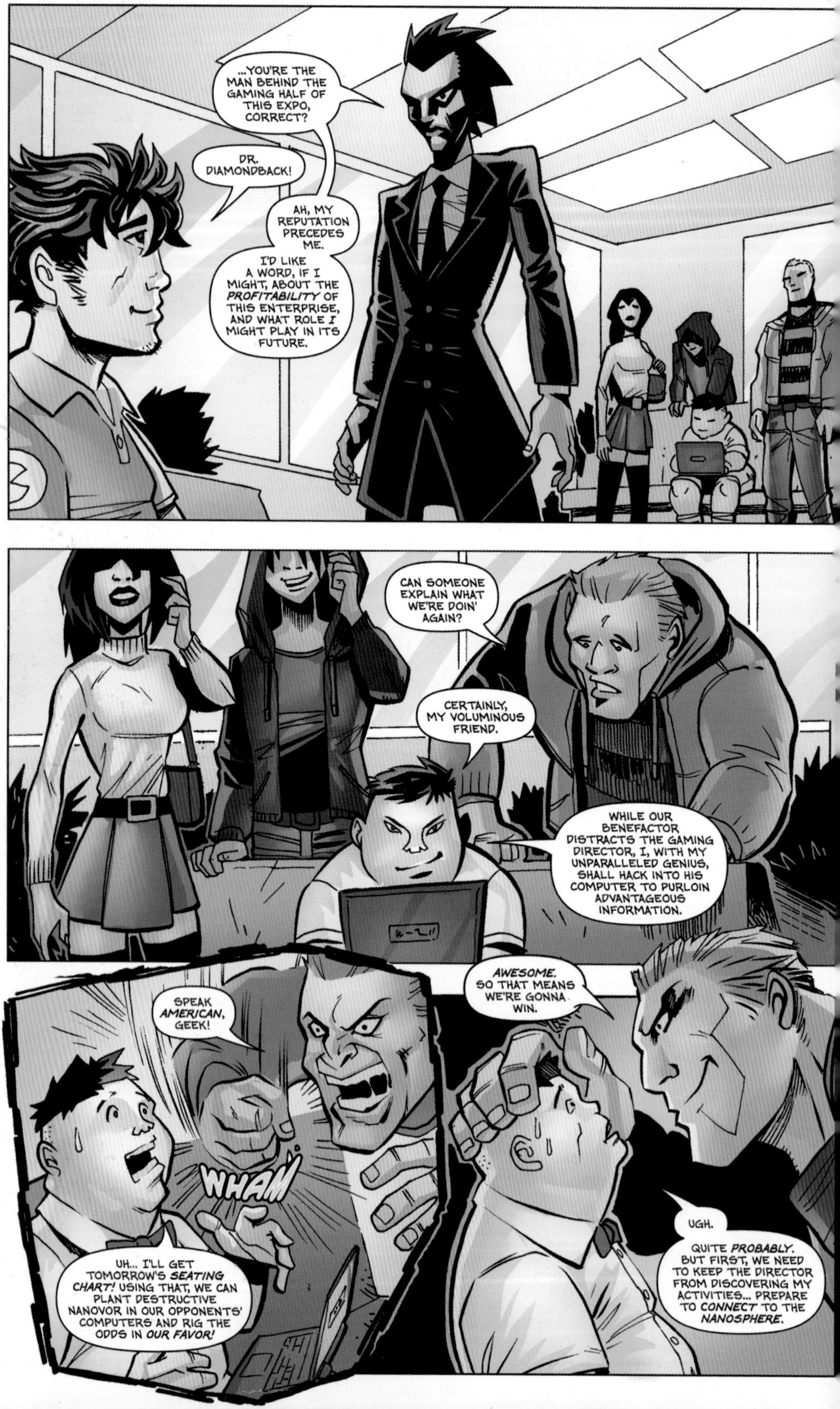
...YOU'RE THE MAN BEHIND THE GAMING HALF OF THIS EXPO, CORRECT?
DR. DIAMONDBACK!
AH, MY REPUTATION PRECEDES ME.
I'D LIKE A WORD, IF I MIGHT, ABOUT THE *PROFITABILITY* OF THIS ENTERPRISE, AND WHAT ROLE *I* MIGHT PLAY IN ITS FUTURE.
CAN SOMEONE EXPLAIN WHAT WE'RE DOIN' AGAIN?
CERTAINLY, MY VOLUMINOUS FRIEND.
WHILE OUR BENEFACTOR DISTRACTS THE GAMING DIRECTOR, I, WITH MY UNPARALLELED GENIUS, SHALL HACK INTO HIS COMPUTER TO PURLOIN ADVANTAGEOUS INFORMATION.
SPEAK *AMERICAN*, GEEK!
WHAM
UH... I'LL GET TOMORROW'S *SEATING CHART!* USING THAT, WE CAN PLANT DESTRUCTIVE NANOVOR IN OUR OPPONENTS' COMPUTERS AND RIG THE ODDS IN *OUR FAVOR!*
AWESOME. SO THAT MEANS WE'RE GONNA WIN.
UGH.
QUITE *PROBABLY*. BUT FIRST, WE NEED TO KEEP THE DIRECTOR FROM DISCOVERING MY ACTIVITIES... PREPARE TO *CONNECT* TO THE *NANOSPHERE*.

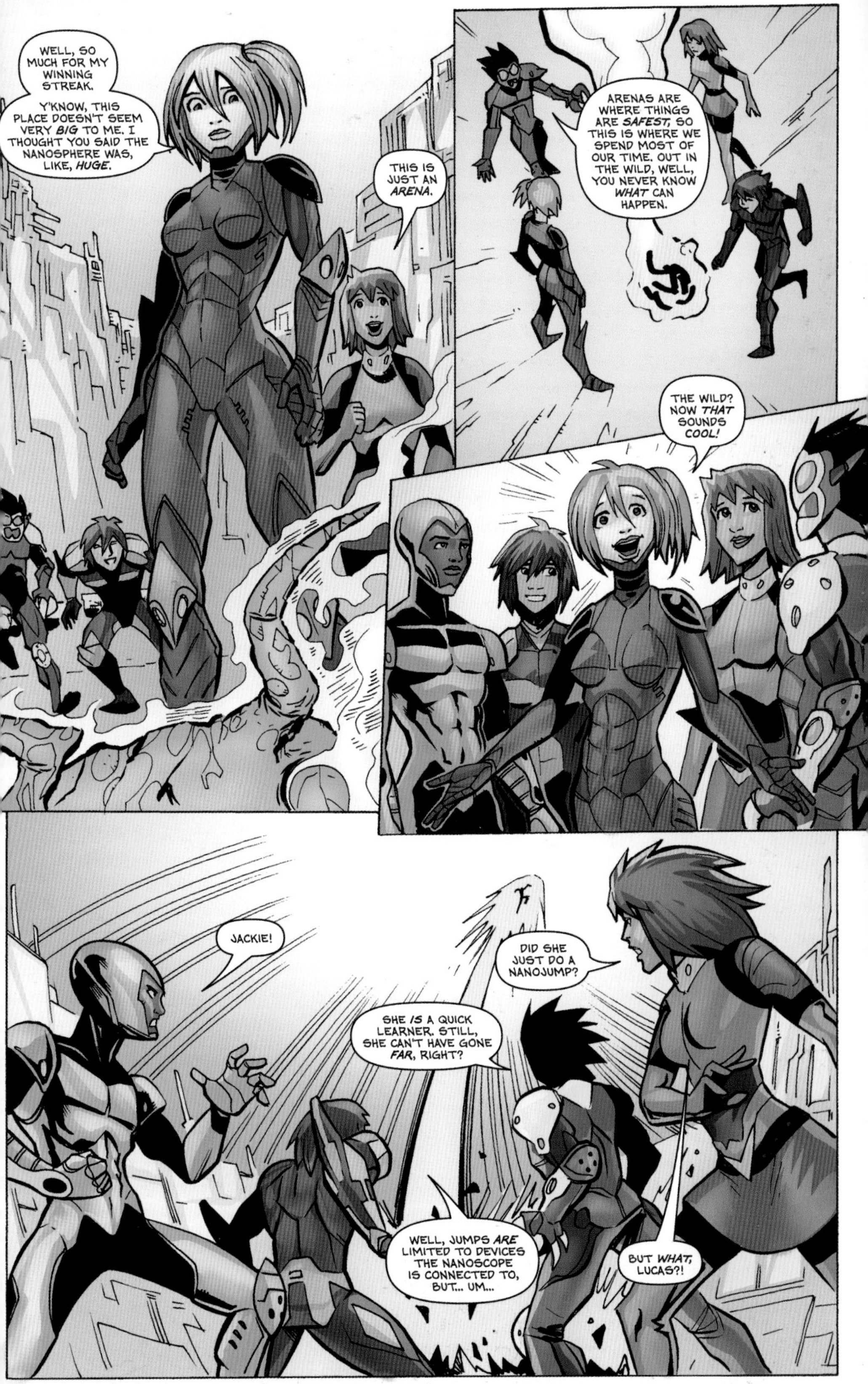
WELL, SO MUCH FOR MY WINNING STREAK.
Y'KNOW, THIS PLACE DOESN'T SEEM VERY BIG TO ME. I THOUGHT YOU SAID THE NANOSPHERE WAS, LIKE, HUGE.
THIS IS JUST AN ARENA.
ARENAS ARE WHERE THINGS ARE SAFEST, SO THIS IS WHERE WE SPEND MOST OF OUR TIME. OUT IN THE WILD, WELL, YOU NEVER KNOW WHAT CAN HAPPEN.
THE WILD? NOW THAT SOUNDS COOL!
JACKIE!
DID SHE JUST DO A NANOJUMP?
SHE IS A QUICK LEARNER. STILL, SHE CAN'T HAVE GONE FAR, RIGHT?
WELL, JUMPS ARE LIMITED TO DEVICES THE NANOSCOPE IS CONNECTED TO, BUT... UM...
BUT WHAT, LUCAS?!

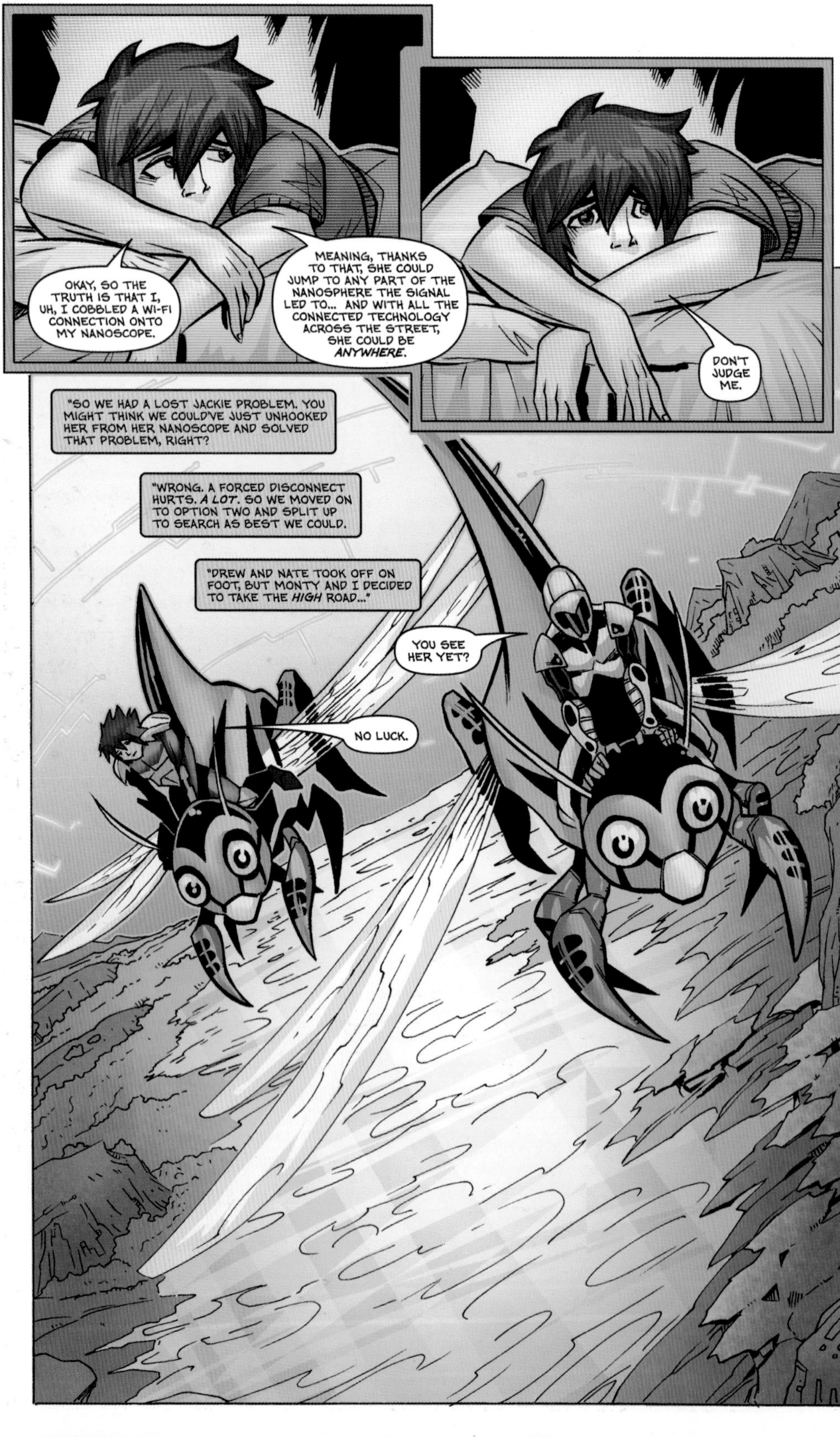
OKAY, SO THE TRUTH IS THAT I, UH, I COBBLED A WI-FI CONNECTION ONTO MY NANOSCOPE.
MEANING, THANKS TO THAT, SHE COULD JUMP TO ANY PART OF THE NANOSPHERE THE SIGNAL LED TO... AND WITH ALL THE CONNECTED TECHNOLOGY ACROSS THE STREET, SHE COULD BE *ANYWHERE*.
DON'T JUDGE ME.
"SO WE HAD A LOST JACKIE PROBLEM. YOU MIGHT THINK WE COULD'VE JUST UNHOOKED HER FROM HER NANOSCOPE AND SOLVED THAT PROBLEM, RIGHT?
"WRONG. A FORCED DISCONNECT HURTS. *A LOT*. SO WE MOVED ON TO OPTION TWO AND SPLIT UP TO SEARCH AS BEST WE COULD.
"DREW AND NATE TOOK OFF ON FOOT, BUT MONTY AND I DECIDED TO TAKE THE *HIGH* ROAD..."
YOU SEE HER YET?
NO LUCK.

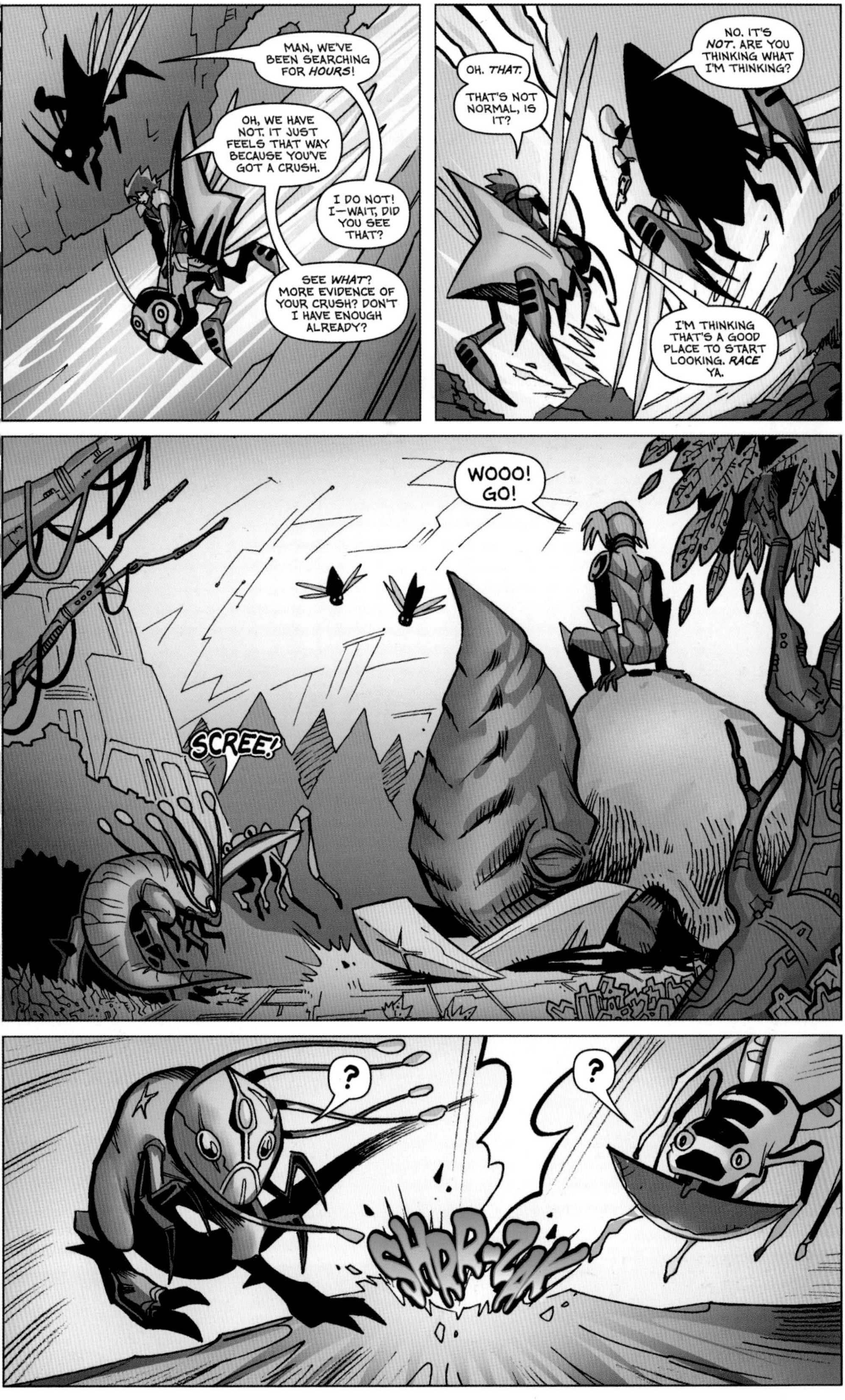
MAN, WE'VE BEEN SEARCHING FOR *HOURS*!
OH, WE HAVE NOT. IT JUST FEELS THAT WAY BECAUSE YOU'VE GOT A CRUSH.
I DO NOT! I—WAIT, DID YOU SEE THAT?
SEE *WHAT*? MORE EVIDENCE OF YOUR CRUSH? DON'T I HAVE ENOUGH ALREADY?
OH. *THAT.*
THAT'S NOT NORMAL, IS IT?
NO, IT'S *NOT*. ARE YOU THINKING WHAT I'M THINKING?
I'M THINKING THAT'S A GOOD PLACE TO START LOOKING. *RACE* YA.
WOOO! GO!
SCREE!
?
?
SHRR-ZAK

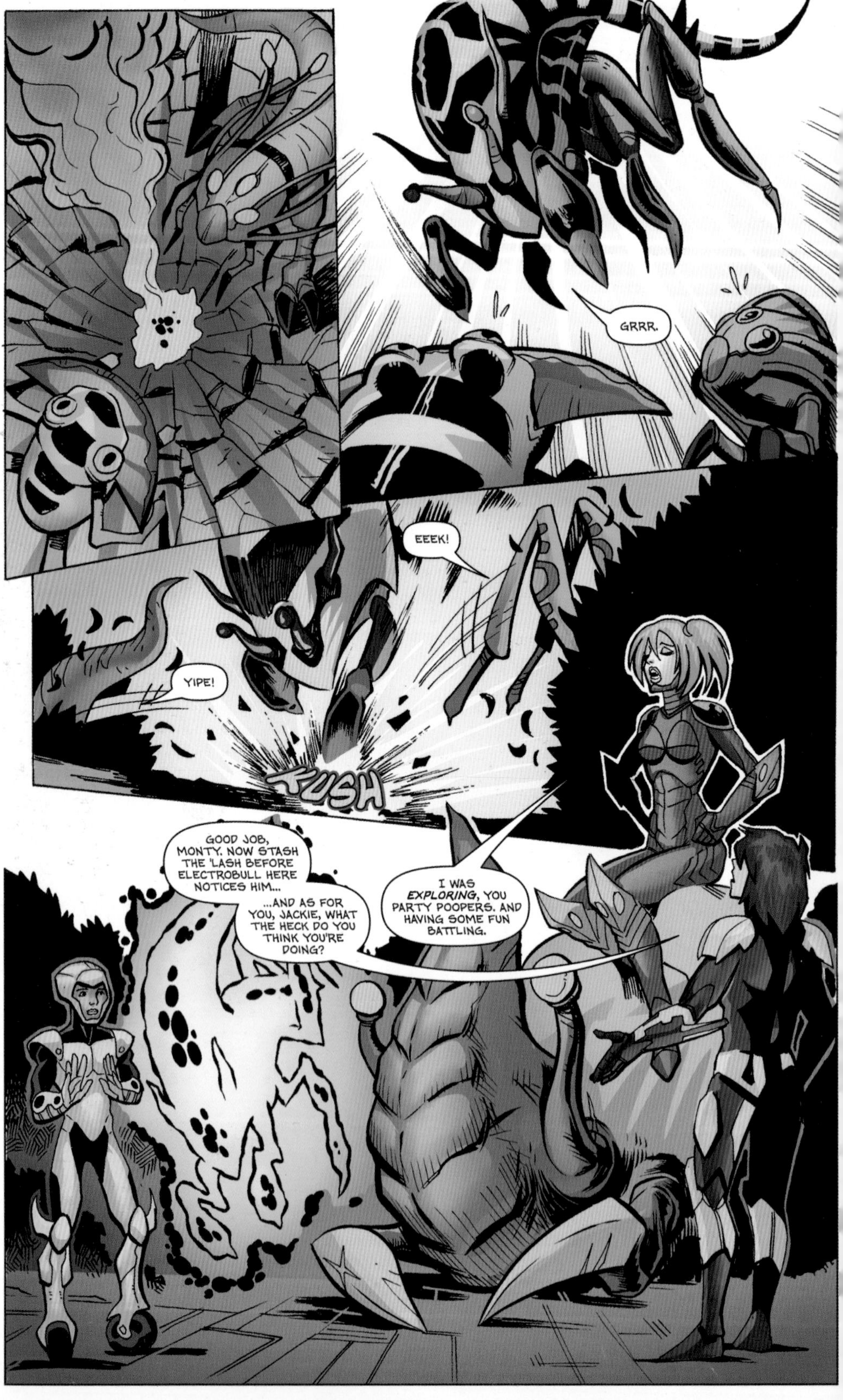
GRRR.
EEEK!
YIPE!
KUSH
GOOD JOB, MONTY. NOW STASH THE 'LASH BEFORE ELECTROBULL HERE NOTICES HIM...
...AND AS FOR YOU, JACKIE, WHAT THE HECK DO YOU THINK YOU'RE DOING?
I WAS *EXPLORING*, YOU PARTY POOPERS. AND HAVING SOME FUN BATTLING.

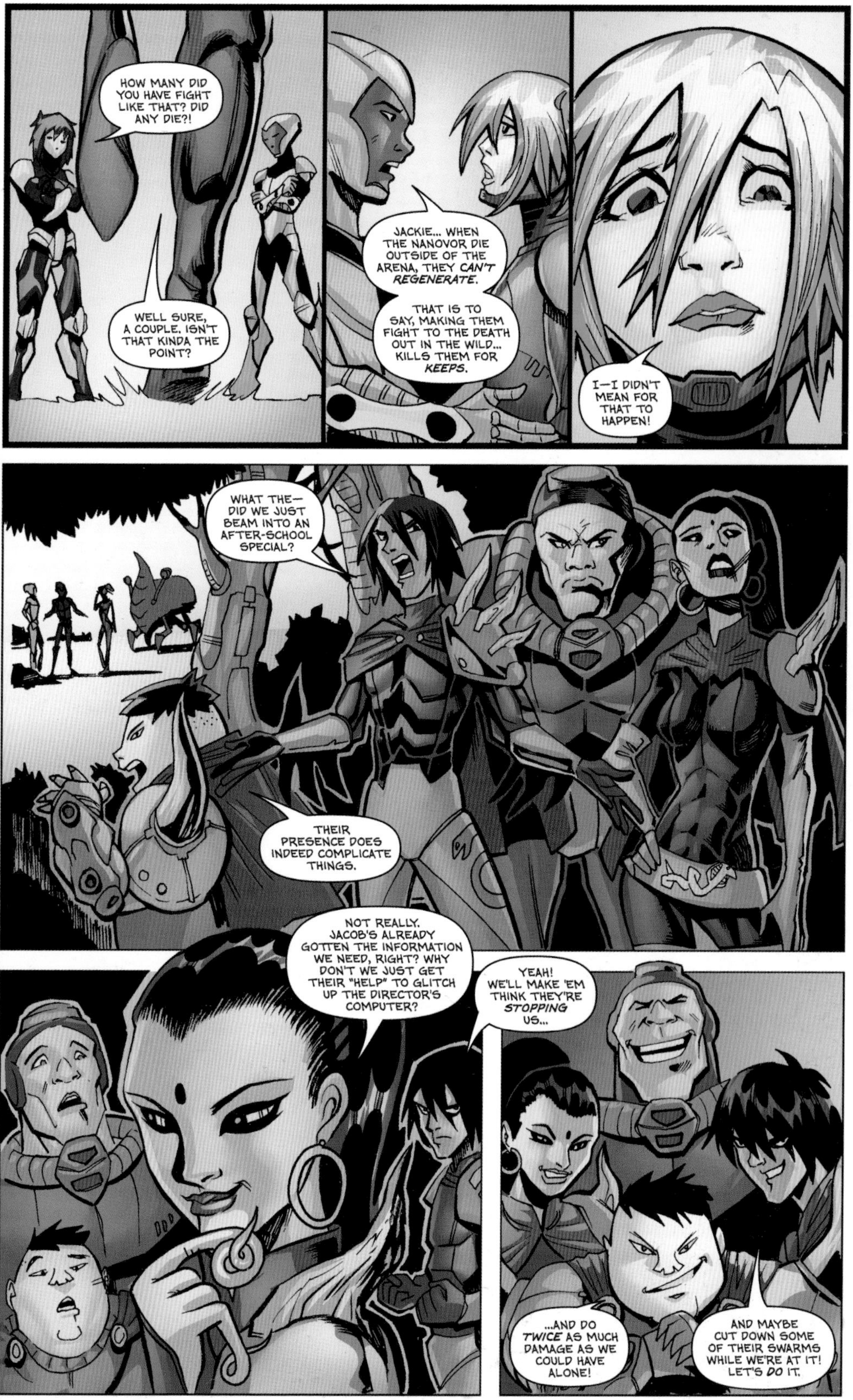

HOW MANY DID YOU HAVE FIGHT LIKE THAT? DID ANY DIE?!
WELL SURE, A COUPLE. ISN'T THAT KINDA THE POINT?
JACKIE... WHEN THE NANOVOR DIE OUTSIDE OF THE ARENA, THEY CAN'T REGENERATE.
THAT IS TO SAY, MAKING THEM FIGHT TO THE DEATH OUT IN THE WILD... KILLS THEM FOR KEEPS.
I—I DIDN'T MEAN FOR THAT TO HAPPEN!
WHAT THE— DID WE JUST BEAM INTO AN AFTER-SCHOOL SPECIAL?
THEIR PRESENCE DOES INDEED COMPLICATE THINGS.
NOT REALLY. JACOB'S ALREADY GOTTEN THE INFORMATION WE NEED, RIGHT? WHY DON'T WE JUST GET THEIR "HELP" TO GLITCH UP THE DIRECTOR'S COMPUTER?
YEAH! WE'LL MAKE 'EM THINK THEY'RE STOPPING US...
...AND DO TWICE AS MUCH DAMAGE AS WE COULD HAVE ALONE!
AND MAYBE CUT DOWN SOME OF THEIR SWARMS WHILE WE'RE AT IT! LET'S DO IT.

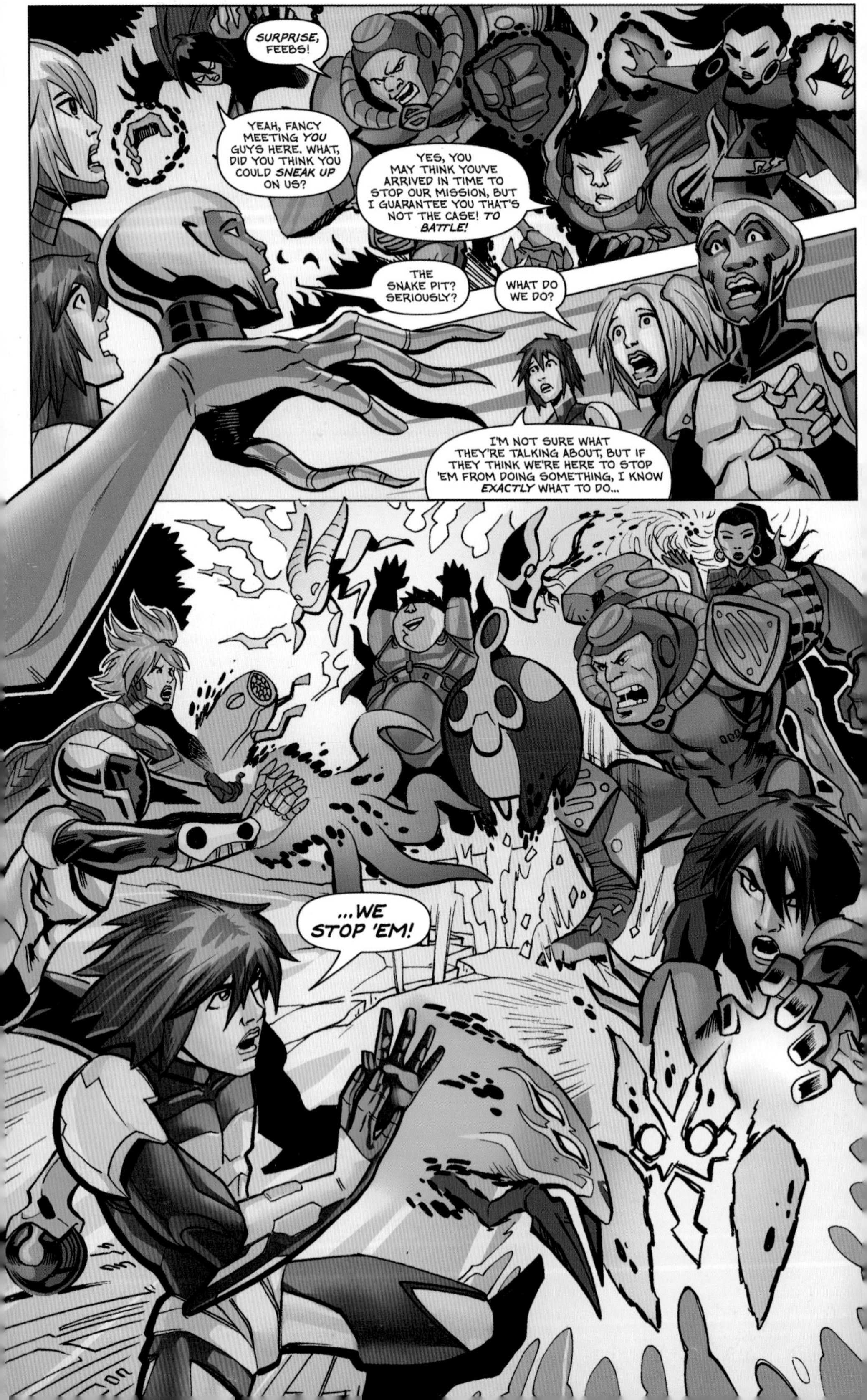
SURPRISE, FEEBS!
YEAH, FANCY MEETING YOU GUYS HERE. WHAT, DID YOU THINK YOU COULD SNEAK UP ON US?
YES, YOU MAY THINK YOU'VE ARRIVED IN TIME TO STOP OUR MISSION, BUT I GUARANTEE YOU THAT'S NOT THE CASE! TO BATTLE!
THE SNAKE PIT? SERIOUSLY?
WHAT DO WE DO?
I'M NOT SURE WHAT THEY'RE TALKING ABOUT, BUT IF THEY THINK WE'RE HERE TO STOP 'EM FROM DOING SOMETHING, I KNOW EXACTLY WHAT TO DO...
...WE STOP 'EM!

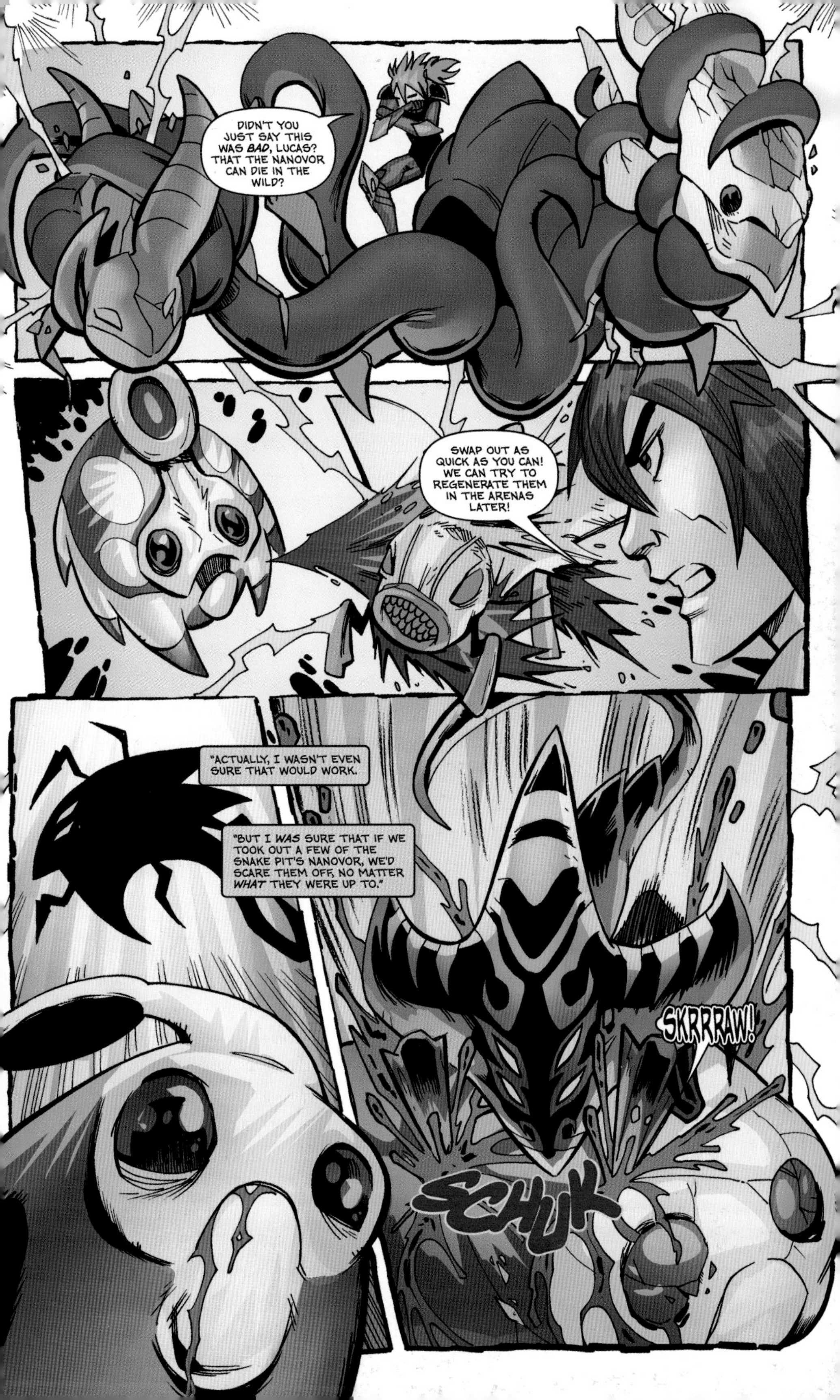

DIDN'T YOU JUST SAY THIS WAS *BAD*, LUCAS? THAT THE NANOVOR CAN DIE IN THE WILD?
SWAP OUT AS QUICK AS YOU CAN! WE CAN TRY TO REGENERATE THEM IN THE ARENAS LATER!
"ACTUALLY, I WASN'T EVEN SURE THAT WOULD WORK.
"BUT I *WAS* SURE THAT IF WE TOOK OUT A FEW OF THE SNAKE PIT'S NANOVOR, WE'D SCARE THEM OFF, NO MATTER *WHAT* THEY WERE UP TO."
SKRRRAW!
SCHUK

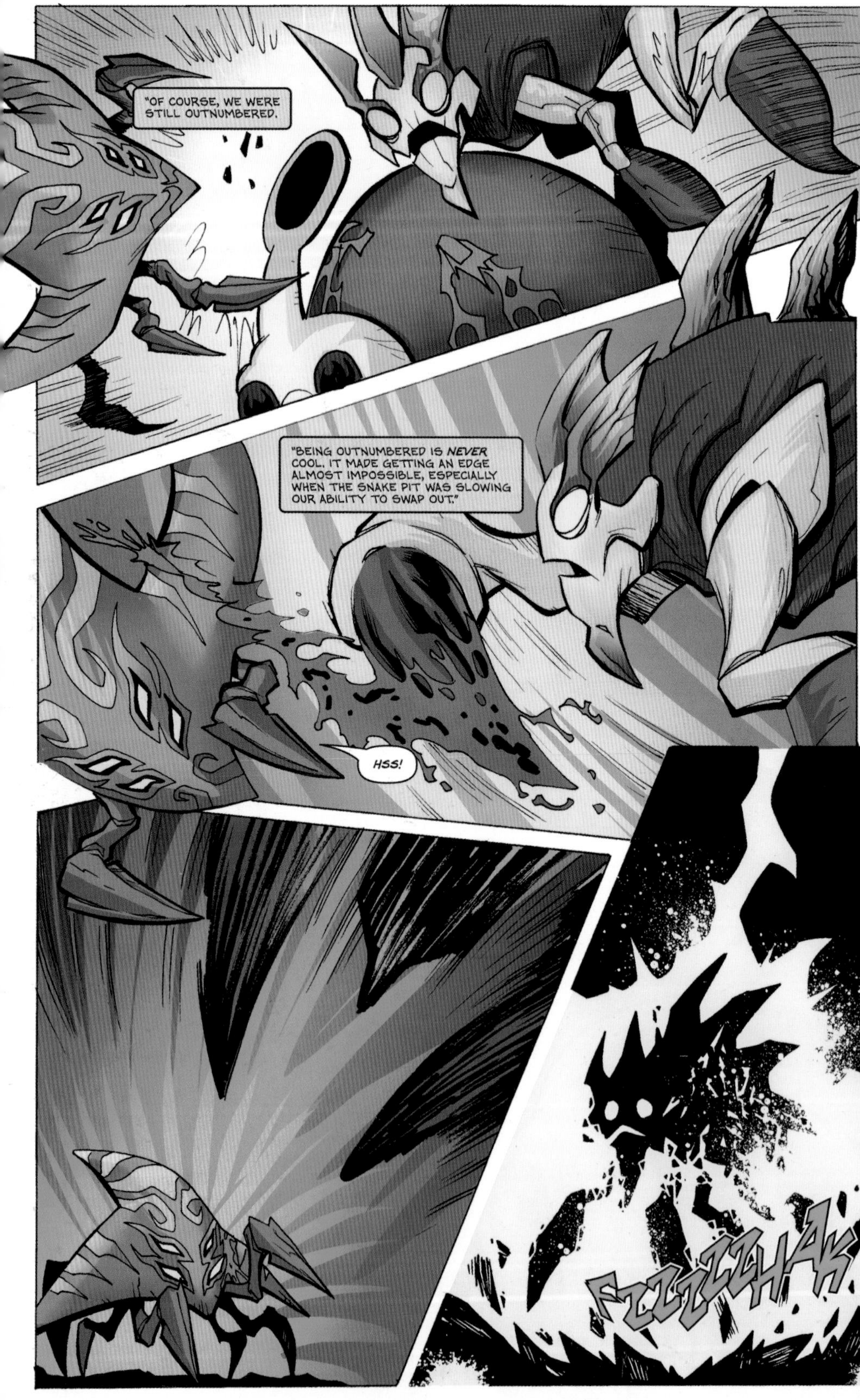
"OF COURSE, WE WERE STILL OUTNUMBERED.
"BEING OUTNUMBERED IS *NEVER* COOL. IT MADE GETTING AN EDGE ALMOST IMPOSSIBLE, ESPECIALLY WHEN THE SNAKE PIT WAS SLOWING OUR ABILITY TO SWAP OUT."
HSS!
FZZZZZHAK

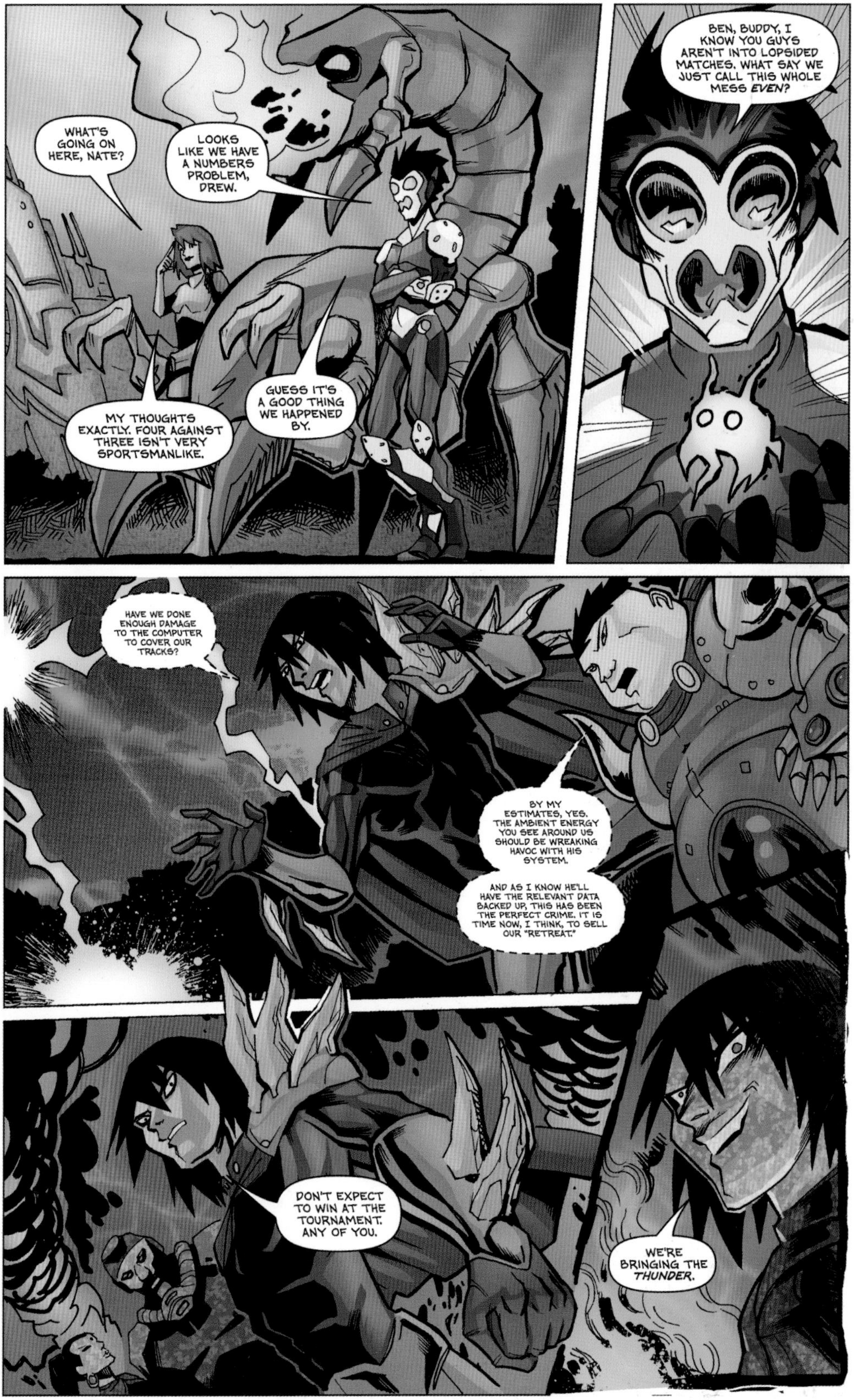
WHAT'S GOING ON HERE, NATE?
LOOKS LIKE WE HAVE A NUMBERS PROBLEM, DREW.
MY THOUGHTS EXACTLY. FOUR AGAINST THREE ISN'T VERY SPORTSMANLIKE.
GUESS IT'S A GOOD THING WE HAPPENED BY.
BEN, BUDDY, I KNOW YOU GUYS AREN'T INTO LOPSIDED MATCHES. WHAT SAY WE JUST CALL THIS WHOLE MESS *EVEN*?
HAVE WE DONE ENOUGH DAMAGE TO THE COMPUTER TO COVER OUR TRACKS?
BY MY ESTIMATES, YES. THE AMBIENT ENERGY YOU SEE AROUND US SHOULD BE WREAKING HAVOC WITH HIS SYSTEM.
AND AS I KNOW HE'LL HAVE THE RELEVANT DATA BACKED UP, THIS HAS BEEN THE PERFECT CRIME. IT IS TIME NOW, I THINK, TO SELL OUR "RETREAT."
DON'T EXPECT TO WIN AT THE TOURNAMENT. ANY OF YOU.
WE'RE BRINGING THE *THUNDER*.

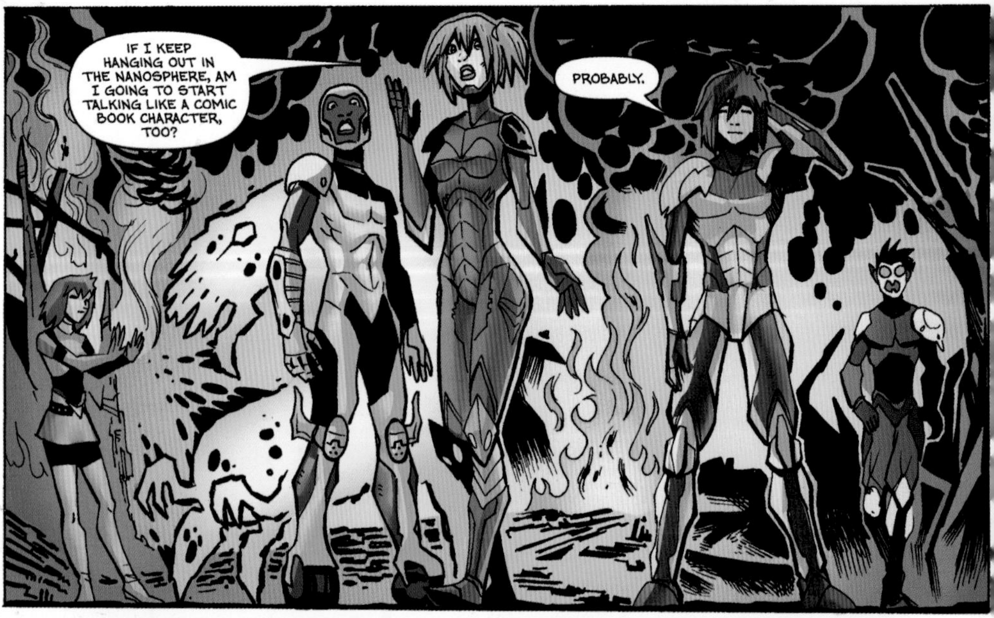
IF I KEEP HANGING OUT IN THE NANOSPHERE, AM I GOING TO START TALKING LIKE A COMIC BOOK CHARACTER, TOO?
PROBABLY.

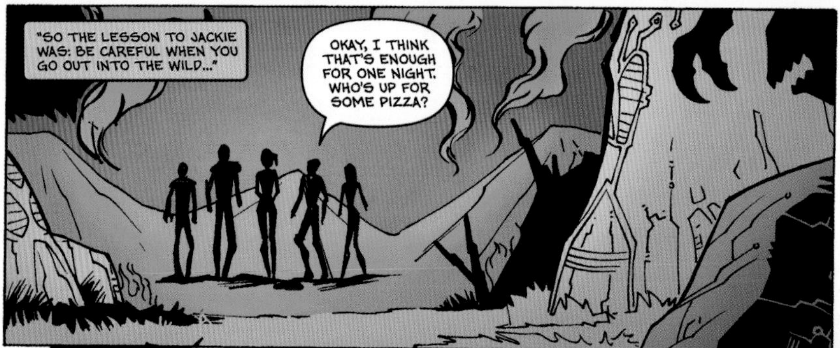
"SO THE LESSON TO JACKIE WAS: BE CAREFUL WHEN YOU GO OUT INTO THE WILD..."
OKAY, I THINK THAT'S ENOUGH FOR ONE NIGHT. WHO'S UP FOR SOME PIZZA?

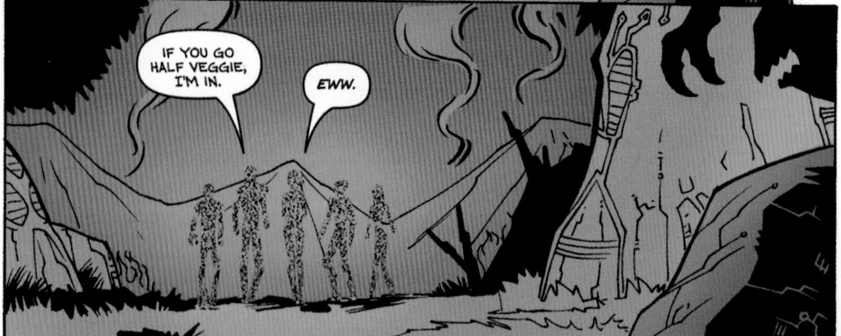
IF YOU GO HALF VEGGIE, I'M IN.
EWW.

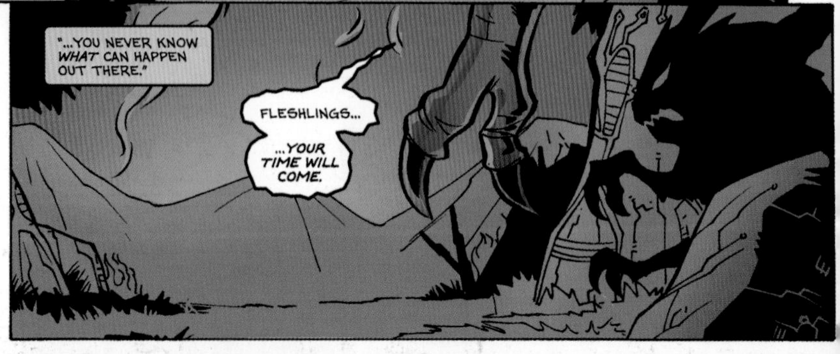
"...YOU NEVER KNOW WHAT CAN HAPPEN OUT THERE."
FLESHLINGS...
...YOUR TIME WILL COME.

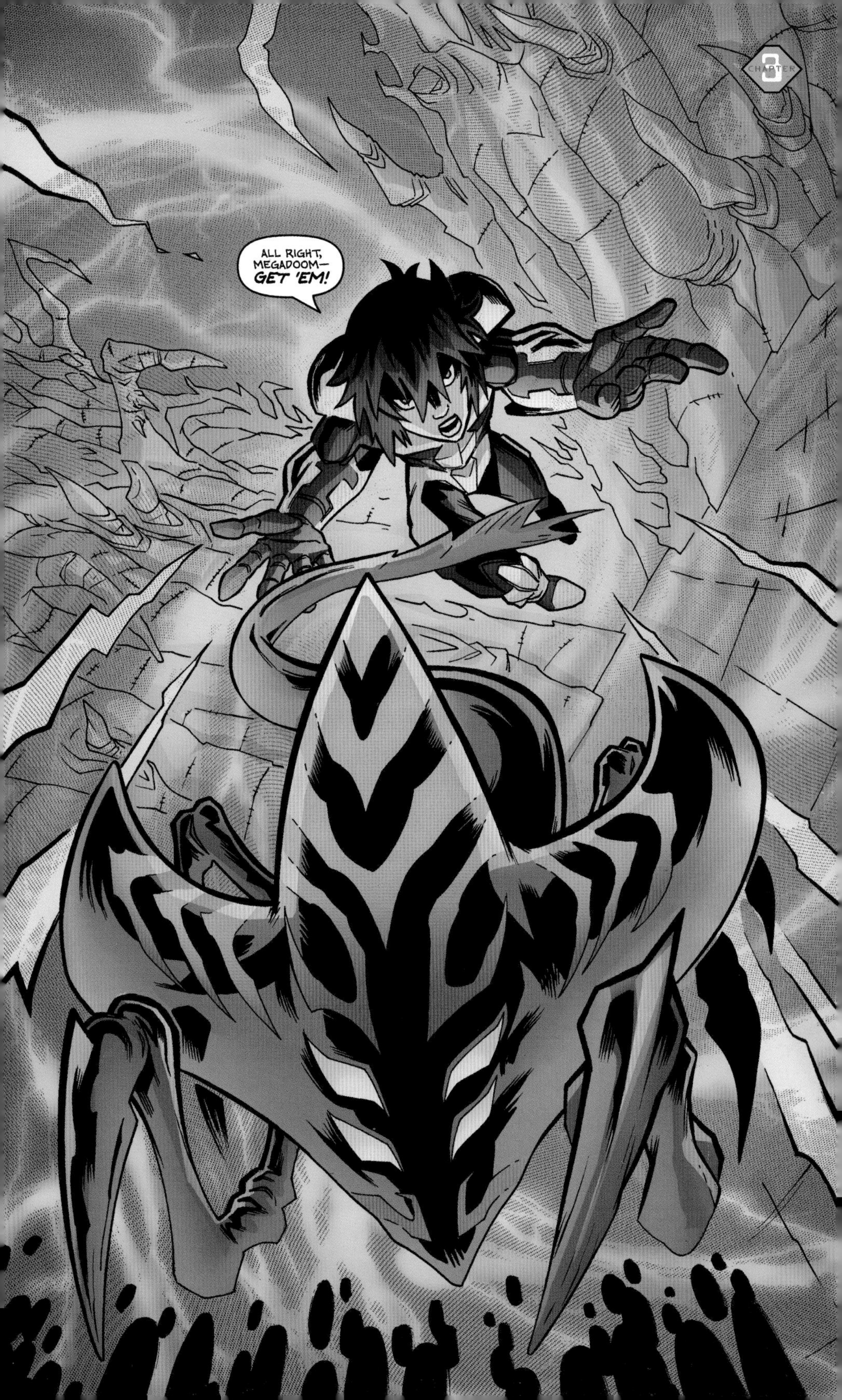
CHAPTER 3
ALL RIGHT, MEGADOOM— GET 'EM!

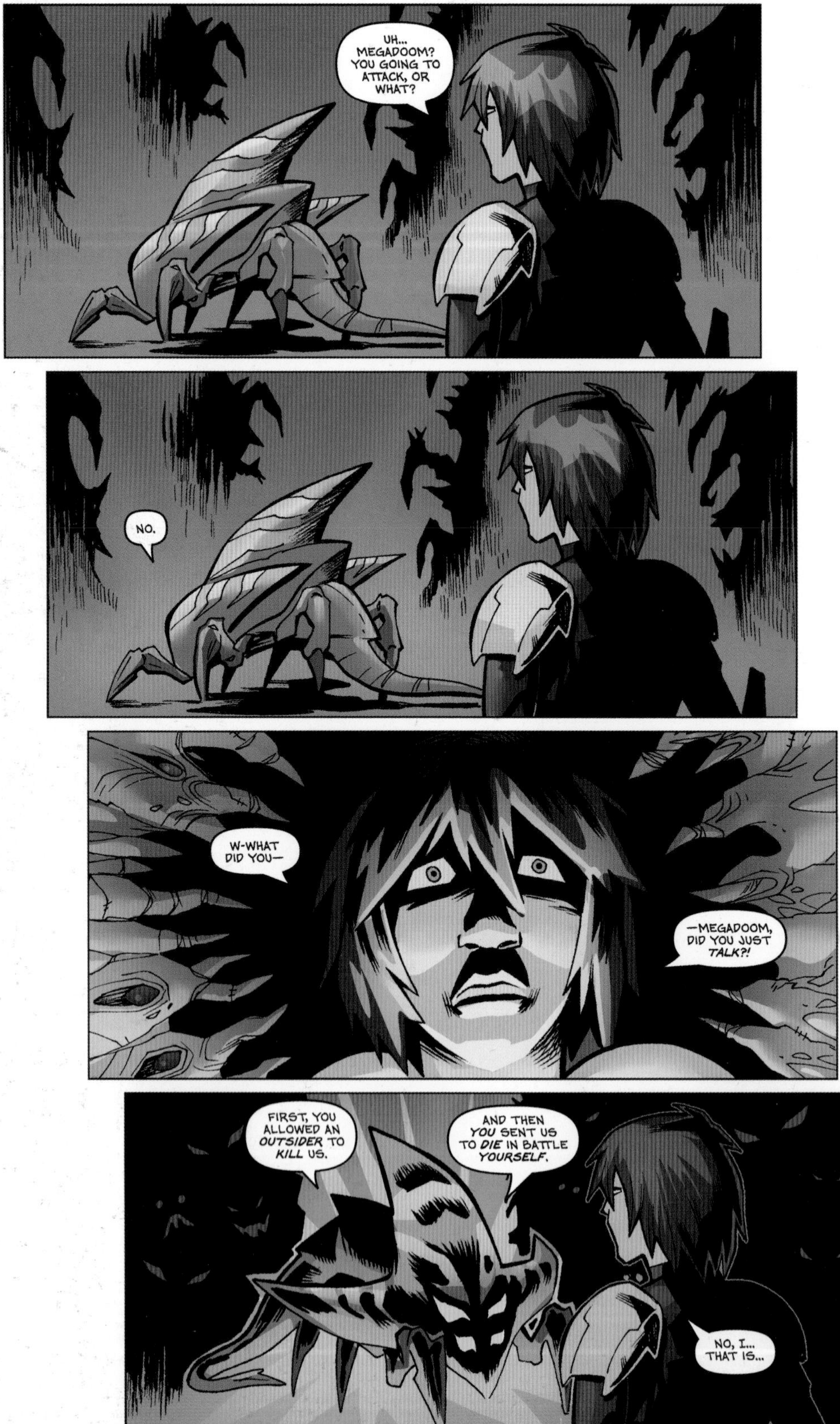
UH... MEGADOOM? YOU GOING TO ATTACK, OR WHAT?
NO.
W-WHAT DID YOU—
—MEGADOOM, DID YOU JUST *TALK*?!
FIRST, YOU ALLOWED AN *OUTSIDER* TO *KILL* US.
AND THEN *YOU* SENT US TO *DIE* IN BATTLE *YOURSELF*.
NO, I... THAT IS...

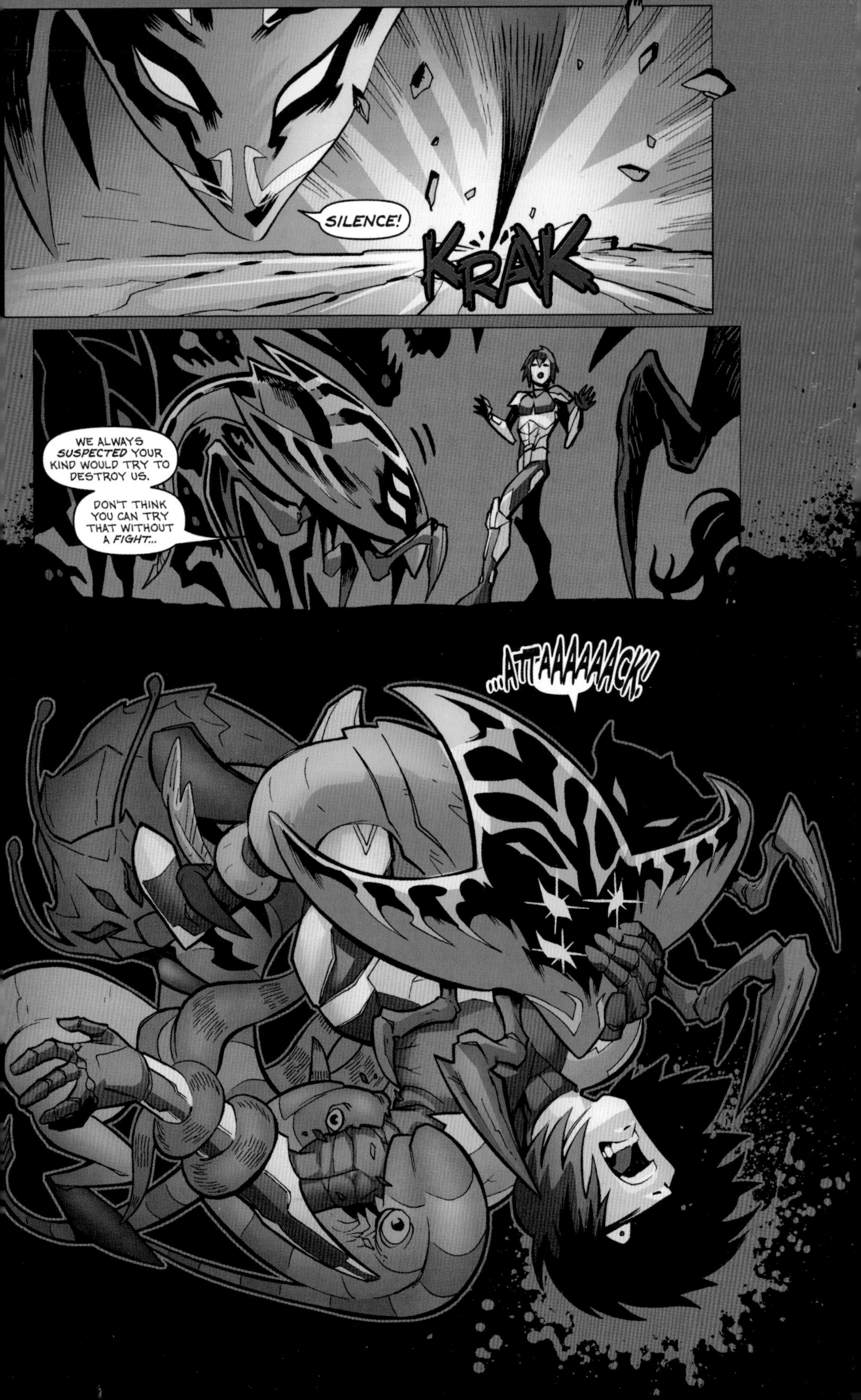
SILENCE!
KRAK
WE ALWAYS SUSPECTED YOUR KIND WOULD TRY TO DESTROY US.
DON'T THINK YOU CAN TRY THAT WITHOUT A FIGHT...
...ATTAAAAAACK!

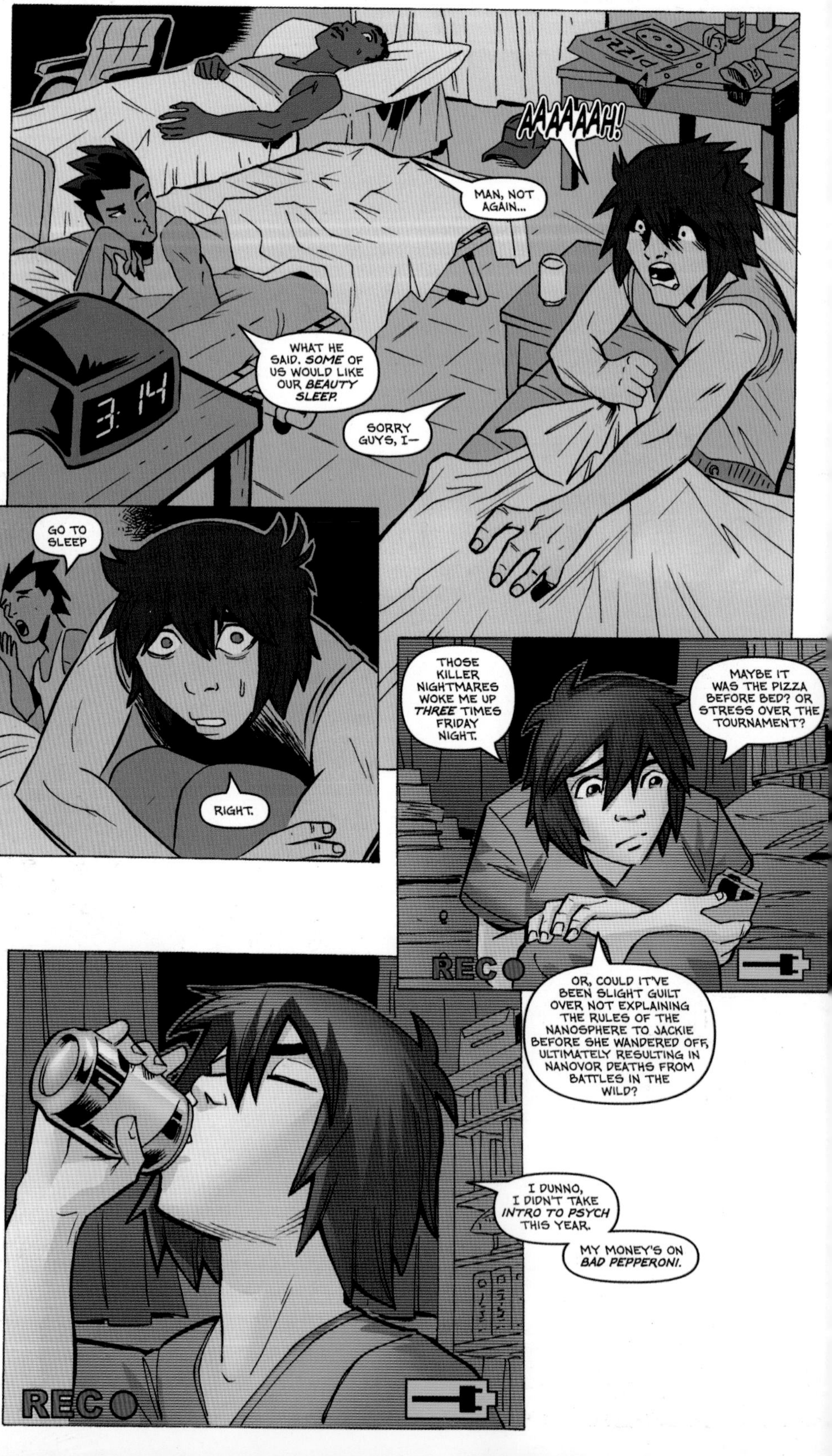
AAAAAAH!
MAN, NOT AGAIN...
WHAT HE SAID. SOME OF US WOULD LIKE OUR BEAUTY SLEEP.
SORRY GUYS, I—
3:14
GO TO SLEEP
RIGHT.
THOSE KILLER NIGHTMARES WOKE ME UP THREE TIMES FRIDAY NIGHT.
MAYBE IT WAS THE PIZZA BEFORE BED? OR STRESS OVER THE TOURNAMENT?
REC
OR, COULD IT'VE BEEN SLIGHT GUILT OVER NOT EXPLAINING THE RULES OF THE NANOSPHERE TO JACKIE BEFORE SHE WANDERED OFF, ULTIMATELY RESULTING IN NANOVOR DEATHS FROM BATTLES IN THE WILD?
I DUNNO, I DIDN'T TAKE INTRO TO PSYCH THIS YEAR.
MY MONEY'S ON BAD PEPPERONI.
REC

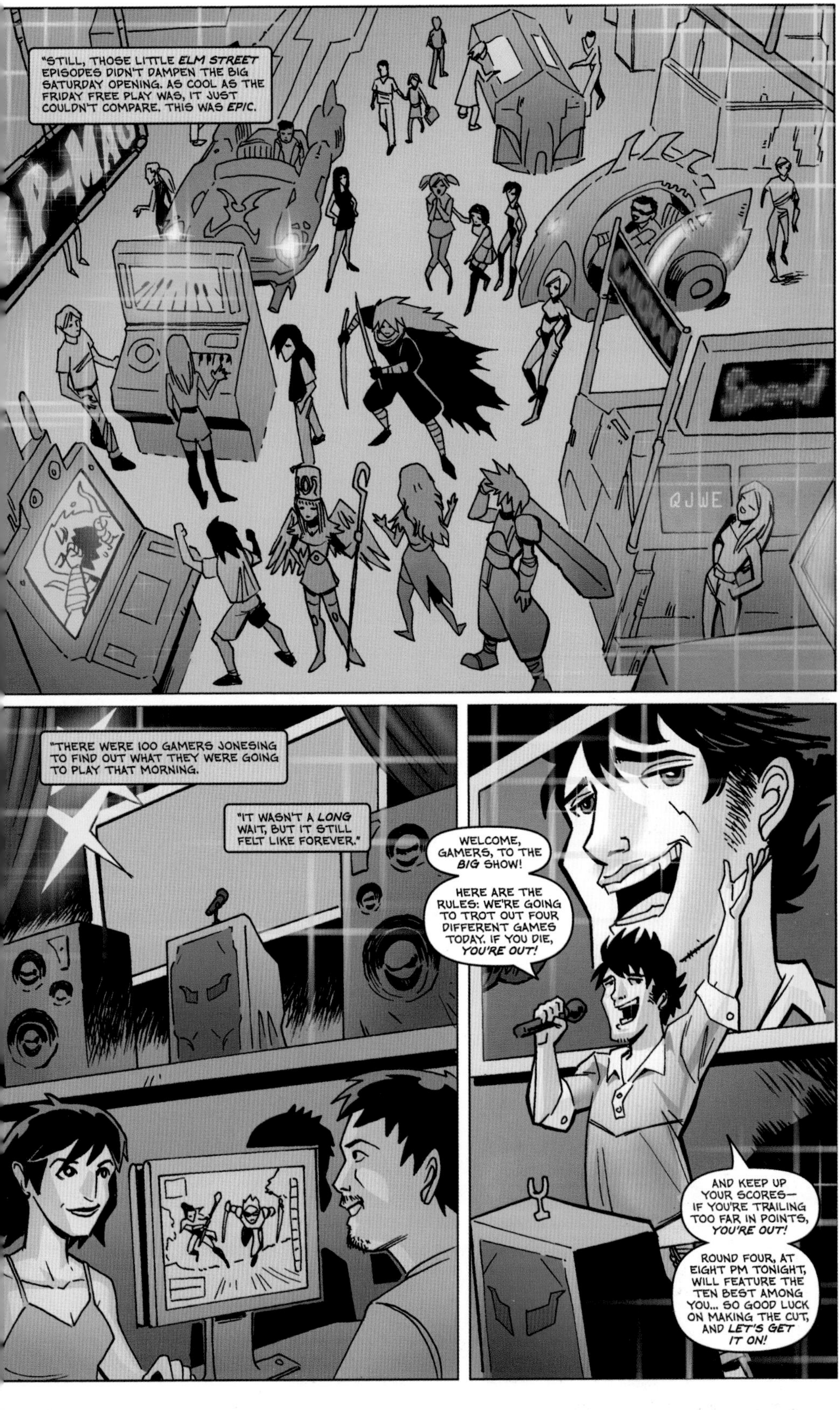
"STILL, THOSE LITTLE *ELM STREET* EPISODES DIDN'T DAMPEN THE BIG SATURDAY OPENING. AS COOL AS THE FRIDAY FREE PLAY WAS, IT JUST COULDN'T COMPARE. THIS WAS *EPIC*.
QJWE
"THERE WERE 100 GAMERS JONESING TO FIND OUT WHAT THEY WERE GOING TO PLAY THAT MORNING.
"IT WASN'T A *LONG* WAIT, BUT IT STILL FELT LIKE FOREVER."
WELCOME, GAMERS, TO THE *BIG* SHOW!
HERE ARE THE RULES: WE'RE GOING TO TROT OUT FOUR DIFFERENT GAMES TODAY. IF YOU DIE, *YOU'RE OUT!*
AND KEEP UP YOUR SCORES— IF YOU'RE TRAILING TOO FAR IN POINTS, *YOU'RE OUT!*
ROUND FOUR, AT EIGHT PM TONIGHT, WILL FEATURE THE TEN BEST AMONG YOU... SO GOOD LUCK ON MAKING THE CUT, AND *LET'S GET IT ON!*

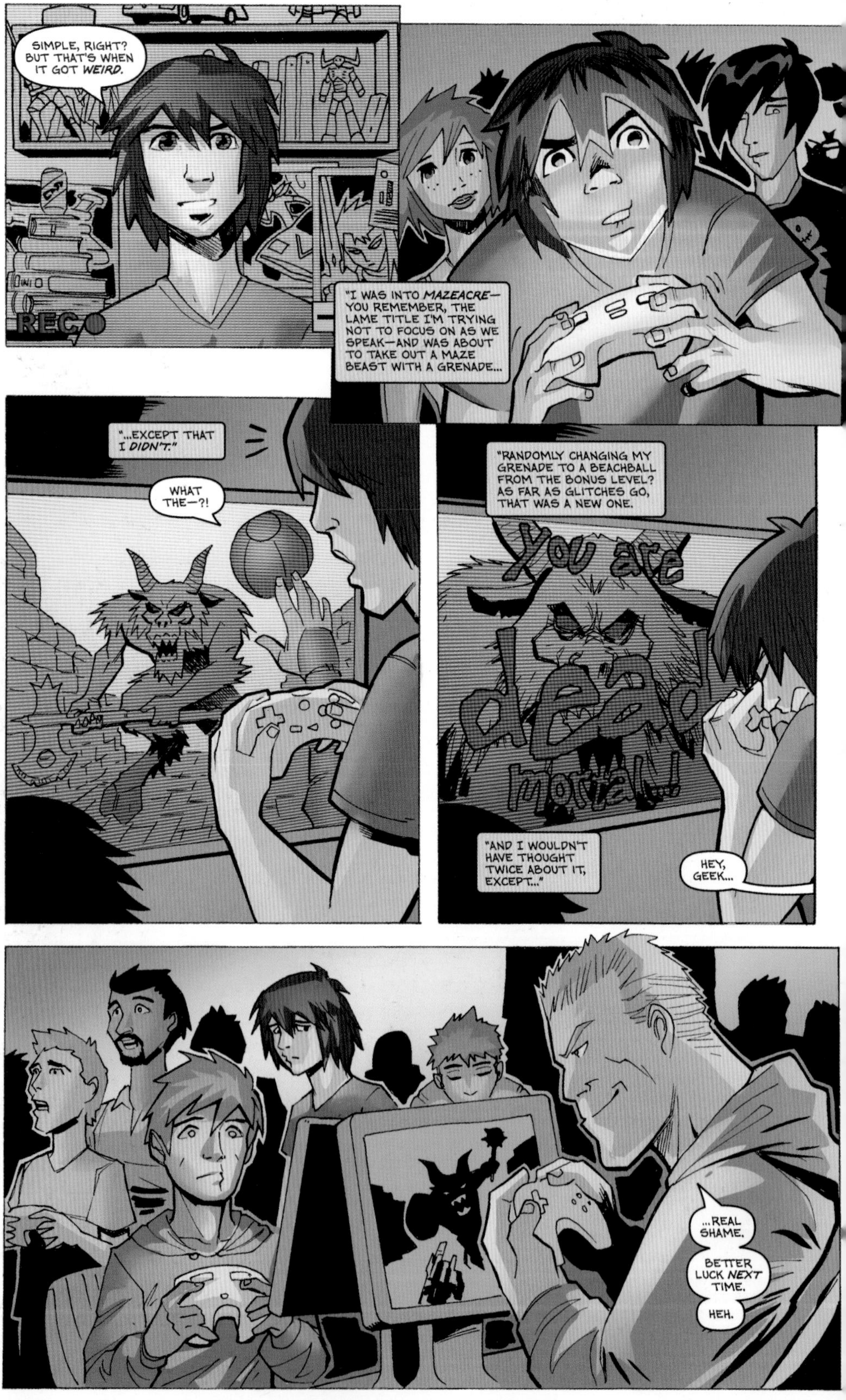

SIMPLE, RIGHT? BUT THAT'S WHEN IT GOT *WEIRD.*
REC
"I WAS INTO *MAZEACRE*—YOU REMEMBER, THE LAME TITLE I'M TRYING NOT TO FOCUS ON AS WE SPEAK—AND WAS ABOUT TO TAKE OUT A MAZE BEAST WITH A GRENADE...
"...EXCEPT THAT I *DIDN'T.*"
WHAT THE—?!
"RANDOMLY CHANGING MY GRENADE TO A BEACHBALL FROM THE BONUS LEVEL? AS FAR AS GLITCHES GO, THAT WAS A NEW ONE.
You are dead, mortal...!
"AND I WOULDN'T HAVE THOUGHT TWICE ABOUT IT, EXCEPT..."
HEY, GEEK...
...REAL SHAME.
BETTER LUCK *NEXT* TIME.
HEH.

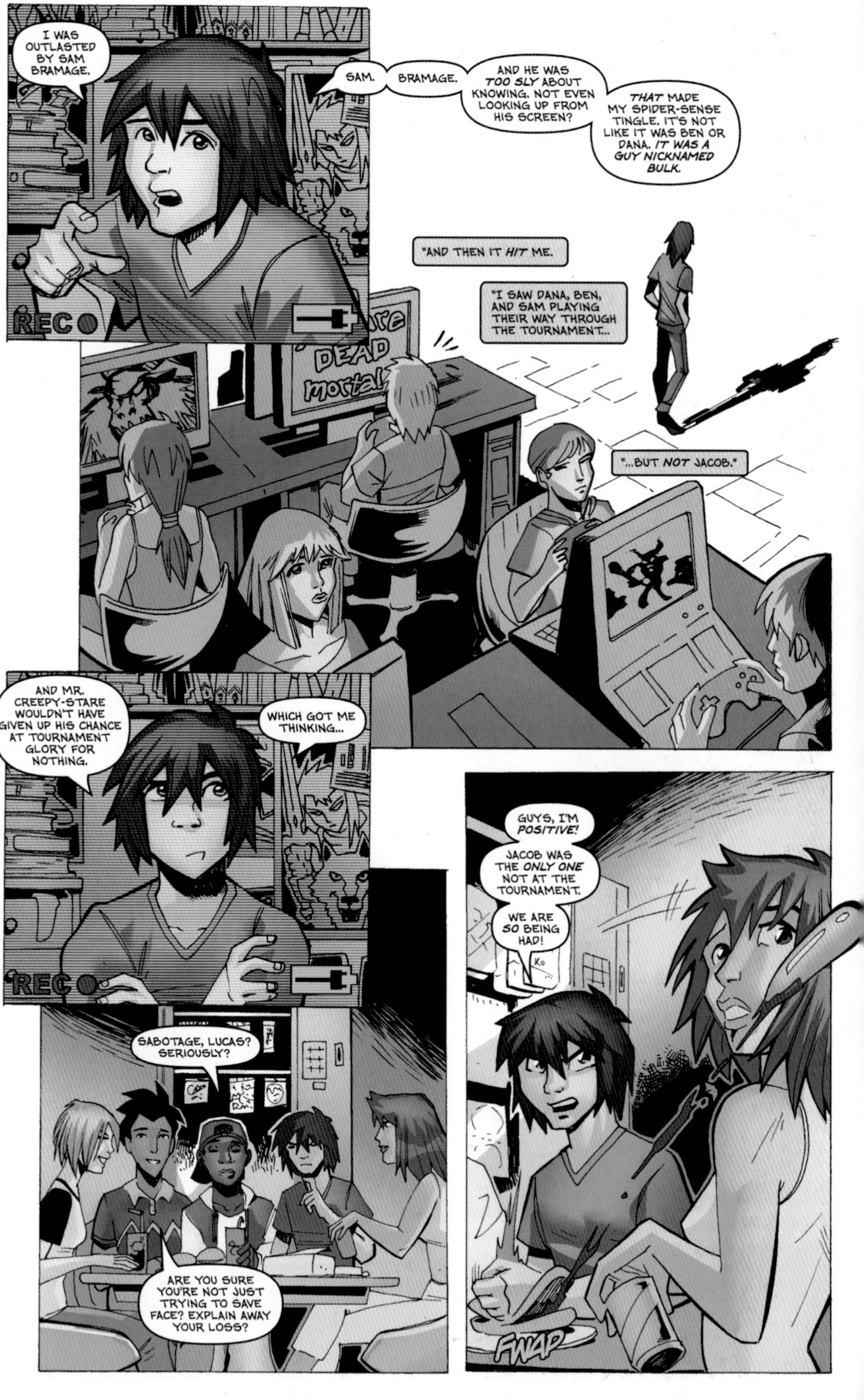

I WAS OUTLASTED BY SAM BRAMAGE.
REC
SAM.
BRAMAGE.
AND HE WAS TOO SLY ABOUT KNOWING. NOT EVEN LOOKING UP FROM HIS SCREEN?
THAT MADE MY SPIDER-SENSE TINGLE. IT'S NOT LIKE IT WAS BEN OR DANA. IT WAS A GUY NICKNAMED BULK.
"AND THEN IT HIT ME.
"I SAW DANA, BEN, AND SAM PLAYING THEIR WAY THROUGH THE TOURNAMENT...
"...BUT NOT JACOB."
DEAD mortal!
AND MR. CREEPY-STARE WOULDN'T HAVE GIVEN UP HIS CHANCE AT TOURNAMENT GLORY FOR NOTHING.
WHICH GOT ME THINKING...
REC
SABOTAGE, LUCAS? SERIOUSLY?
ARE YOU SURE YOU'RE NOT JUST TRYING TO SAVE FACE? EXPLAIN AWAY YOUR LOSS?
GUYS, I'M POSITIVE!
JACOB WAS THE ONLY ONE NOT AT THE TOURNAMENT.
WE ARE SO BEING HAD!
FWAP

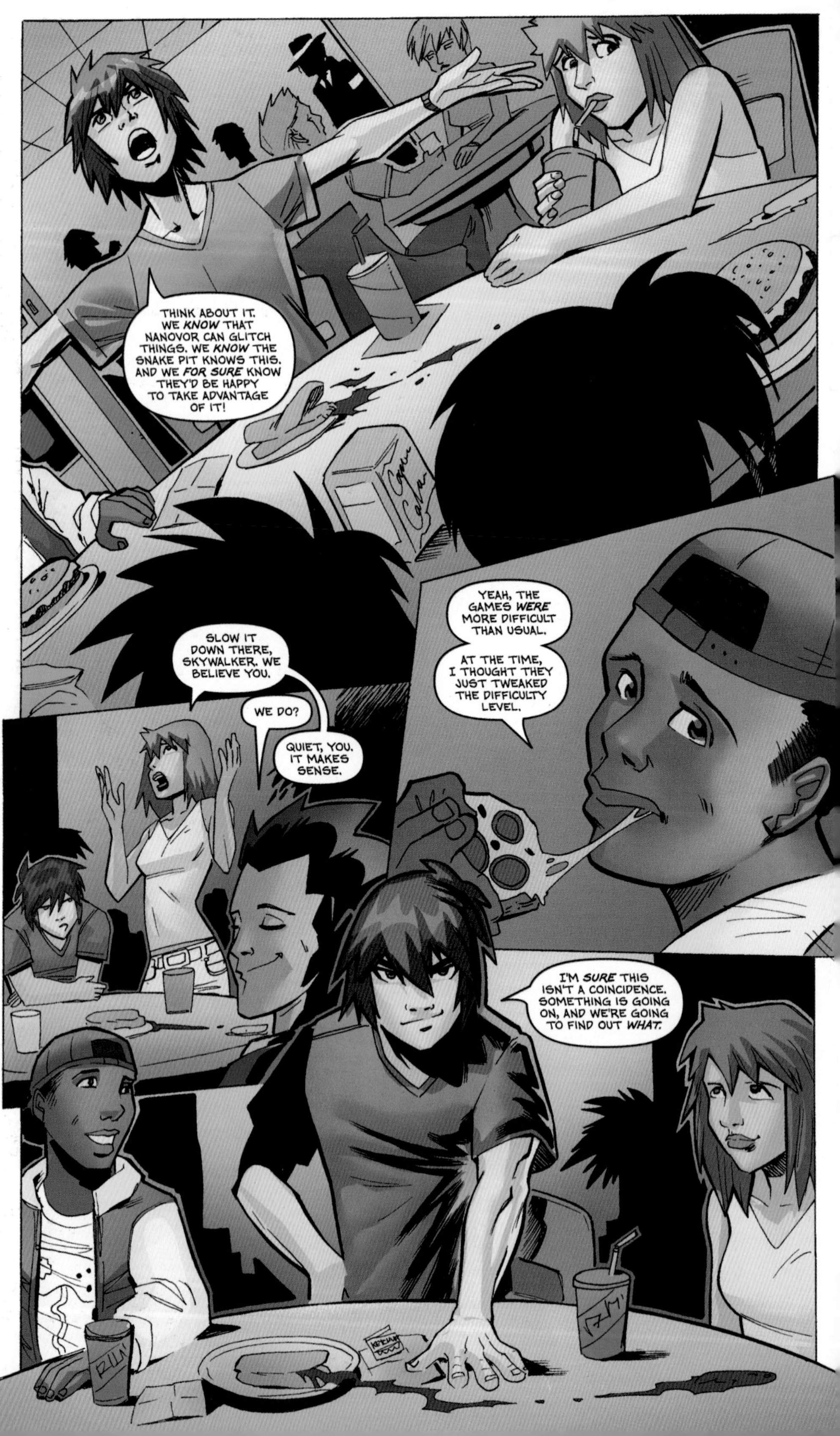
THINK ABOUT IT. WE *KNOW* THAT NANOVOR CAN GLITCH THINGS. WE *KNOW* THE SNAKE PIT KNOWS THIS. AND WE *FOR SURE* KNOW THEY'D BE HAPPY TO TAKE ADVANTAGE OF IT!
YEAH, THE GAMES *WERE* MORE DIFFICULT THAN USUAL.
AT THE TIME, I THOUGHT THEY JUST TWEAKED THE DIFFICULTY LEVEL.
SLOW IT DOWN THERE, SKYWALKER. WE BELIEVE YOU.
WE DO?
QUIET, YOU. IT MAKES SENSE.
I'M *SURE* THIS ISN'T A COINCIDENCE. SOMETHING IS GOING ON, AND WE'RE GOING TO FIND OUT *WHAT*.

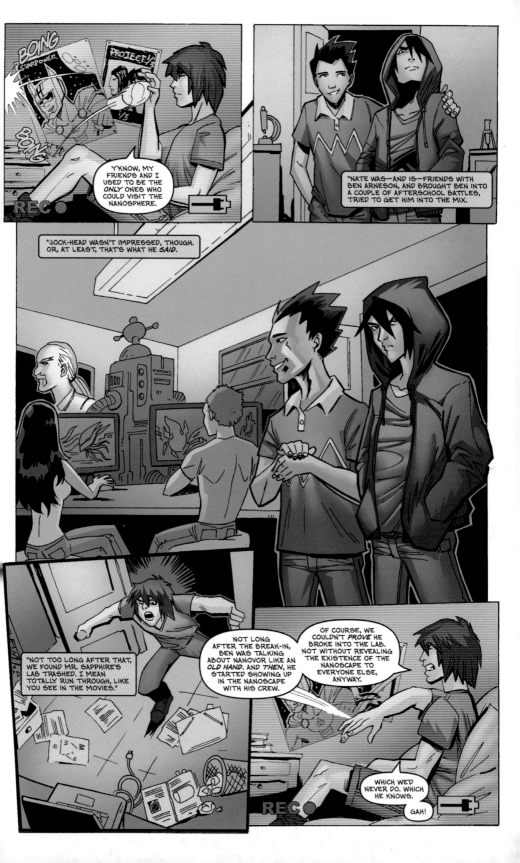

BOING

STARPOWER

PROJECT V3

REC

Y'KNOW, MY FRIENDS AND I USED TO BE THE *ONLY* ONES WHO COULD VISIT THE NANOSPHERE.

"NATE WAS—AND IS—FRIENDS WITH BEN ARNESON, AND BROUGHT BEN INTO A COUPLE OF AFTERSCHOOL BATTLES, TRIED TO GET HIM INTO THE MIX.

"JOCK-HEAD WASN'T IMPRESSED, THOUGH. OR, AT LEAST, THAT'S WHAT HE *SAID*.

"NOT TOO LONG AFTER THAT, WE FOUND MR. SAPPHIRE'S LAB TRASHED. I MEAN TOTALLY RUN THROUGH, LIKE YOU SEE IN THE MOVIES."

NOT LONG AFTER THE BREAK-IN, BEN WAS TALKING ABOUT NANOVOR LIKE AN *OLD HAND*. AND *THEN*, HE STARTED SHOWING UP IN THE NANOSCAPE WITH HIS CREW.

OF COURSE, WE COULDN'T *PROVE* HE BROKE INTO THE LAB. NOT WITHOUT REVEALING THE EXISTENCE OF THE NANOSCAPE TO EVERYONE ELSE, ANYWAY.

WHICH WE'D NEVER DO. WHICH HE KNOWS.

GAH!

REC

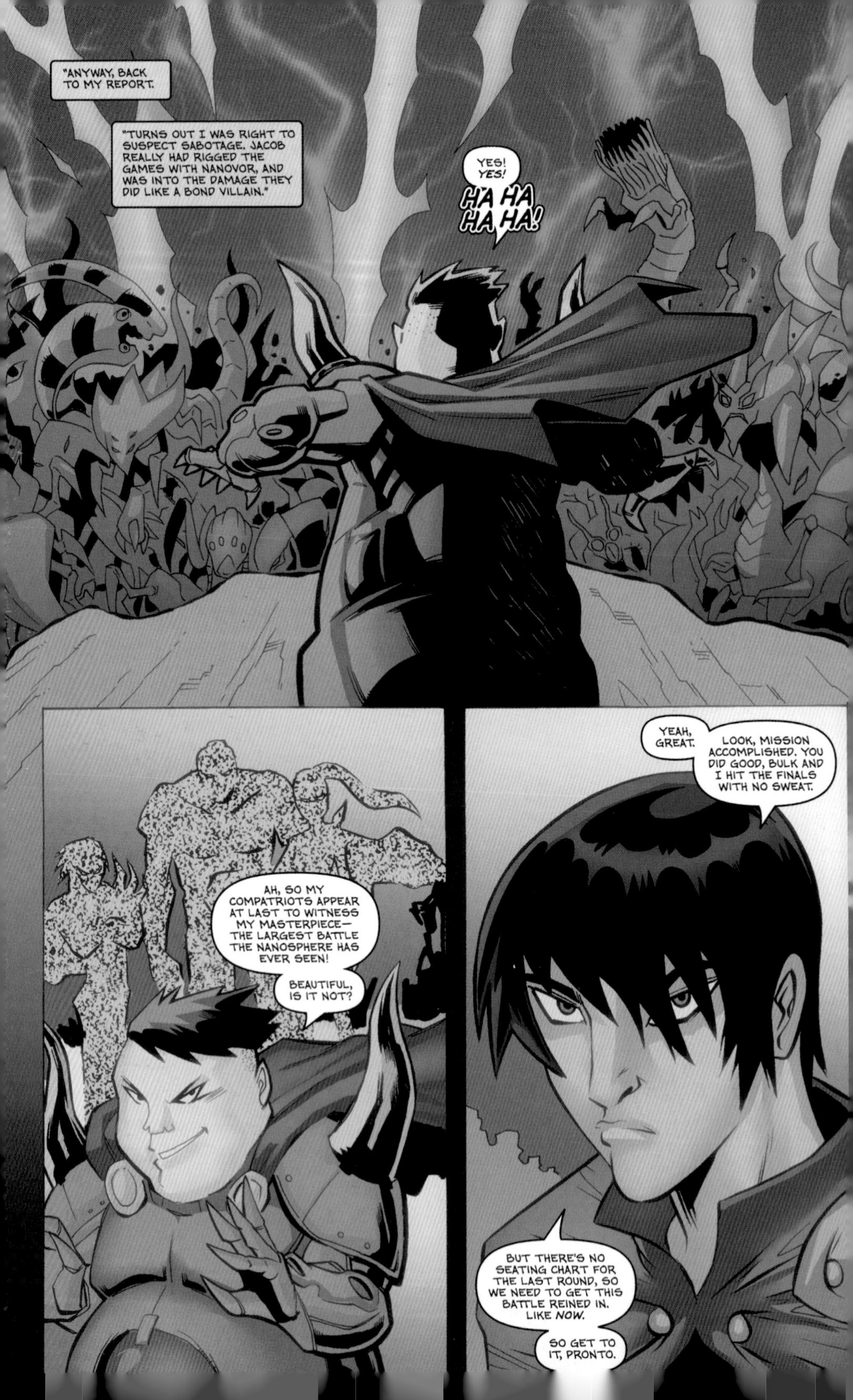
"ANYWAY, BACK TO MY REPORT.
"TURNS OUT I WAS RIGHT TO SUSPECT SABOTAGE. JACOB REALLY HAD RIGGED THE GAMES WITH NANOVOR, AND WAS INTO THE DAMAGE THEY DID LIKE A BOND VILLAIN."
YES! YES! HA HA HA HA!
AH, SO MY COMPATRIOTS APPEAR AT LAST TO WITNESS MY MASTERPIECE— THE LARGEST BATTLE THE NANOSPHERE HAS EVER SEEN!
BEAUTIFUL, IS IT NOT?
YEAH, GREAT.
LOOK, MISSION ACCOMPLISHED. YOU DID GOOD, BULK AND I HIT THE FINALS WITH NO SWEAT.
BUT THERE'S NO SEATING CHART FOR THE LAST ROUND, SO WE NEED TO GET THIS BATTLE REINED IN. LIKE *NOW*.
SO GET TO IT, PRONTO.

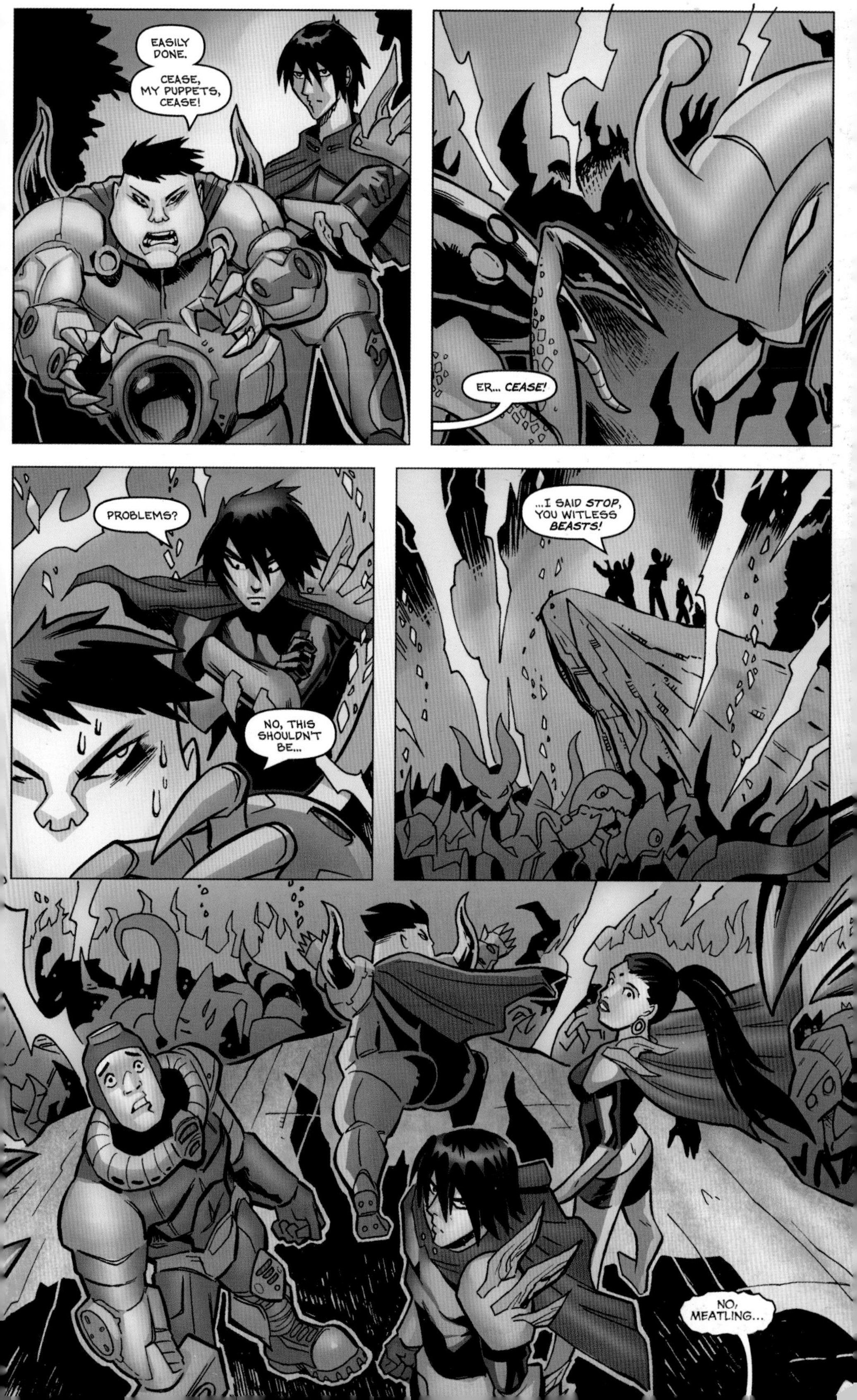
EASILY DONE.
CEASE, MY PUPPETS, CEASE!
ER... CEASE!
PROBLEMS?
NO, THIS SHOULDN'T BE...
...I SAID STOP, YOU WITLESS BEASTS!
NO, MEATLING...

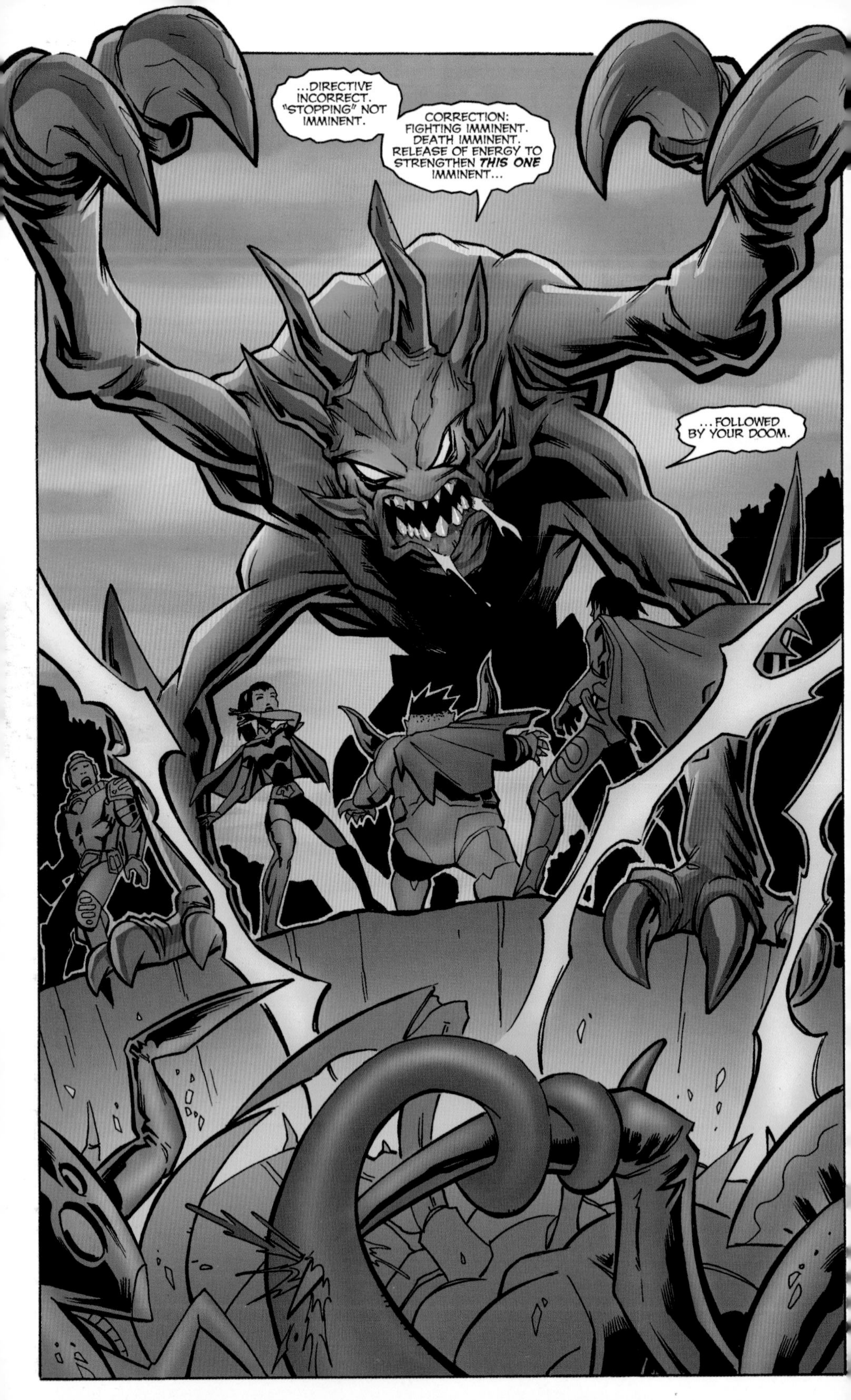
...DIRECTIVE INCORRECT. "STOPPING" NOT IMMINENT.
CORRECTION: FIGHTING IMMINENT. DEATH IMMINENT. RELEASE OF ENERGY TO STRENGTHEN *THIS ONE* IMMINENT...
...FOLLOWED BY YOUR DOOM.

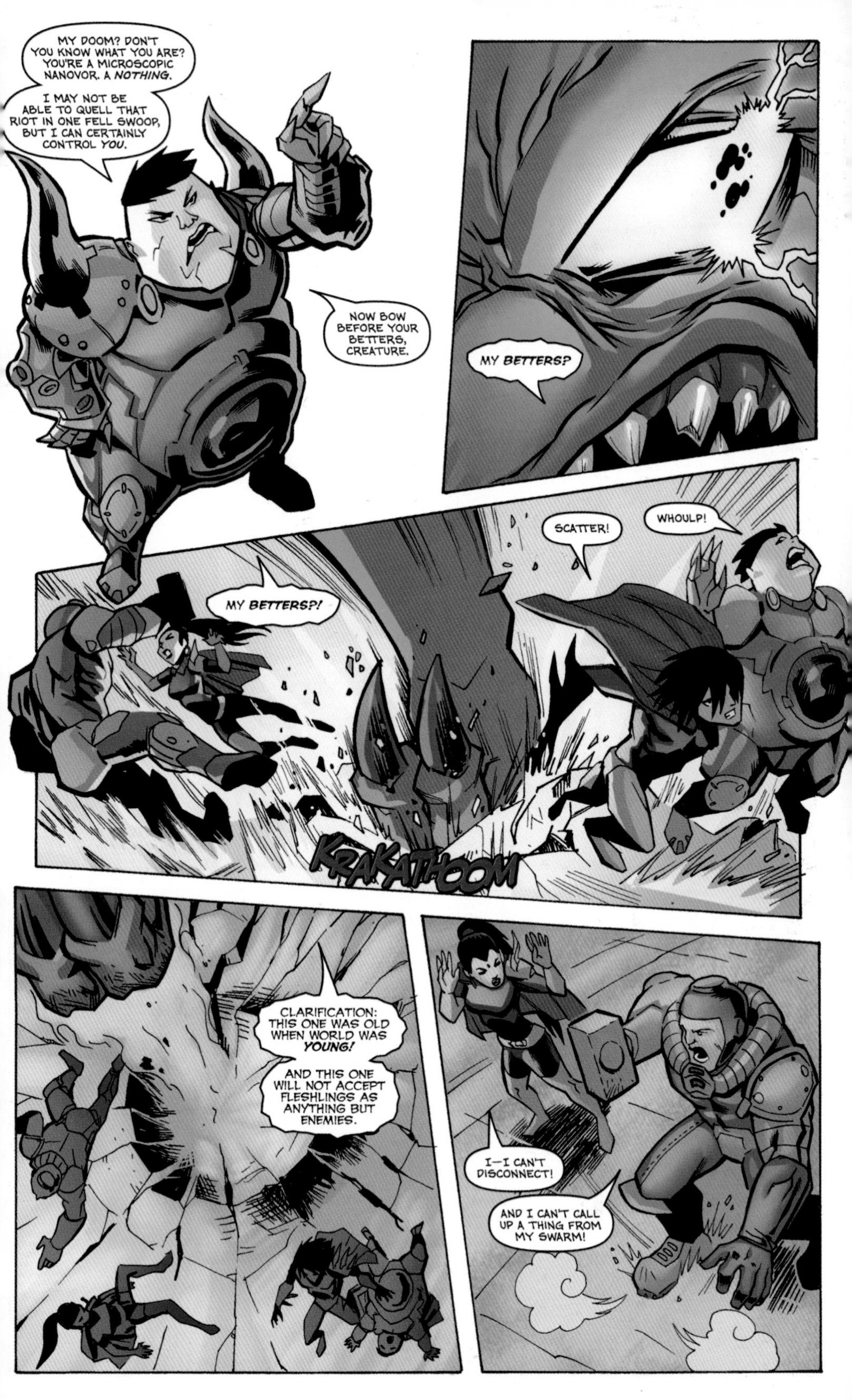

MY DOOM? DON'T YOU KNOW WHAT YOU ARE? YOU'RE A MICROSCOPIC NANOVOR. A *NOTHING*.
I MAY NOT BE ABLE TO QUELL THAT RIOT IN ONE FELL SWOOP, BUT I CAN CERTAINLY CONTROL *YOU*.
NOW BOW BEFORE YOUR BETTERS, CREATURE.
MY *BETTERS?*
MY *BETTERS?!*
SCATTER!
WHOULP!
KRAKATHOOM
CLARIFICATION: THIS ONE WAS OLD WHEN WORLD WAS *YOUNG!*
AND THIS ONE WILL NOT ACCEPT FLESHLINGS AS ANYTHING BUT ENEMIES.
I—I CAN'T DISCONNECT!
AND I CAN'T CALL UP A THING FROM MY SWARM!

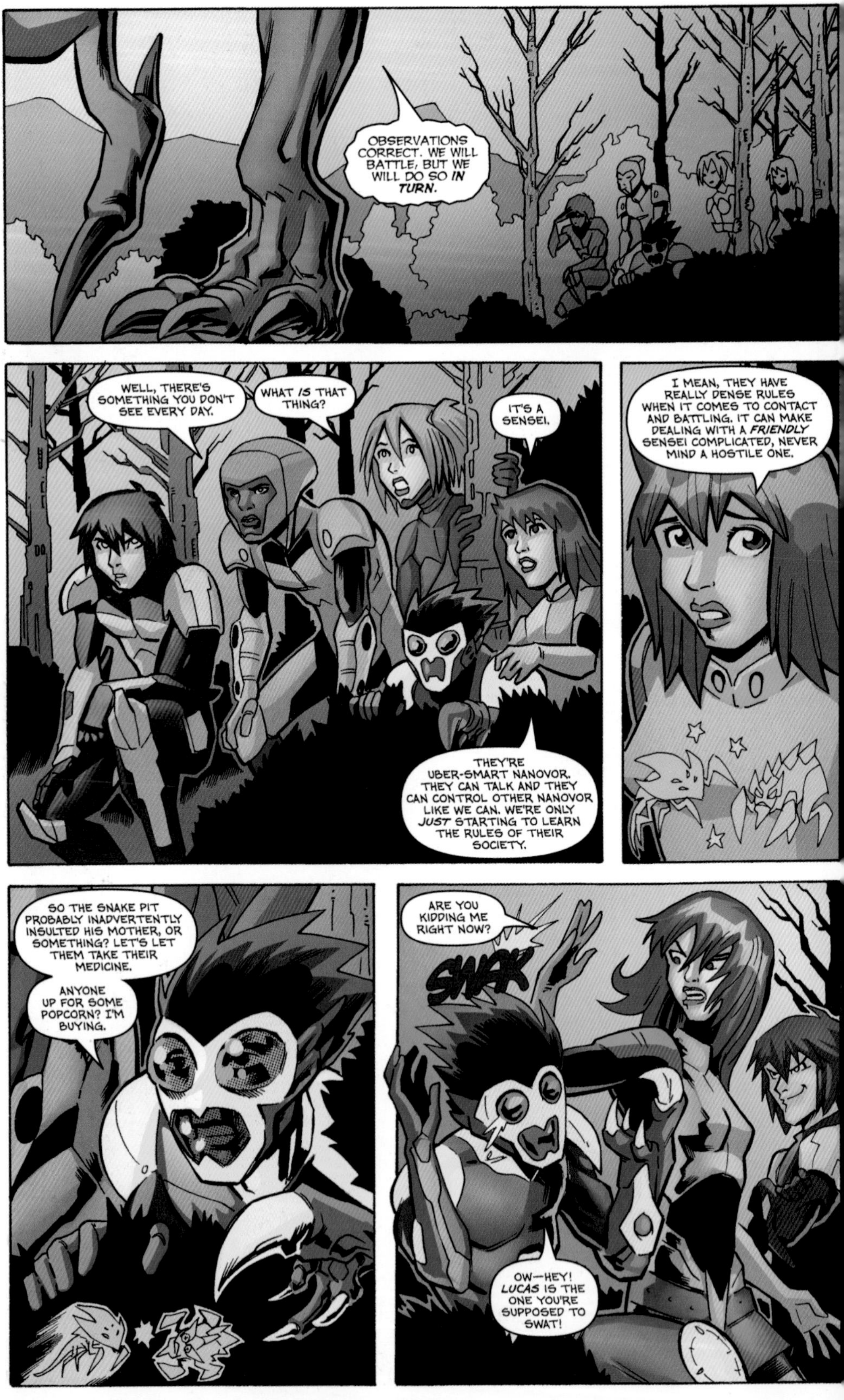

OBSERVATIONS CORRECT. WE WILL BATTLE, BUT WE WILL DO SO *IN TURN.*
WELL, THERE'S SOMETHING YOU DON'T SEE EVERY DAY.
WHAT *IS* THAT THING?
IT'S A SENSEI.
THEY'RE UBER-SMART NANOVOR. THEY CAN TALK AND THEY CAN CONTROL OTHER NANOVOR LIKE WE CAN. WE'RE ONLY *JUST* STARTING TO LEARN THE RULES OF THEIR SOCIETY.
I MEAN, THEY HAVE REALLY DENSE RULES WHEN IT COMES TO CONTACT AND BATTLING. IT CAN MAKE DEALING WITH A *FRIENDLY* SENSEI COMPLICATED, NEVER MIND A HOSTILE ONE.
SO THE SNAKE PIT PROBABLY INADVERTENTLY INSULTED HIS MOTHER, OR SOMETHING? LET'S LET THEM TAKE THEIR MEDICINE.
ANYONE UP FOR SOME POPCORN? I'M BUYING.
ARE YOU KIDDING ME RIGHT NOW?
SWAK
OW—HEY! *LUCAS* IS THE ONE YOU'RE SUPPOSED TO SWAT!

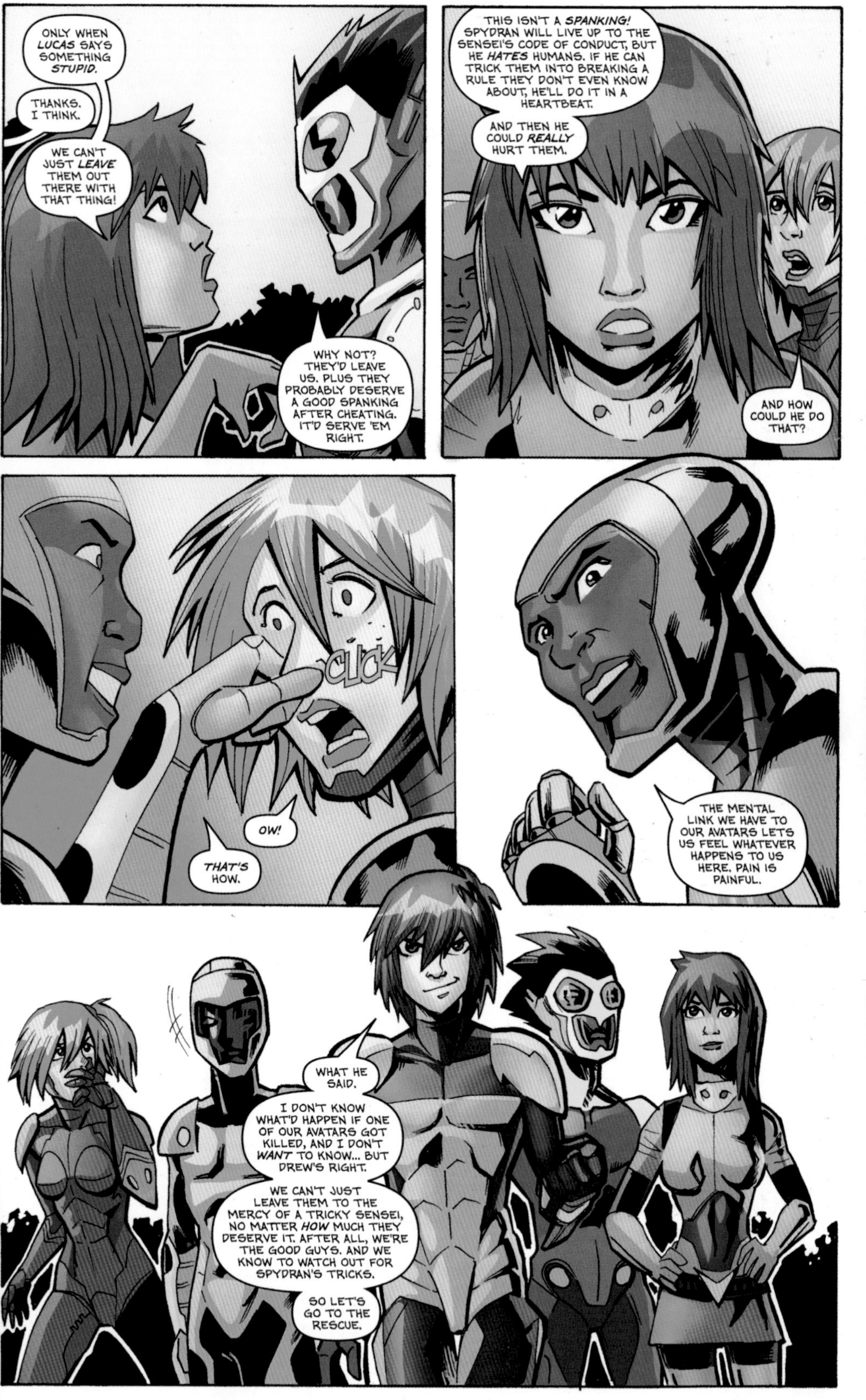

ONLY WHEN LUCAS SAYS SOMETHING STUPID.
THANKS. I THINK.
WE CAN'T JUST LEAVE THEM OUT THERE WITH THAT THING!
WHY NOT? THEY'D LEAVE US. PLUS THEY PROBABLY DESERVE A GOOD SPANKING AFTER CHEATING. IT'D SERVE 'EM RIGHT.
THIS ISN'T A SPANKING! SPYDRAN WILL LIVE UP TO THE SENSEI'S CODE OF CONDUCT, BUT HE HATES HUMANS. IF HE CAN TRICK THEM INTO BREAKING A RULE THEY DON'T EVEN KNOW ABOUT, HE'LL DO IT IN A HEARTBEAT.
AND THEN HE COULD REALLY HURT THEM.
AND HOW COULD HE DO THAT?
CLICK
OW!
THAT'S HOW.
THE MENTAL LINK WE HAVE TO OUR AVATARS LETS US FEEL WHATEVER HAPPENS TO US HERE. PAIN IS PAINFUL.
WHAT HE SAID.
I DON'T KNOW WHAT'D HAPPEN IF ONE OF OUR AVATARS GOT KILLED, AND I DON'T WANT TO KNOW... BUT DREW'S RIGHT.
WE CAN'T JUST LEAVE THEM TO THE MERCY OF A TRICKY SENSEI, NO MATTER HOW MUCH THEY DESERVE IT. AFTER ALL, WE'RE THE GOOD GUYS. AND WE KNOW TO WATCH OUT FOR SPYDRAN'S TRICKS.
SO LET'S GO TO THE RESCUE.

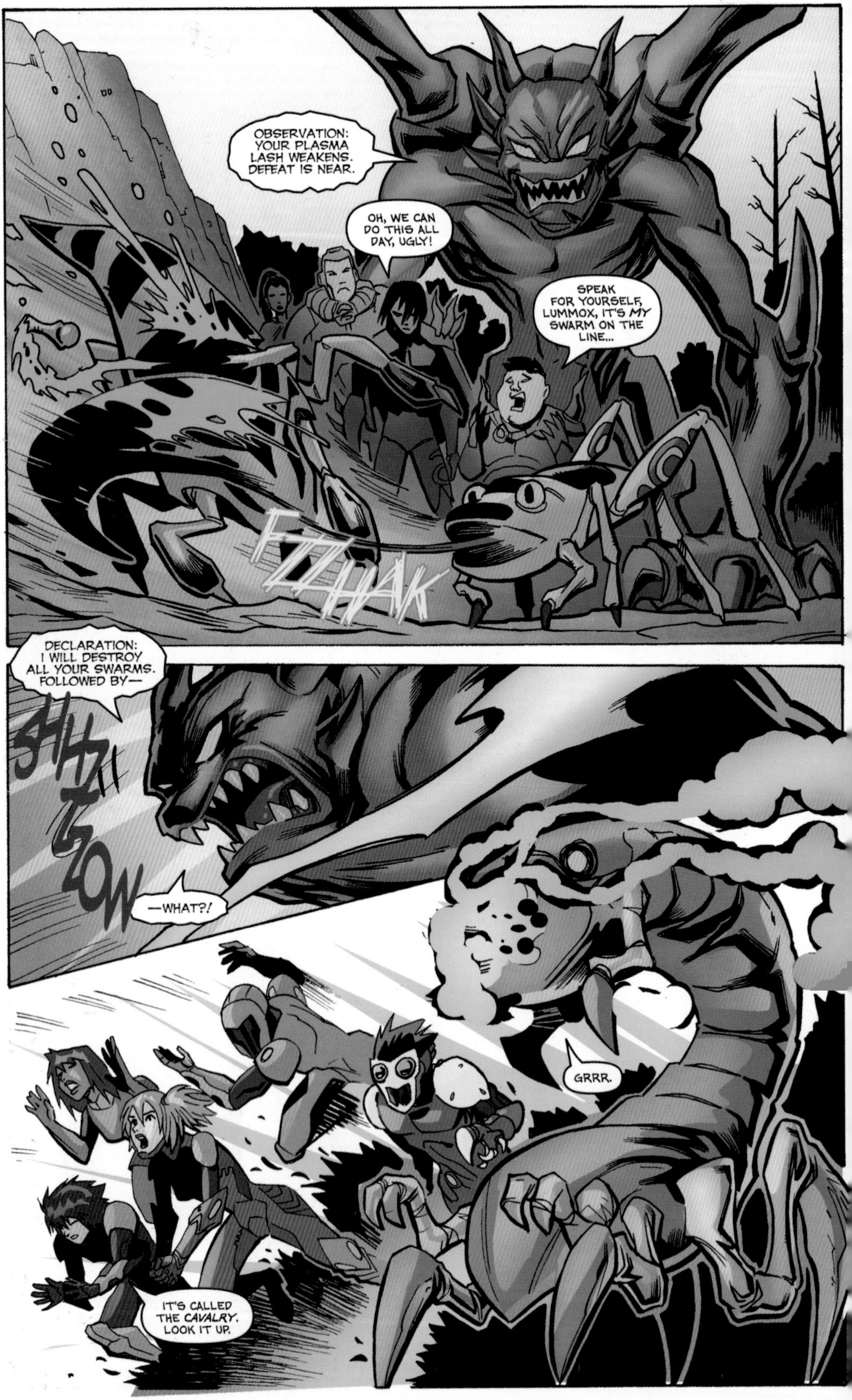

OBSERVATION: YOUR PLASMA LASH WEAKENS. DEFEAT IS NEAR.
OH, WE CAN DO THIS ALL DAY, UGLY!
SPEAK FOR YOURSELF, LUMMOX, IT'S MY SWARM ON THE LINE...
FZZHAK
DECLARATION: I WILL DESTROY ALL YOUR SWARMS. FOLLOWED BY—
SHHZZZOW
—WHAT?!
GRRR.
IT'S CALLED THE CAVALRY. LOOK IT UP.

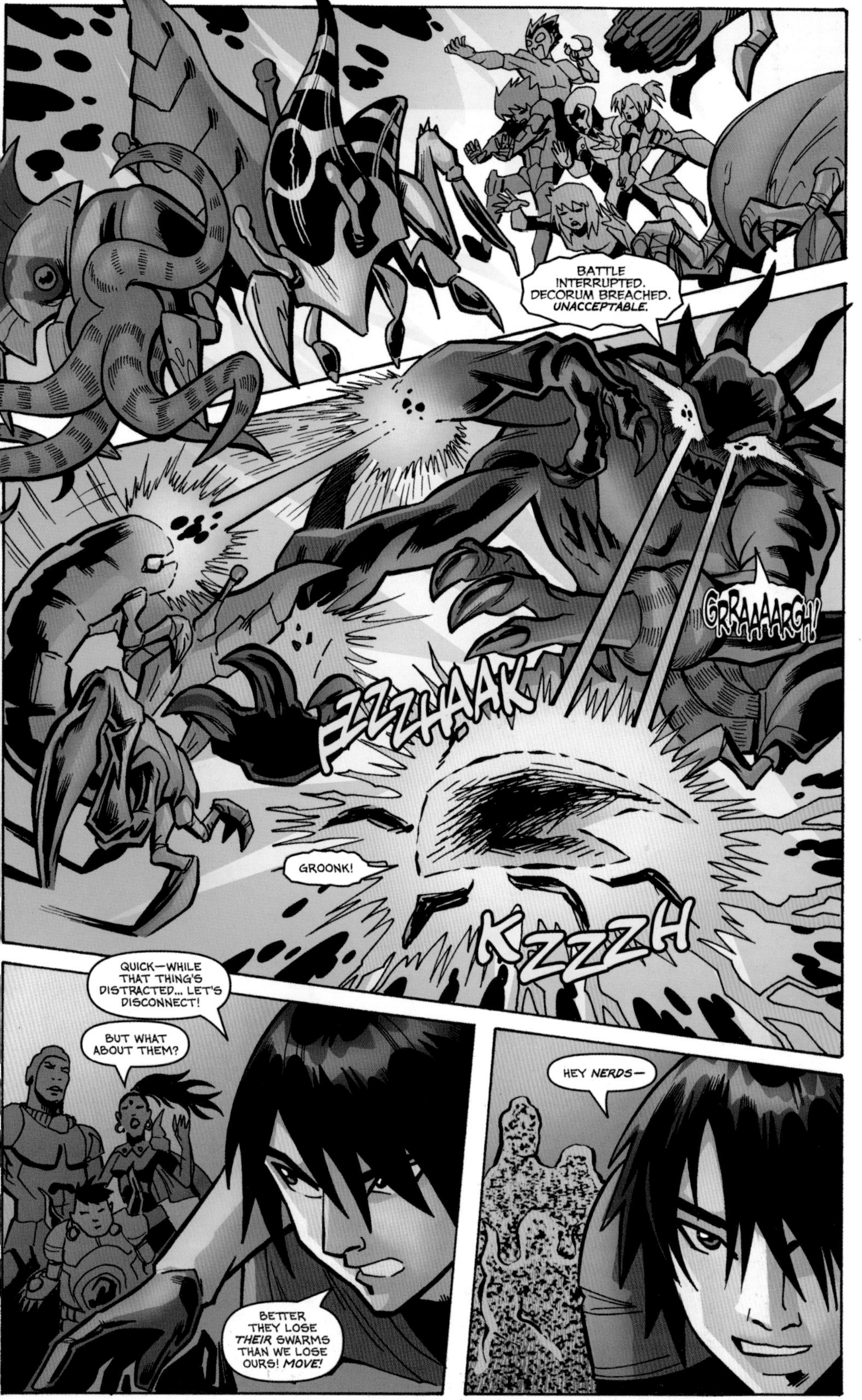
BATTLE INTERRUPTED. DECORUM BREACHED. *UNACCEPTABLE.*
GRRAAAARGH!
ZZZHAAK
GROONK!
KZZZH
QUICK—WHILE THAT THING'S DISTRACTED... LET'S DISCONNECT!
BUT WHAT ABOUT THEM?
BETTER THEY LOSE *THEIR* SWARMS THAN WE LOSE OURS! *MOVE!*
HEY *NERDS*—

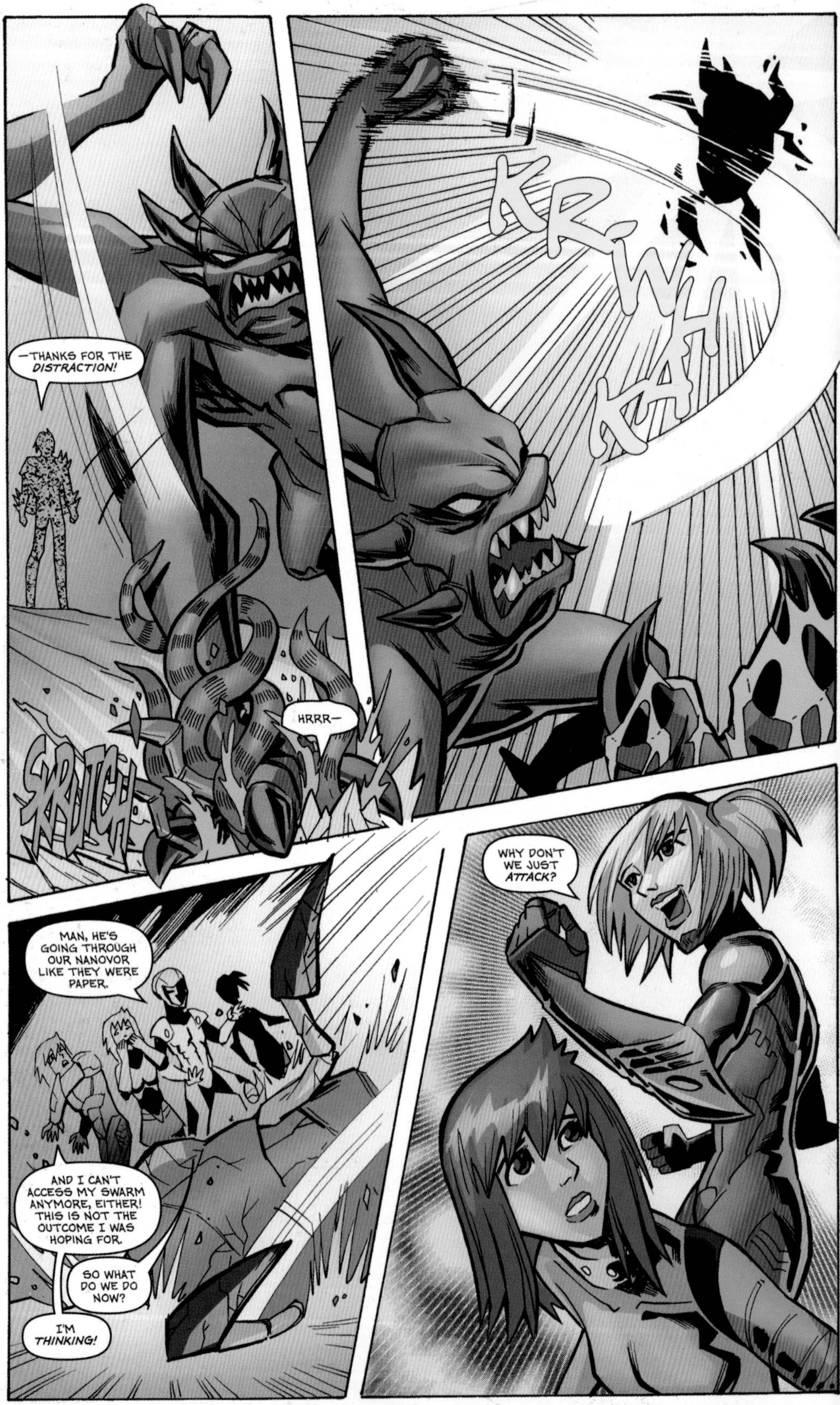
—THANKS FOR THE *DISTRACTION!*
KR-WH KA!
HRRR—
SKRUTCH
MAN, HE'S GOING THROUGH OUR NANOVOR LIKE THEY WERE PAPER.
AND I CAN'T ACCESS MY SWARM ANYMORE, EITHER! THIS IS NOT THE OUTCOME I WAS HOPING FOR.
SO WHAT DO WE DO NOW?
I'M *THINKING!*
WHY DON'T WE JUST *ATTACK?*

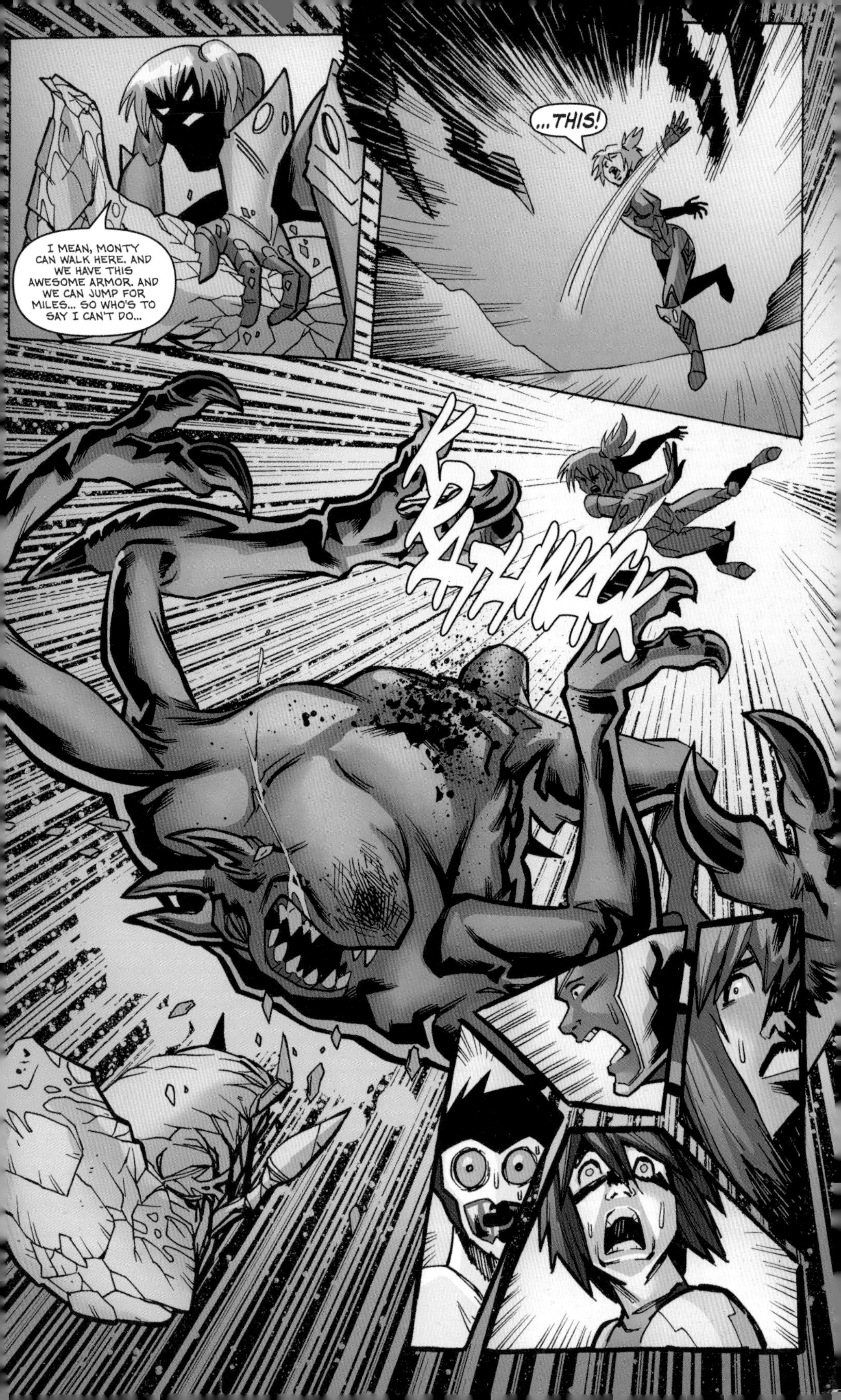
I MEAN, MONTY CAN WALK HERE. AND WE HAVE THIS AWESOME ARMOR. AND WE CAN JUMP FOR MILES... SO WHO'S TO SAY I CAN'T DO...
...THIS!
KRAKHWACK

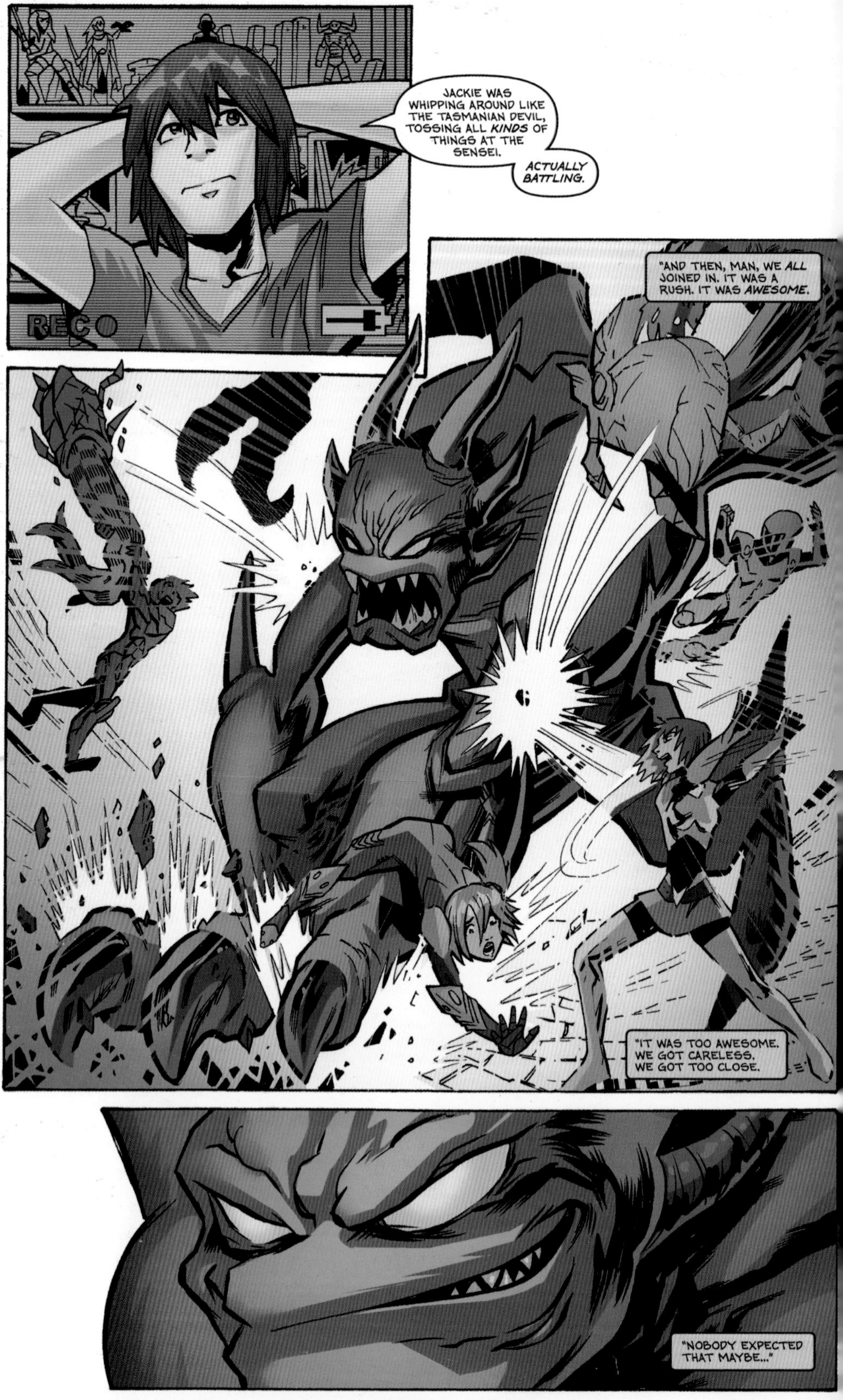
JACKIE WAS WHIPPING AROUND LIKE THE TASMANIAN DEVIL, TOSSING ALL *KINDS* OF THINGS AT THE SENSEI.
ACTUALLY BATTLING.
RECO
"AND THEN, MAN, WE *ALL* JOINED IN. IT WAS A RUSH. IT WAS *AWESOME.*
"IT WAS TOO AWESOME. WE GOT CARELESS. WE GOT TOO CLOSE.
"NOBODY EXPECTED THAT MAYBE..."

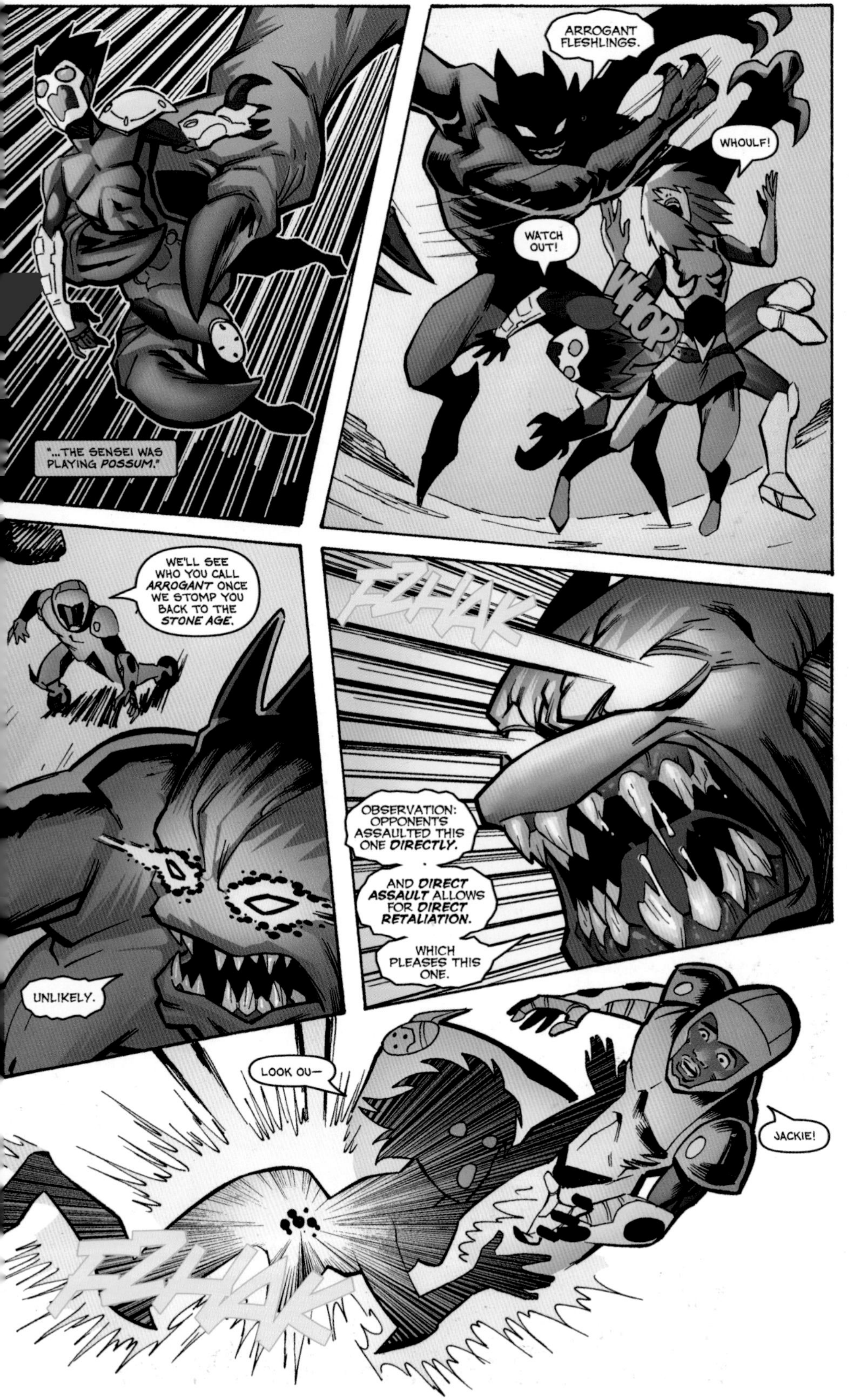

"...THE SENSEI WAS PLAYING POSSUM."
ARROGANT FLESHLINGS.
WHOULF!
WATCH OUT!
WHOP
WE'LL SEE WHO YOU CALL ARROGANT ONCE WE STOMP YOU BACK TO THE STONE AGE.
UNLIKELY.
FZHAK
OBSERVATION: OPPONENTS ASSAULTED THIS ONE DIRECTLY.
AND DIRECT ASSAULT ALLOWS FOR DIRECT RETALIATION.
WHICH PLEASES THIS ONE.
LOOK OU—
JACKIE!
FZHAK

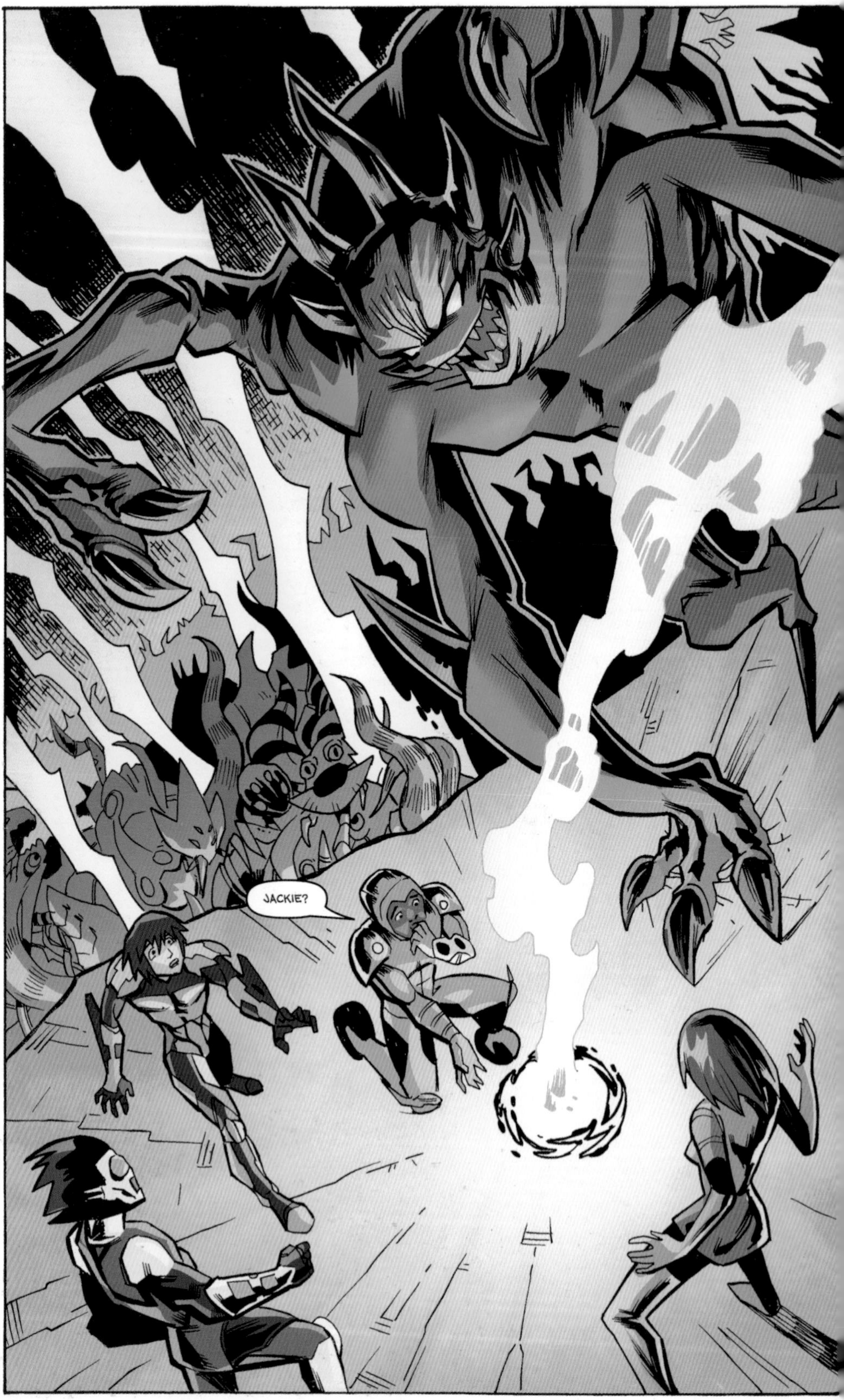
JACKIE?

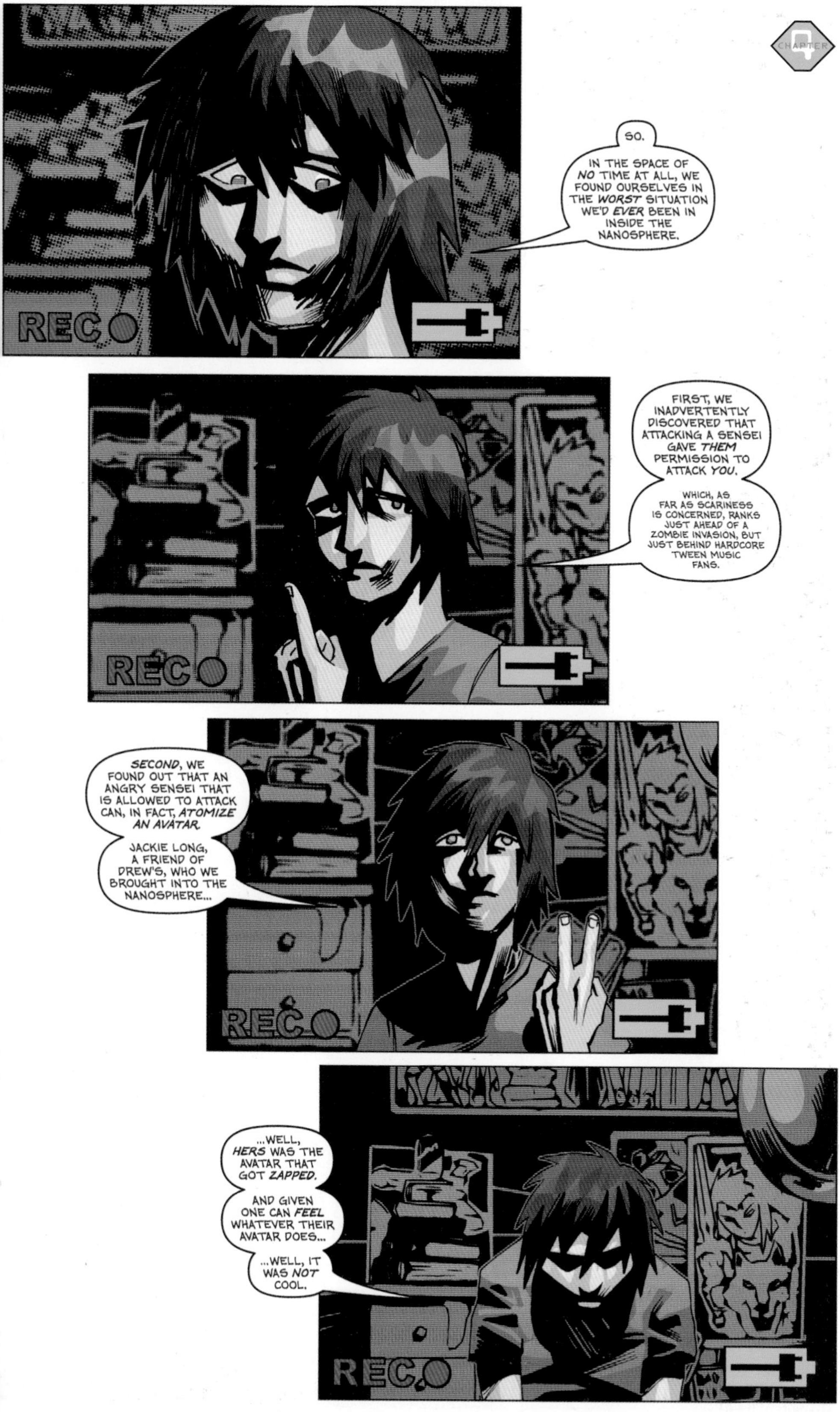
SO.
IN THE SPACE OF NO TIME AT ALL, WE FOUND OURSELVES IN THE WORST SITUATION WE'D EVER BEEN IN INSIDE THE NANOSPHERE.
REC
FIRST, WE INADVERTENTLY DISCOVERED THAT ATTACKING A SENSEI GAVE THEM PERMISSION TO ATTACK YOU.
WHICH, AS FAR AS SCARINESS IS CONCERNED, RANKS JUST AHEAD OF A ZOMBIE INVASION, BUT JUST BEHIND HARDCORE TWEEN MUSIC FANS.
REC
SECOND, WE FOUND OUT THAT AN ANGRY SENSEI THAT IS ALLOWED TO ATTACK CAN, IN FACT, ATOMIZE AN AVATAR.
JACKIE LONG, A FRIEND OF DREW'S, WHO WE BROUGHT INTO THE NANOSPHERE...
REC
...WELL, HERS WAS THE AVATAR THAT GOT ZAPPED.
AND GIVEN ONE CAN FEEL WHATEVER THEIR AVATAR DOES...
...WELL, IT WAS NOT COOL.
REC

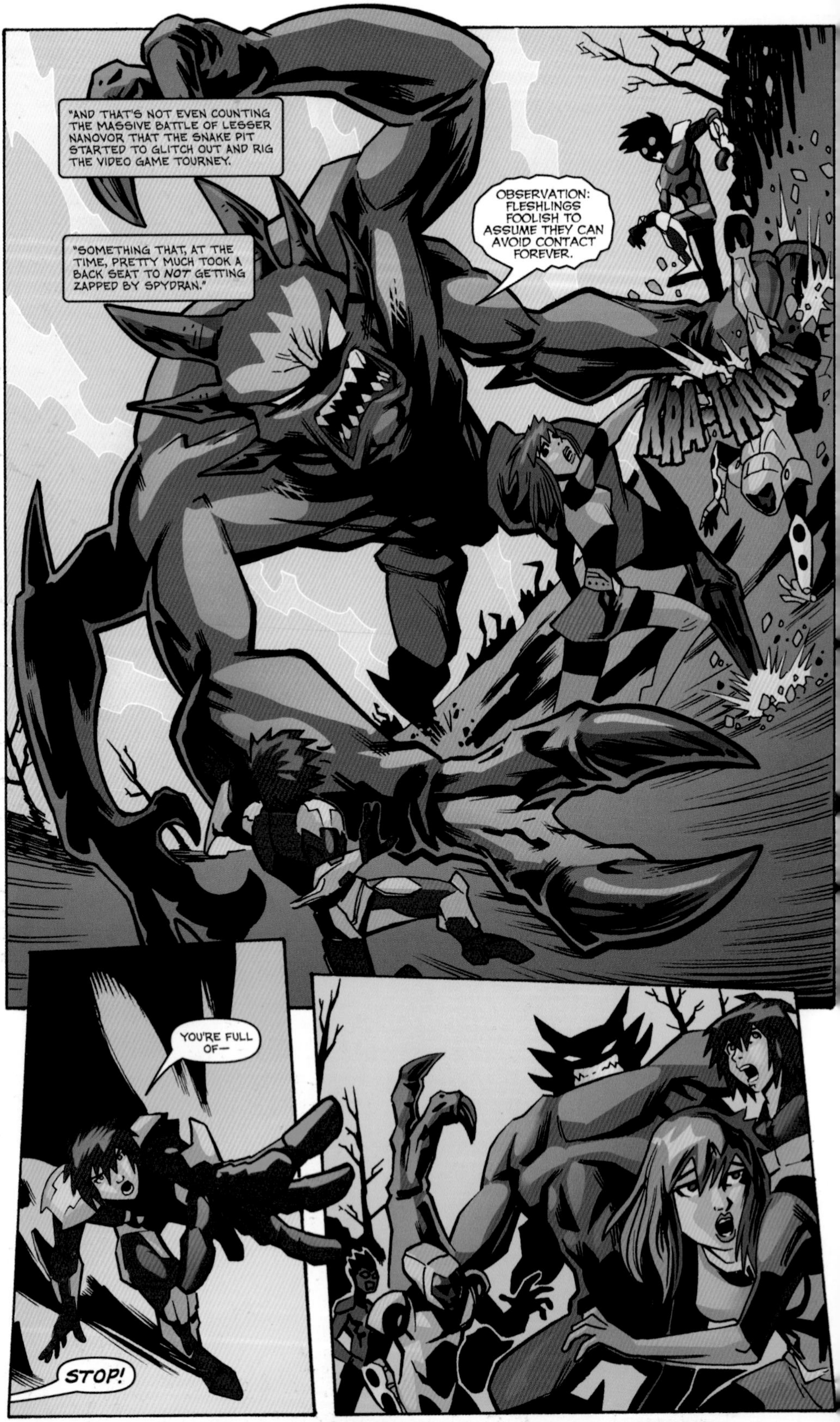
"AND THAT'S NOT EVEN COUNTING THE MASSIVE BATTLE OF LESSER NANOVOR THAT THE SNAKE PIT STARTED TO GLITCH OUT AND RIG THE VIDEO GAME TOURNEY.
"SOMETHING THAT, AT THE TIME, PRETTY MUCH TOOK A BACK SEAT TO *NOT* GETTING ZAPPED BY SPYDRAN."
OBSERVATION: FLESHLINGS FOOLISH TO ASSUME THEY CAN AVOID CONTACT FOREVER.
YOU'RE FULL OF—
STOP!

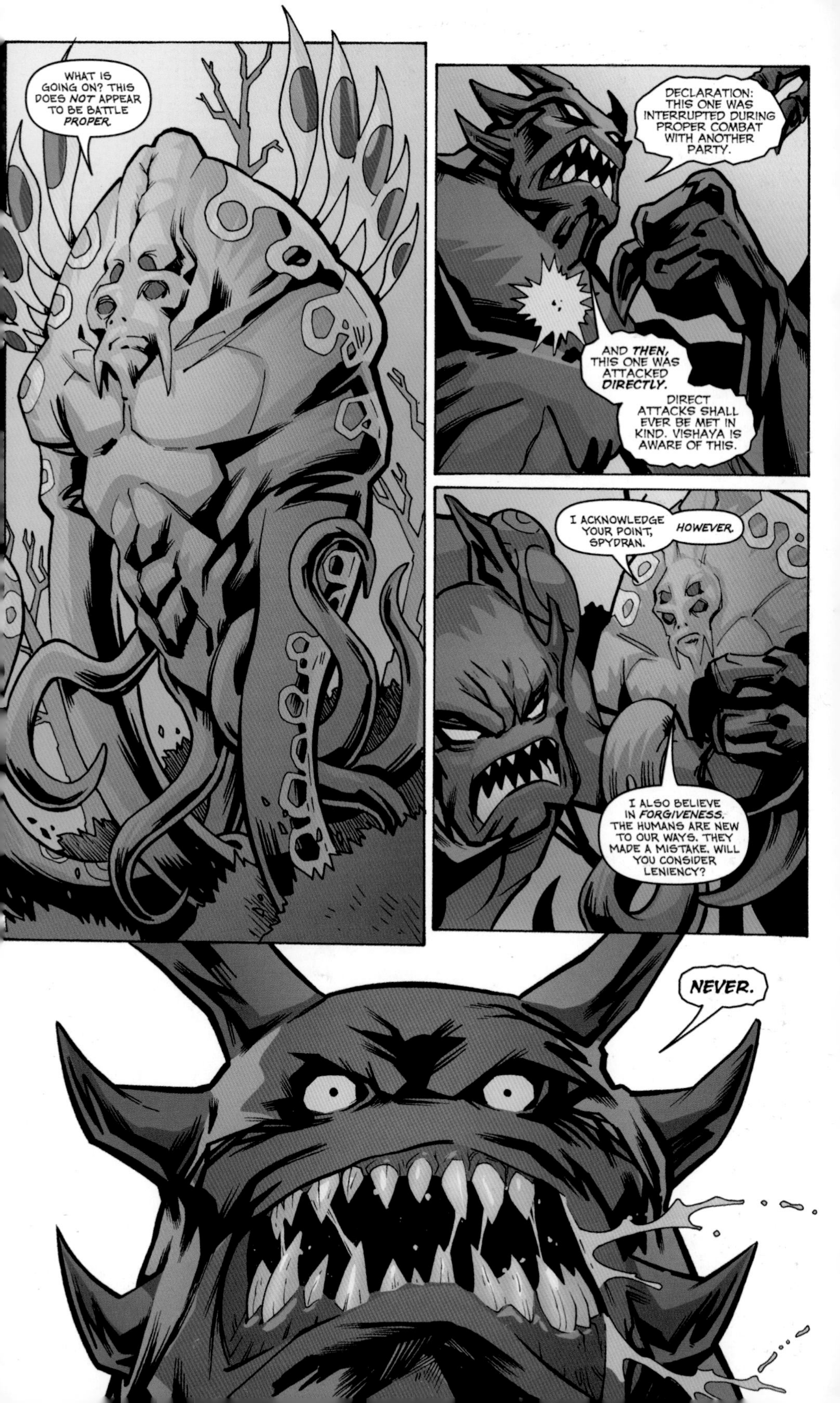
WHAT IS GOING ON? THIS DOES *NOT* APPEAR TO BE BATTLE *PROPER*.
DECLARATION: THIS ONE WAS INTERRUPTED DURING PROPER COMBAT WITH ANOTHER PARTY.
AND *THEN*, THIS ONE WAS ATTACKED ***DIRECTLY***.
DIRECT ATTACKS SHALL EVER BE MET IN KIND. VISHAYA IS AWARE OF THIS.
I ACKNOWLEDGE YOUR POINT, SPYDRAN.
HOWEVER.
I ALSO BELIEVE IN *FORGIVENESS*. THE HUMANS ARE NEW TO OUR WAYS. THEY MADE A MISTAKE. WILL YOU CONSIDER LENIENCY?
NEVER.

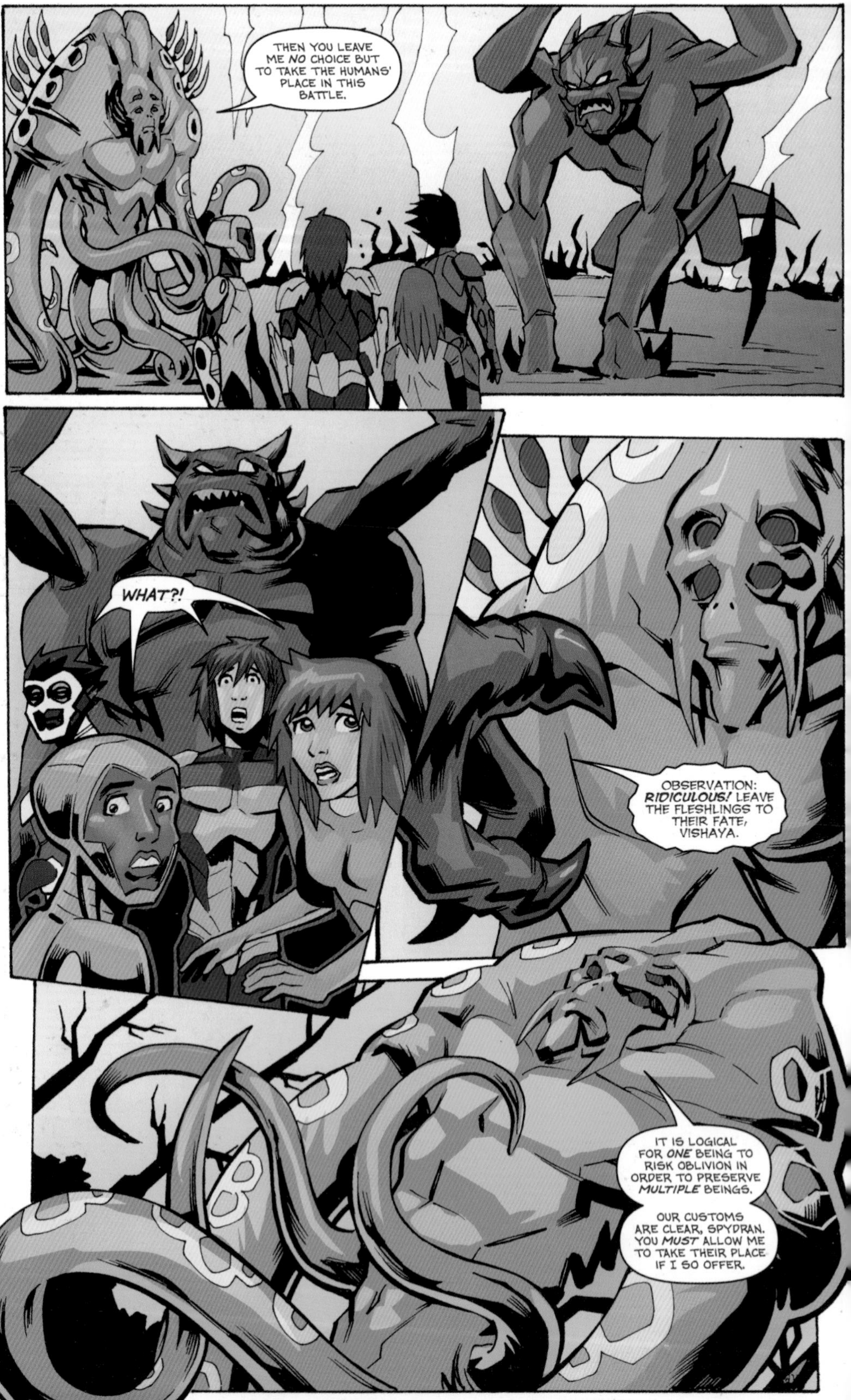
THEN YOU LEAVE ME NO CHOICE BUT TO TAKE THE HUMANS' PLACE IN THIS BATTLE.
WHAT?!
OBSERVATION: RIDICULOUS! LEAVE THE FLESHLINGS TO THEIR FATE, VISHAYA.
IT IS LOGICAL FOR ONE BEING TO RISK OBLIVION IN ORDER TO PRESERVE MULTIPLE BEINGS.
OUR CUSTOMS ARE CLEAR, SPYDRAN. YOU MUST ALLOW ME TO TAKE THEIR PLACE IF I SO OFFER.

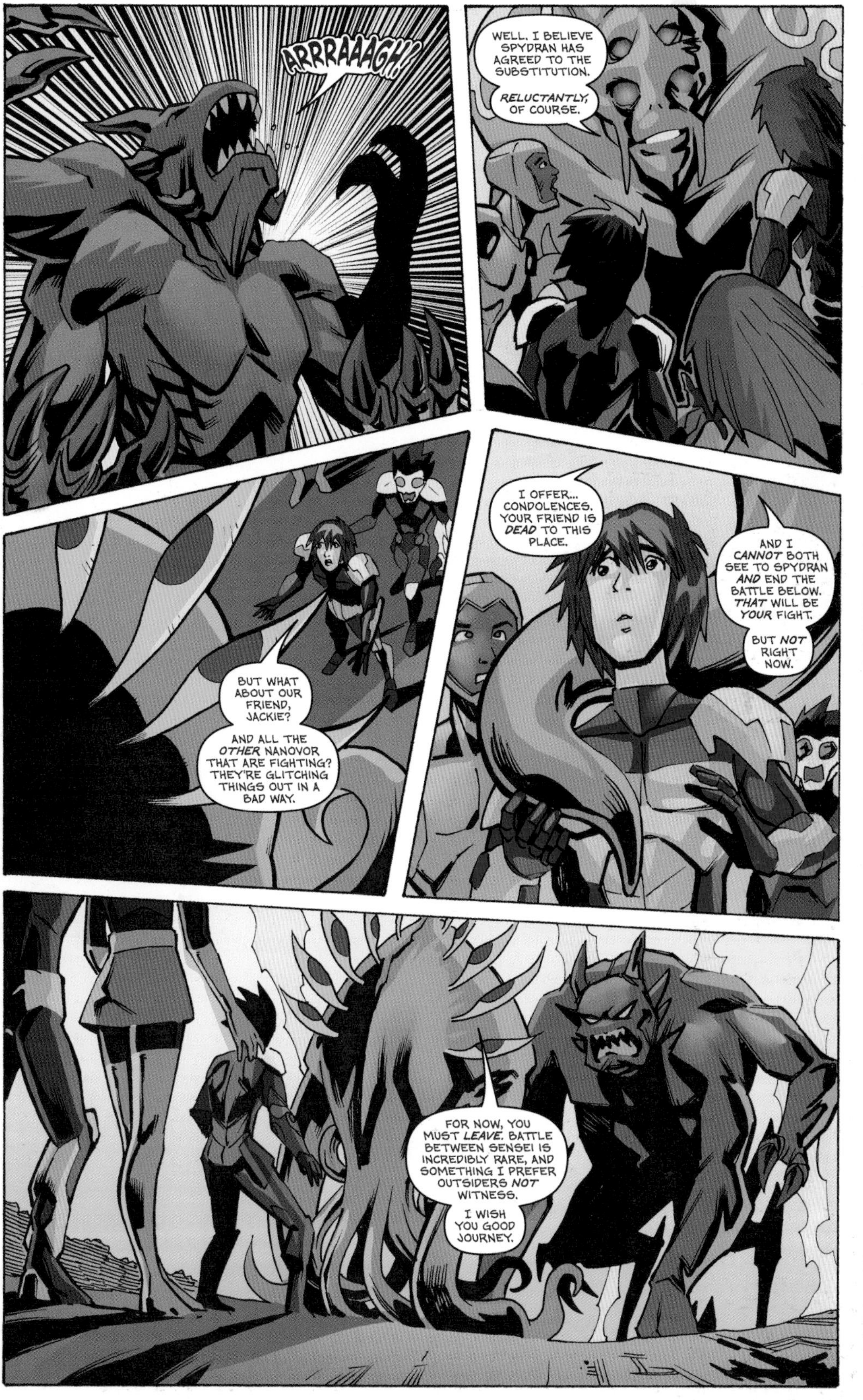
ARRRAAAGH!
WELL. I BELIEVE SPYDRAN HAS AGREED TO THE SUBSTITUTION.
RELUCTANTLY, OF COURSE.
BUT WHAT ABOUT OUR FRIEND, JACKIE?
AND ALL THE OTHER NANOVOR THAT ARE FIGHTING? THEY'RE GLITCHING THINGS OUT IN A BAD WAY.
I OFFER... CONDOLENCES. YOUR FRIEND IS DEAD TO THIS PLACE.
AND I CANNOT BOTH SEE TO SPYDRAN AND END THE BATTLE BELOW. THAT WILL BE YOUR FIGHT.
BUT NOT RIGHT NOW.
FOR NOW, YOU MUST LEAVE. BATTLE BETWEEN SENSEI IS INCREDIBLY RARE, AND SOMETHING I PREFER OUTSIDERS NOT WITNESS.
I WISH YOU GOOD JOURNEY.

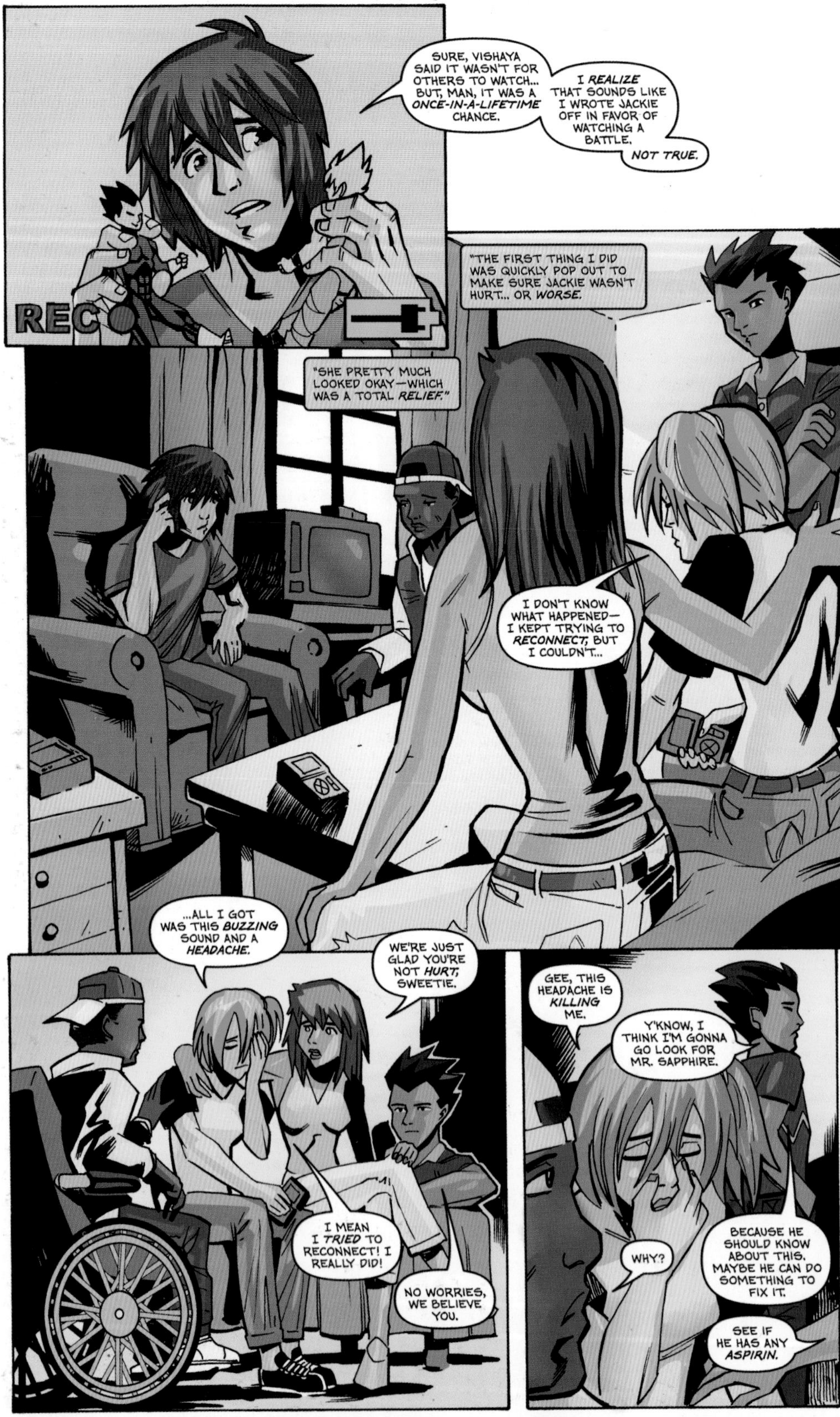

SURE, VISHAYA SAID IT WASN'T FOR OTHERS TO WATCH... BUT, MAN, IT WAS A ONCE-IN-A-LIFETIME CHANCE.
I REALIZE THAT SOUNDS LIKE I WROTE JACKIE OFF IN FAVOR OF WATCHING A BATTLE.
NOT TRUE.
REC
"THE FIRST THING I DID WAS QUICKLY POP OUT TO MAKE SURE JACKIE WASN'T HURT... OR WORSE.
"SHE PRETTY MUCH LOOKED OKAY—WHICH WAS A TOTAL RELIEF."
I DON'T KNOW WHAT HAPPENED— I KEPT TRYING TO RECONNECT, BUT I COULDN'T...
...ALL I GOT WAS THIS BUZZING SOUND AND A HEADACHE.
WE'RE JUST GLAD YOU'RE NOT HURT, SWEETIE.
I MEAN I TRIED TO RECONNECT! I REALLY DID!
NO WORRIES, WE BELIEVE YOU.
GEE, THIS HEADACHE IS KILLING ME.
Y'KNOW, I THINK I'M GONNA GO LOOK FOR MR. SAPPHIRE.
WHY?
BECAUSE HE SHOULD KNOW ABOUT THIS. MAYBE HE CAN DO SOMETHING TO FIX IT.
SEE IF HE HAS ANY ASPIRIN.

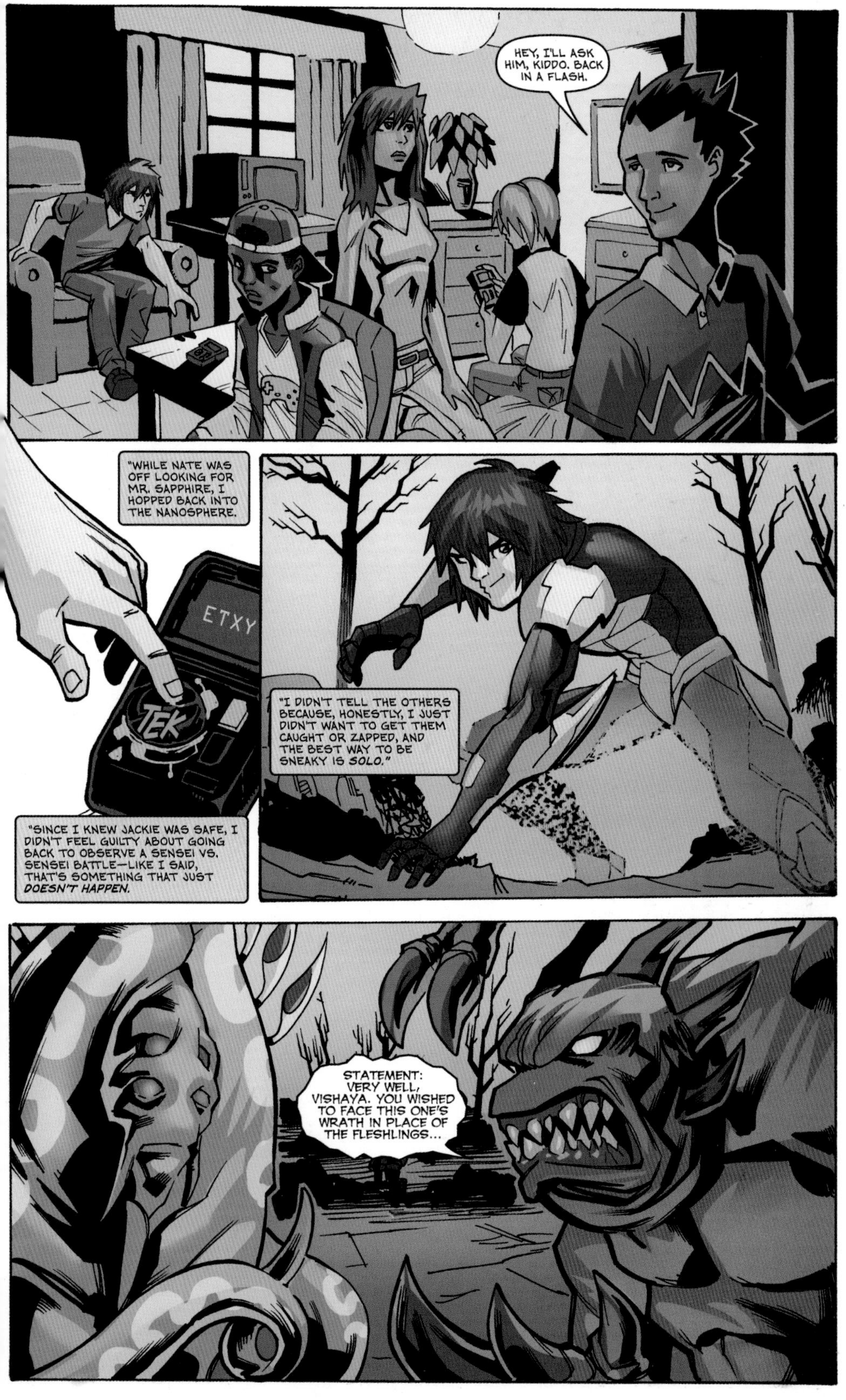
HEY, I'LL ASK HIM, KIDDO. BACK IN A FLASH.
"WHILE NATE WAS OFF LOOKING FOR MR. SAPPHIRE, I HOPPED BACK INTO THE NANOSPHERE.
ETXY
TEK
"I DIDN'T TELL THE OTHERS BECAUSE, HONESTLY, I JUST DIDN'T WANT TO GET THEM CAUGHT OR ZAPPED, AND THE BEST WAY TO BE SNEAKY IS *SOLO*."
"SINCE I KNEW JACKIE WAS SAFE, I DIDN'T FEEL GUILTY ABOUT GOING BACK TO OBSERVE A SENSEI VS. SENSEI BATTLE—LIKE I SAID, THAT'S SOMETHING THAT JUST *DOESN'T HAPPEN.*
STATEMENT: VERY WELL, VISHAYA. YOU WISHED TO FACE THIS ONE'S WRATH IN PLACE OF THE FLESHLINGS...

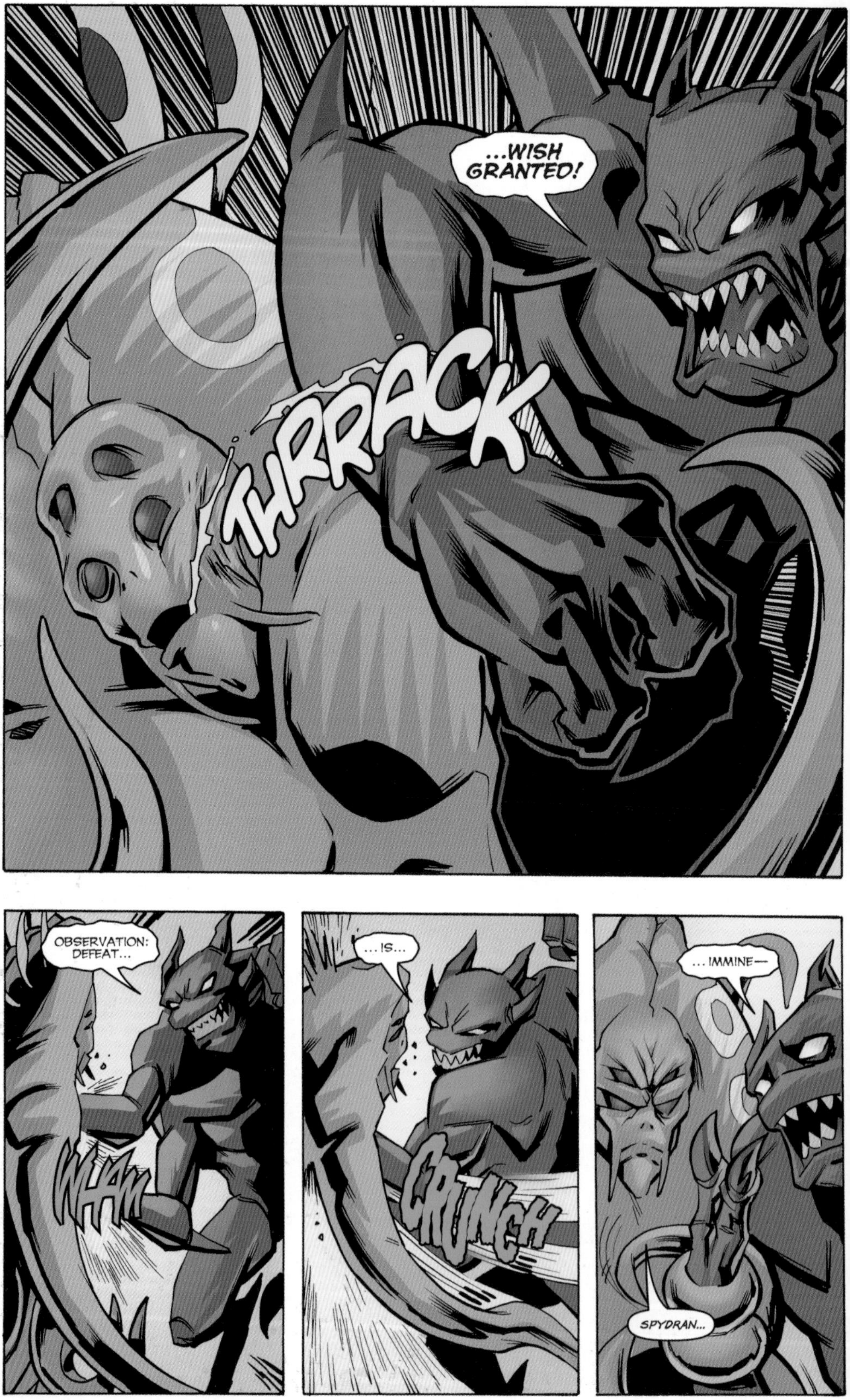
...WISH GRANTED!
THRRACK
OBSERVATION: DEFEAT...
WHAM
...IS...
CRUNCH
...IMMINE—
SPYDRAN...

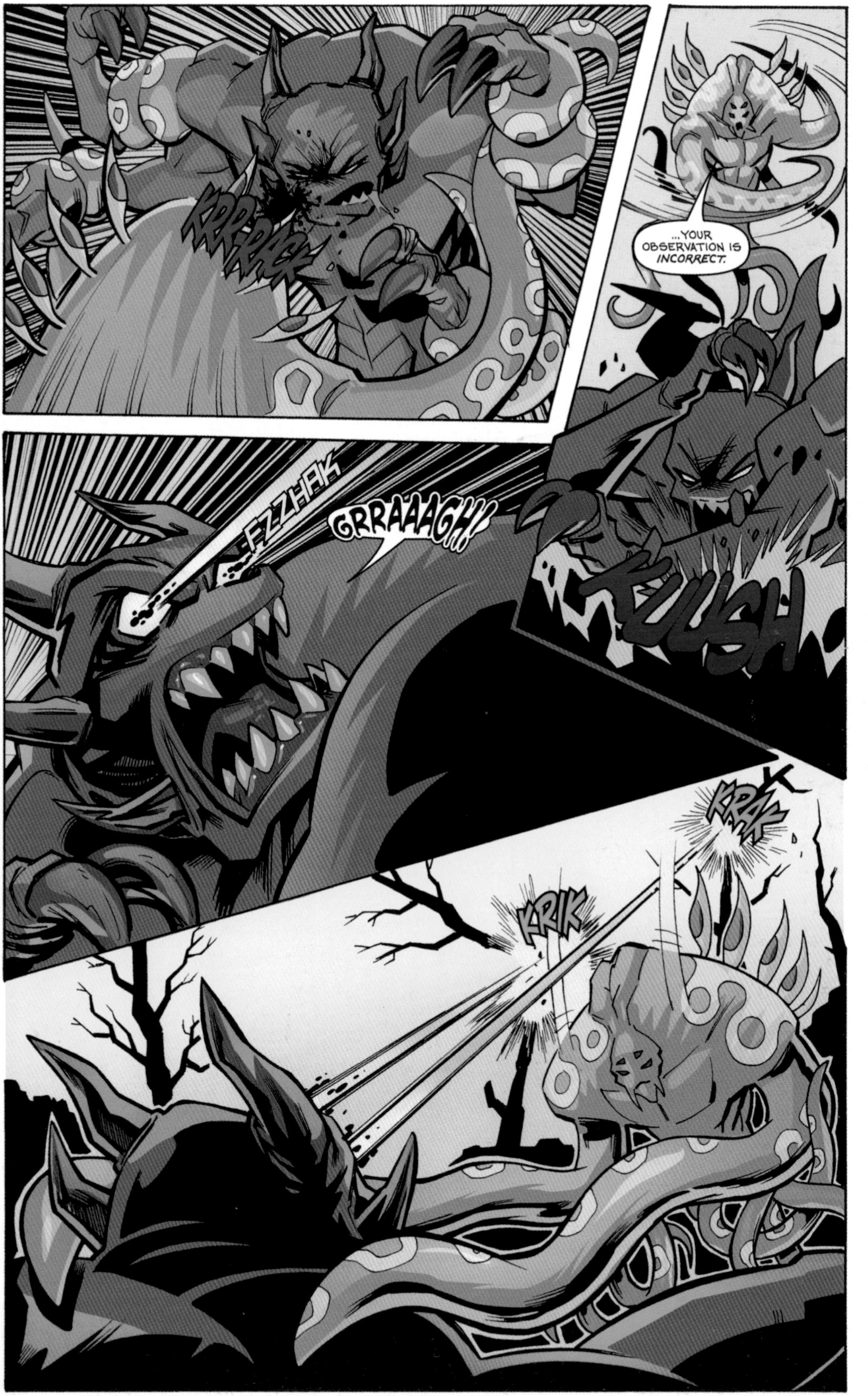
KRRRACK
...YOUR OBSERVATION IS INCORRECT.
FZZHAK
GRRAAAGH!
KRUSH
KRAK
KRIK

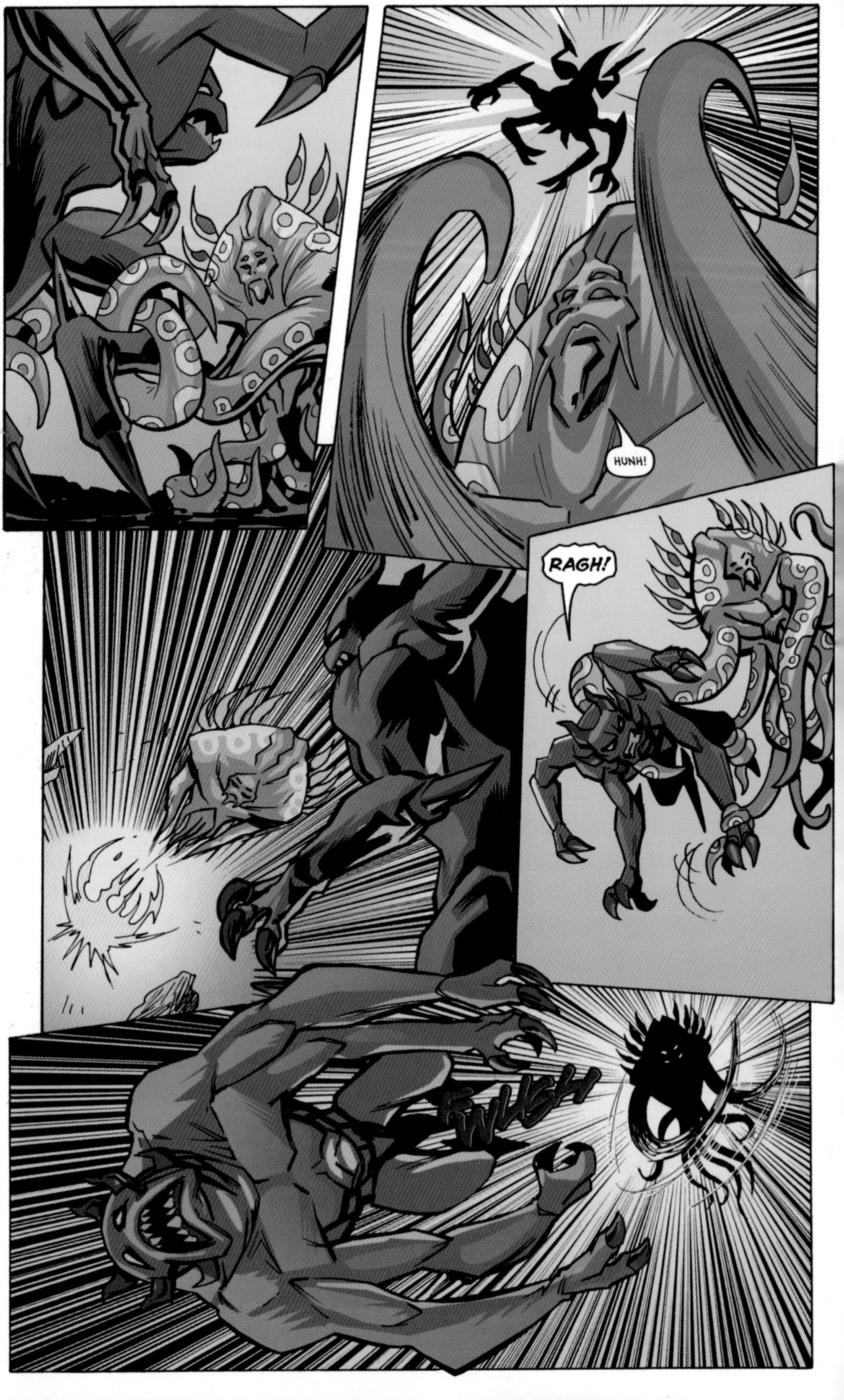
HUNH!
RAGH!
FWUSH

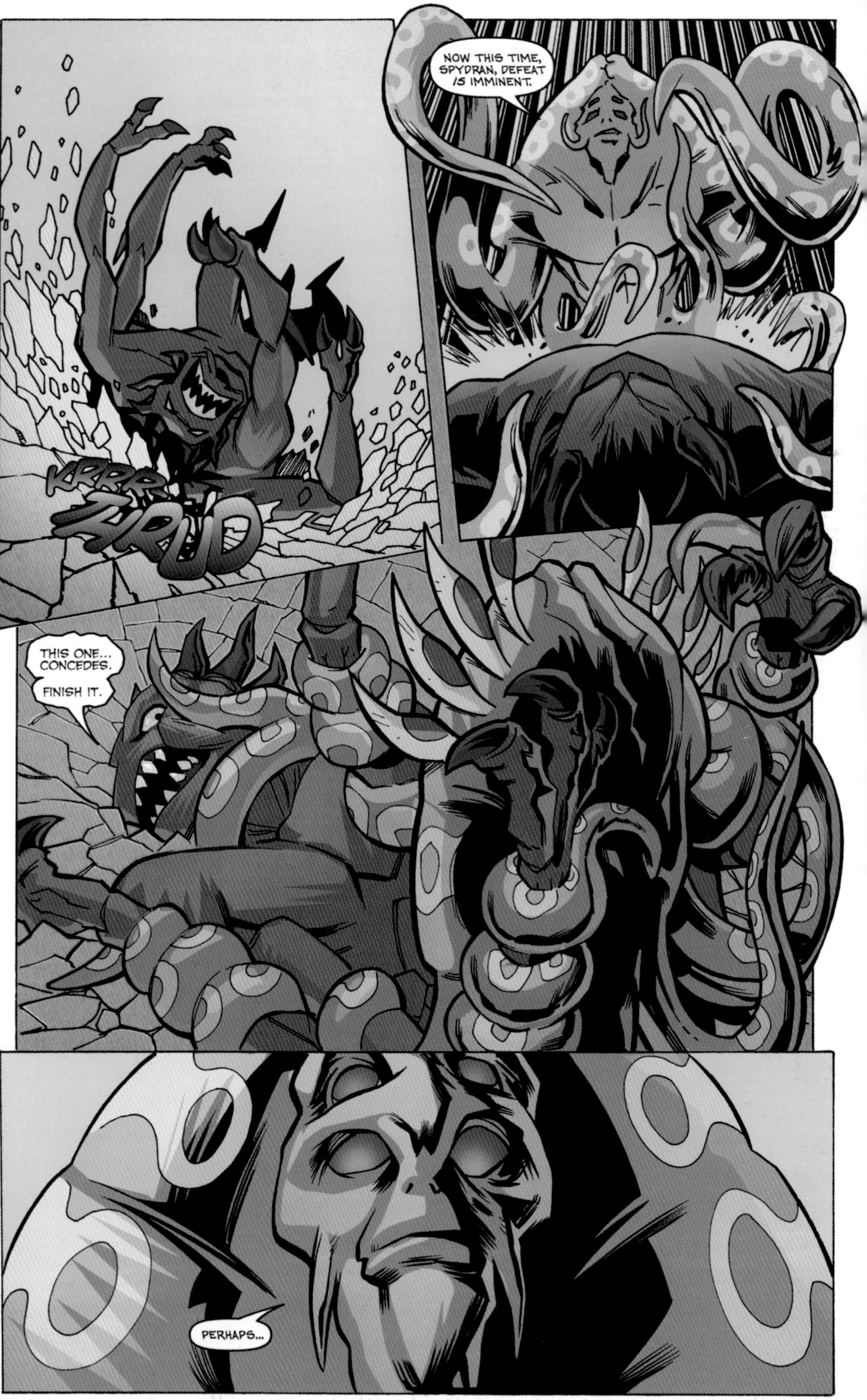
KRRR
THUD
NOW THIS TIME, SPYDRAN, DEFEAT IS IMMINENT.
THIS ONE... CONCEDES.
FINISH IT.
PERHAPS...

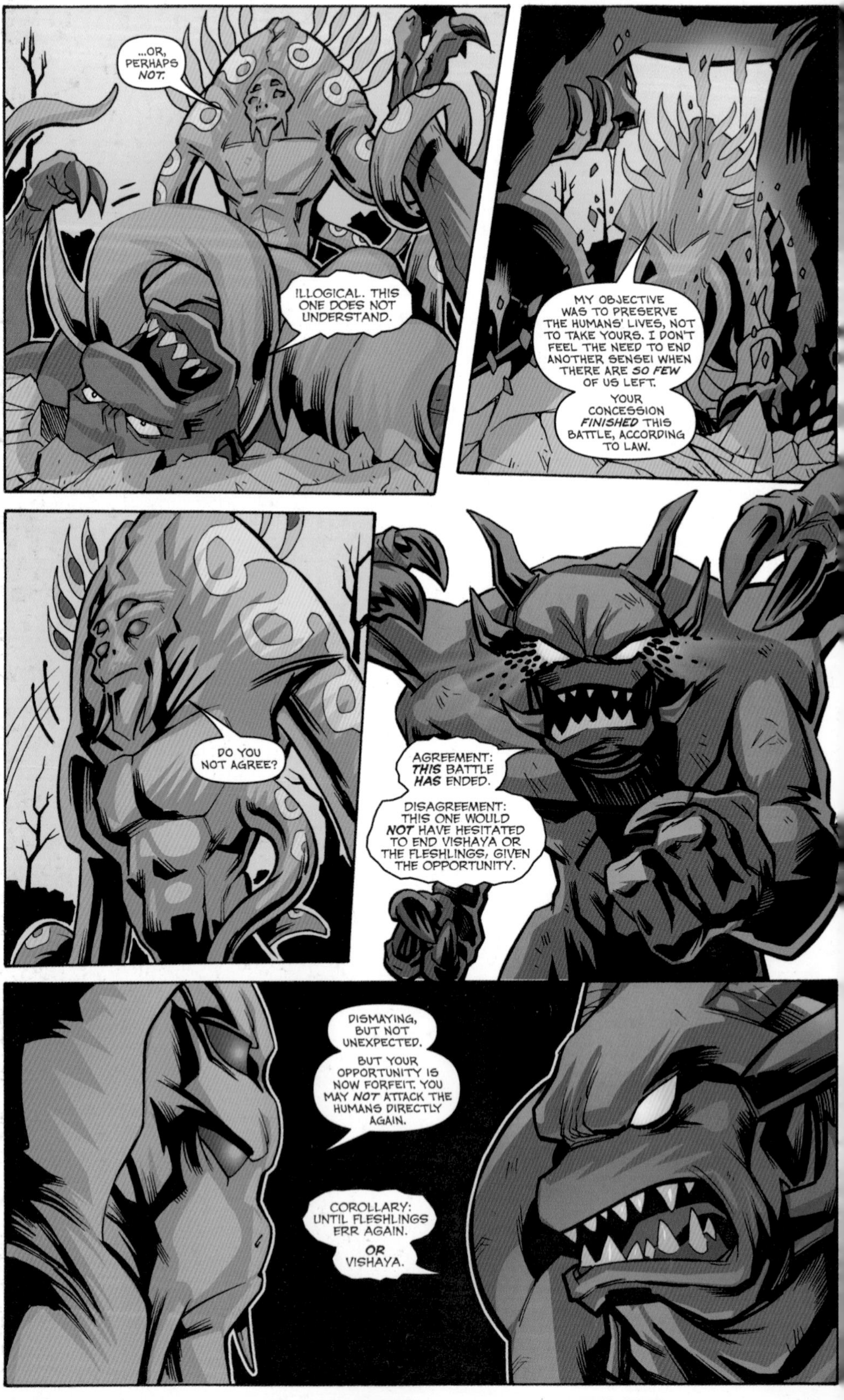
...OR, PERHAPS NOT.
ILLOGICAL. THIS ONE DOES NOT UNDERSTAND.
MY OBJECTIVE WAS TO PRESERVE THE HUMANS' LIVES, NOT TO TAKE YOURS. I DON'T FEEL THE NEED TO END ANOTHER SENSEI WHEN THERE ARE SO FEW OF US LEFT.
YOUR CONCESSION FINISHED THIS BATTLE, ACCORDING TO LAW.
DO YOU NOT AGREE?
AGREEMENT: THIS BATTLE HAS ENDED.
DISAGREEMENT: THIS ONE WOULD NOT HAVE HESITATED TO END VISHAYA OR THE FLESHLINGS, GIVEN THE OPPORTUNITY.
DISMAYING, BUT NOT UNEXPECTED.
BUT YOUR OPPORTUNITY IS NOW FORFEIT. YOU MAY NOT ATTACK THE HUMANS DIRECTLY AGAIN.
COROLLARY: UNTIL FLESHLINGS ERR AGAIN.
OR VISHAYA.

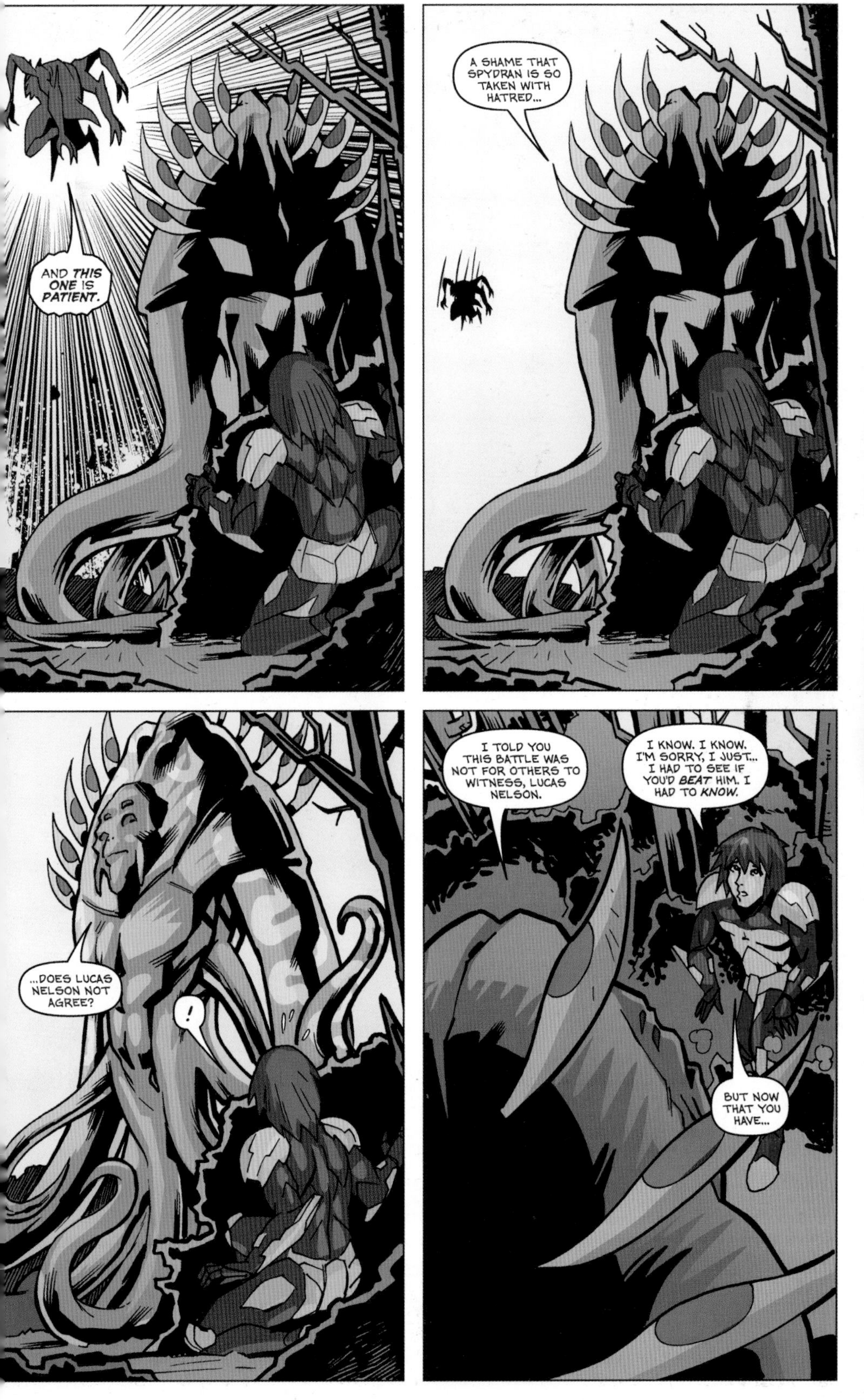
AND THIS ONE IS PATIENT.
A SHAME THAT SPYDRAN IS SO TAKEN WITH HATRED...
...DOES LUCAS NELSON NOT AGREE?
!
I TOLD YOU THIS BATTLE WAS NOT FOR OTHERS TO WITNESS, LUCAS NELSON.
I KNOW. I KNOW. I'M SORRY, I JUST... I HAD TO SEE IF YOU'D BEAT HIM. I HAD TO KNOW.
BUT NOW THAT YOU HAVE...

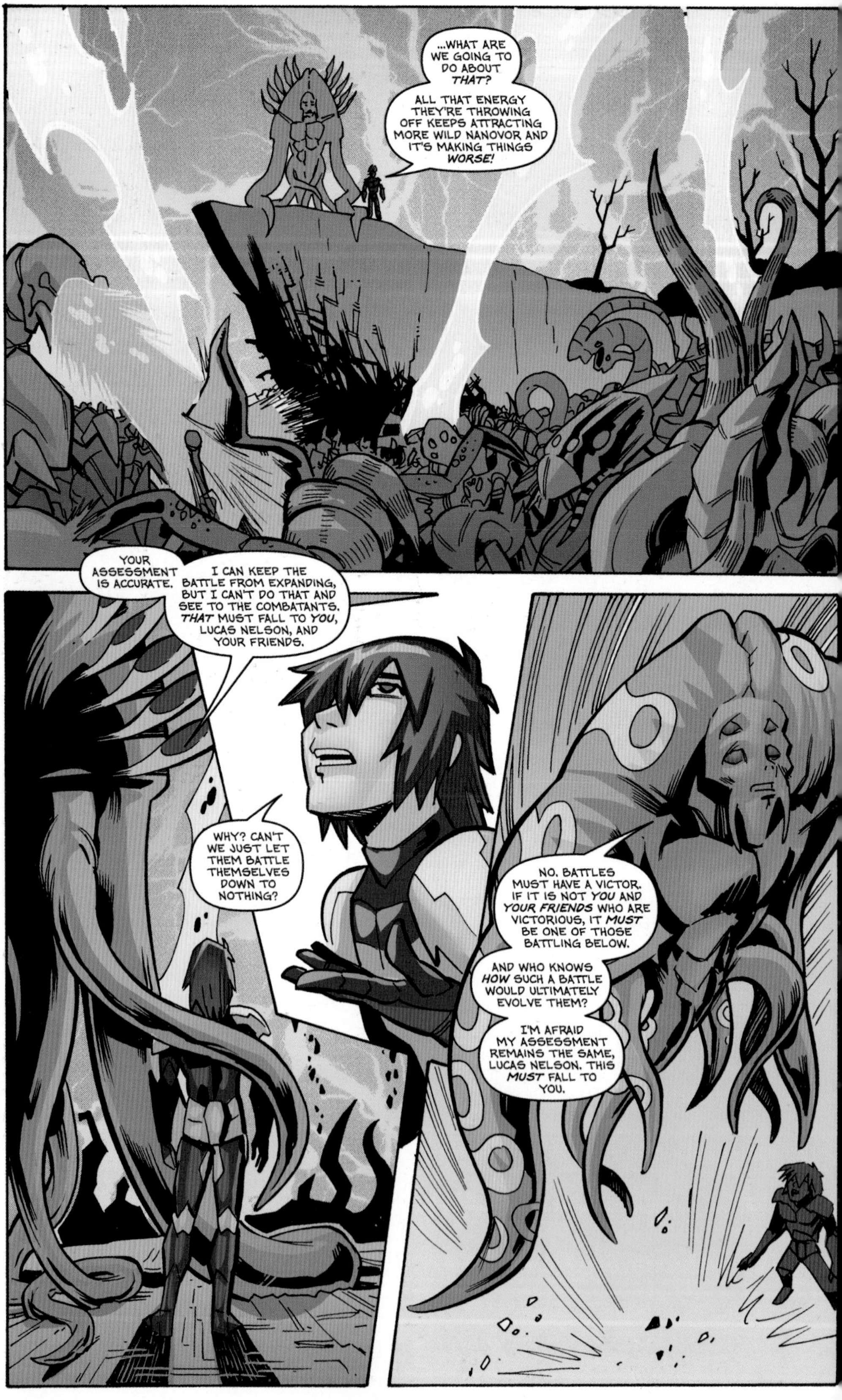
...WHAT ARE WE GOING TO DO ABOUT *THAT?*
ALL THAT ENERGY THEY'RE THROWING OFF KEEPS ATTRACTING MORE WILD NANOVOR AND IT'S MAKING THINGS *WORSE!*
YOUR ASSESSMENT IS ACCURATE.
I CAN KEEP THE BATTLE FROM EXPANDING, BUT I CAN'T DO THAT AND SEE TO THE COMBATANTS. *THAT* MUST FALL TO *YOU*, LUCAS NELSON, AND YOUR FRIENDS.
WHY? CAN'T WE JUST LET THEM BATTLE THEMSELVES DOWN TO NOTHING?
NO. BATTLES MUST HAVE A VICTOR. IF IT IS NOT *YOU* AND *YOUR FRIENDS* WHO ARE VICTORIOUS, IT *MUST* BE ONE OF THOSE BATTLING BELOW.
AND WHO KNOWS *HOW* SUCH A BATTLE WOULD ULTIMATELY EVOLVE THEM?
I'M AFRAID MY ASSESSMENT REMAINS THE SAME, LUCAS NELSON. THIS *MUST* FALL TO YOU.

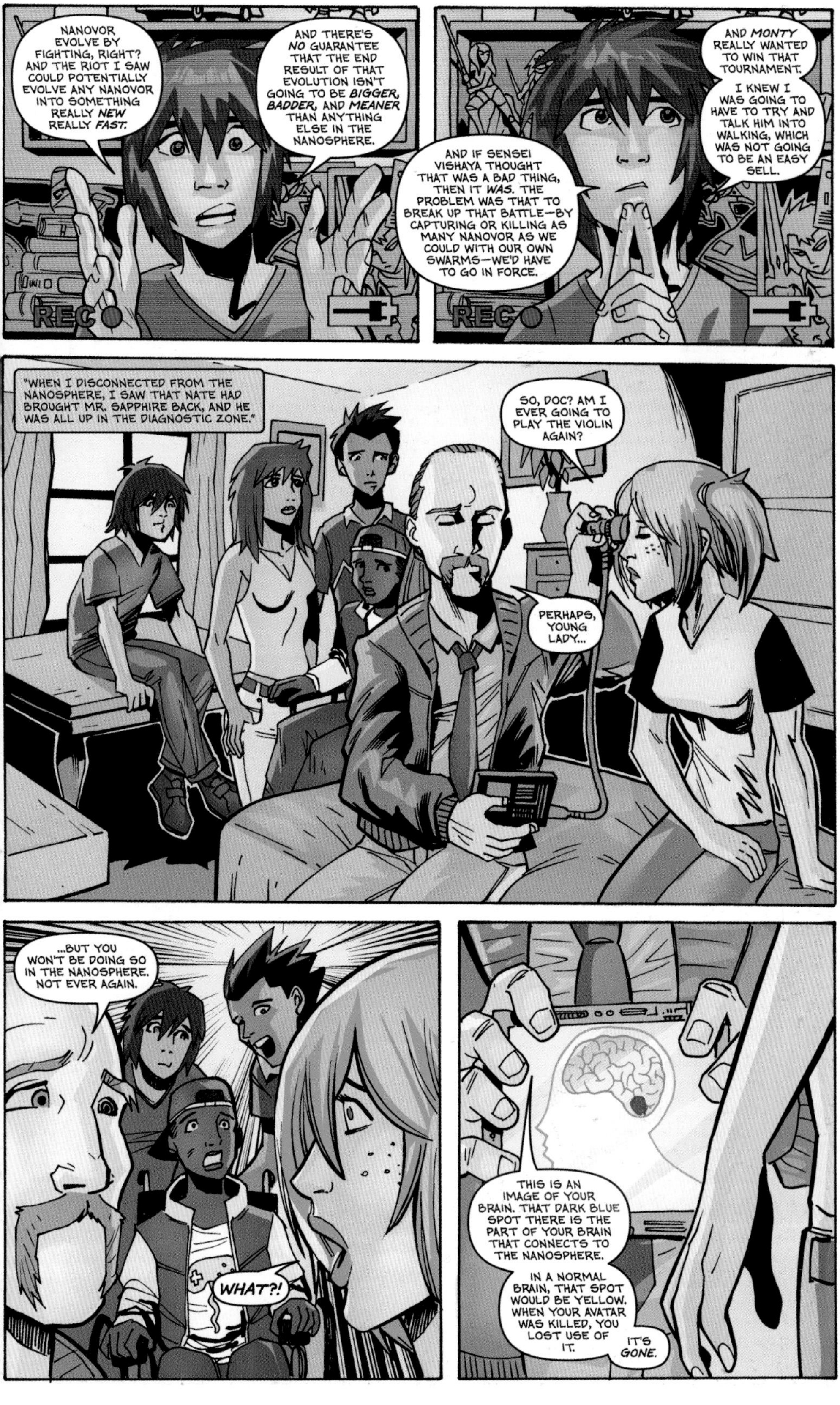
NANOVOR EVOLVE BY FIGHTING, RIGHT? AND THE RIOT I SAW COULD POTENTIALLY EVOLVE ANY NANOVOR INTO SOMETHING REALLY *NEW* REALLY *FAST.*
AND THERE'S *NO* GUARANTEE THAT THE END RESULT OF THAT EVOLUTION ISN'T GOING TO BE *BIGGER, BADDER,* AND *MEANER* THAN ANYTHING ELSE IN THE NANOSPHERE.
REC
AND IF SENSEI VISHAYA THOUGHT THAT WAS A BAD THING, THEN IT *WAS.* THE PROBLEM WAS THAT TO BREAK UP THAT BATTLE—BY CAPTURING OR KILLING AS MANY NANOVOR AS WE COULD WITH OUR OWN SWARMS—WE'D HAVE TO GO IN FORCE.
AND *MONTY* REALLY WANTED TO WIN THAT TOURNAMENT.
I KNEW I WAS GOING TO HAVE TO TRY AND TALK HIM INTO WALKING, WHICH WAS NOT GOING TO BE AN EASY SELL.
REC
"WHEN I DISCONNECTED FROM THE NANOSPHERE, I SAW THAT NATE HAD BROUGHT MR. SAPPHIRE BACK, AND HE WAS ALL UP IN THE DIAGNOSTIC ZONE."
SO, DOC? AM I EVER GOING TO PLAY THE VIOLIN AGAIN?
PERHAPS, YOUNG LADY...
...BUT YOU WON'T BE DOING SO IN THE NANOSPHERE. NOT EVER AGAIN.
WHAT?!
THIS IS AN IMAGE OF YOUR BRAIN. THAT DARK BLUE SPOT THERE IS THE PART OF YOUR BRAIN THAT CONNECTS TO THE NANOSPHERE.
IN A NORMAL BRAIN, THAT SPOT WOULD BE YELLOW. WHEN YOUR AVATAR WAS KILLED, YOU LOST USE OF IT.
IT'S *GONE.*

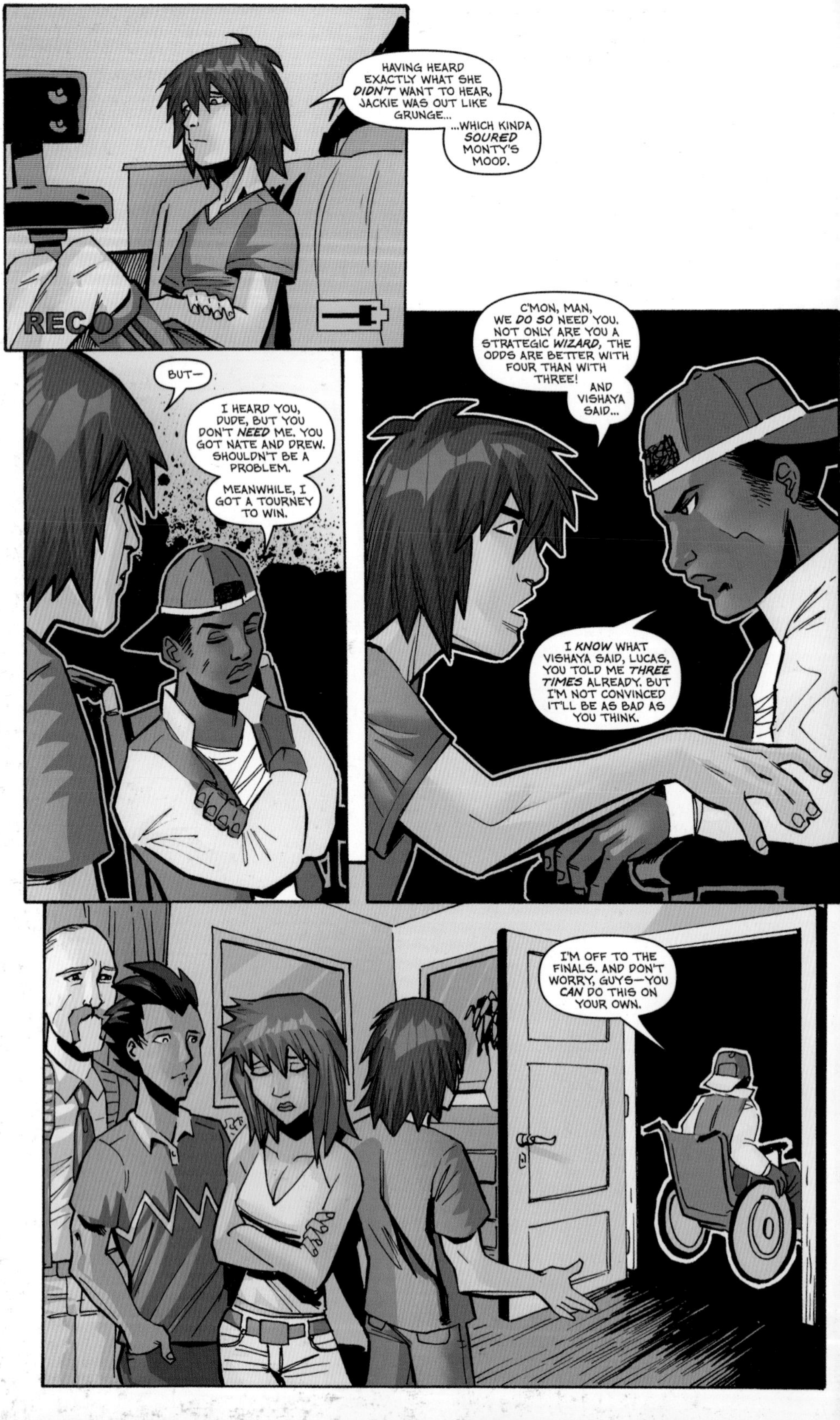
HAVING HEARD EXACTLY WHAT SHE DIDN'T WANT TO HEAR, JACKIE WAS OUT LIKE GRUNGE...
...WHICH KINDA SOURED MONTY'S MOOD.
REC
BUT—
I HEARD YOU, DUDE, BUT YOU DON'T NEED ME. YOU GOT NATE AND DREW. SHOULDN'T BE A PROBLEM.
MEANWHILE, I GOT A TOURNEY TO WIN.
C'MON, MAN, WE DO SO NEED YOU. NOT ONLY ARE YOU A STRATEGIC WIZARD, THE ODDS ARE BETTER WITH FOUR THAN WITH THREE!
AND VISHAYA SAID...
I KNOW WHAT VISHAYA SAID, LUCAS, YOU TOLD ME THREE TIMES ALREADY. BUT I'M NOT CONVINCED IT'LL BE AS BAD AS YOU THINK.
I'M OFF TO THE FINALS. AND DON'T WORRY, GUYS—YOU CAN DO THIS ON YOUR OWN.

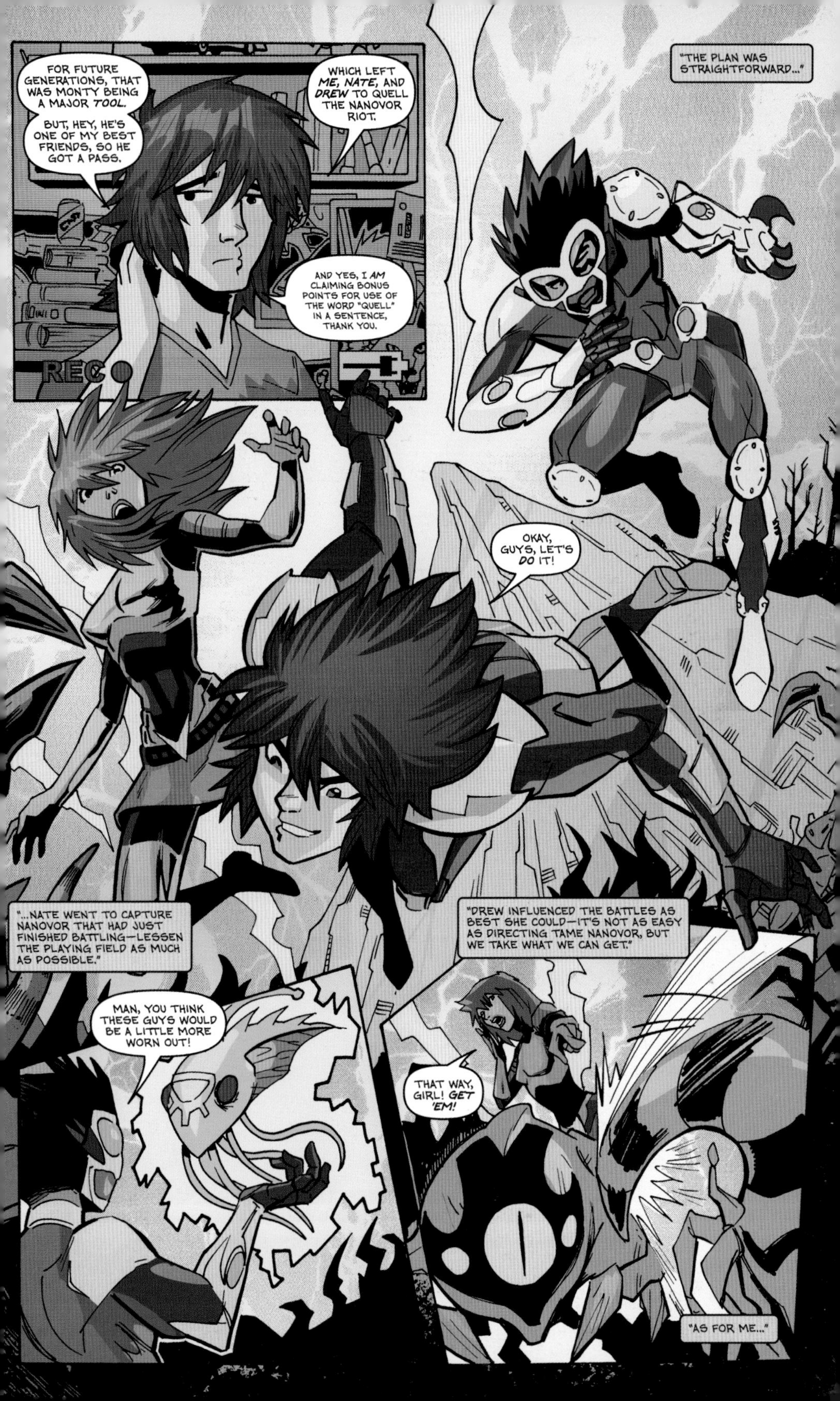

FOR FUTURE GENERATIONS, THAT WAS MONTY BEING A MAJOR TOOL.
BUT, HEY, HE'S ONE OF MY BEST FRIENDS, SO HE GOT A PASS.
WHICH LEFT ME, NATE, AND DREW TO QUELL THE NANOVOR RIOT.
AND YES, I AM CLAIMING BONUS POINTS FOR USE OF THE WORD "QUELL" IN A SENTENCE, THANK YOU.
REC
"THE PLAN WAS STRAIGHTFORWARD..."
OKAY, GUYS, LET'S DO IT!
"...NATE WENT TO CAPTURE NANOVOR THAT HAD JUST FINISHED BATTLING—LESSEN THE PLAYING FIELD AS MUCH AS POSSIBLE."
"DREW INFLUENCED THE BATTLES AS BEST SHE COULD—IT'S NOT AS EASY AS DIRECTING TAME NANOVOR, BUT WE TAKE WHAT WE CAN GET."
MAN, YOU THINK THESE GUYS WOULD BE A LITTLE MORE WORN OUT!
THAT WAY, GIRL! GET 'EM!
"AS FOR ME..."

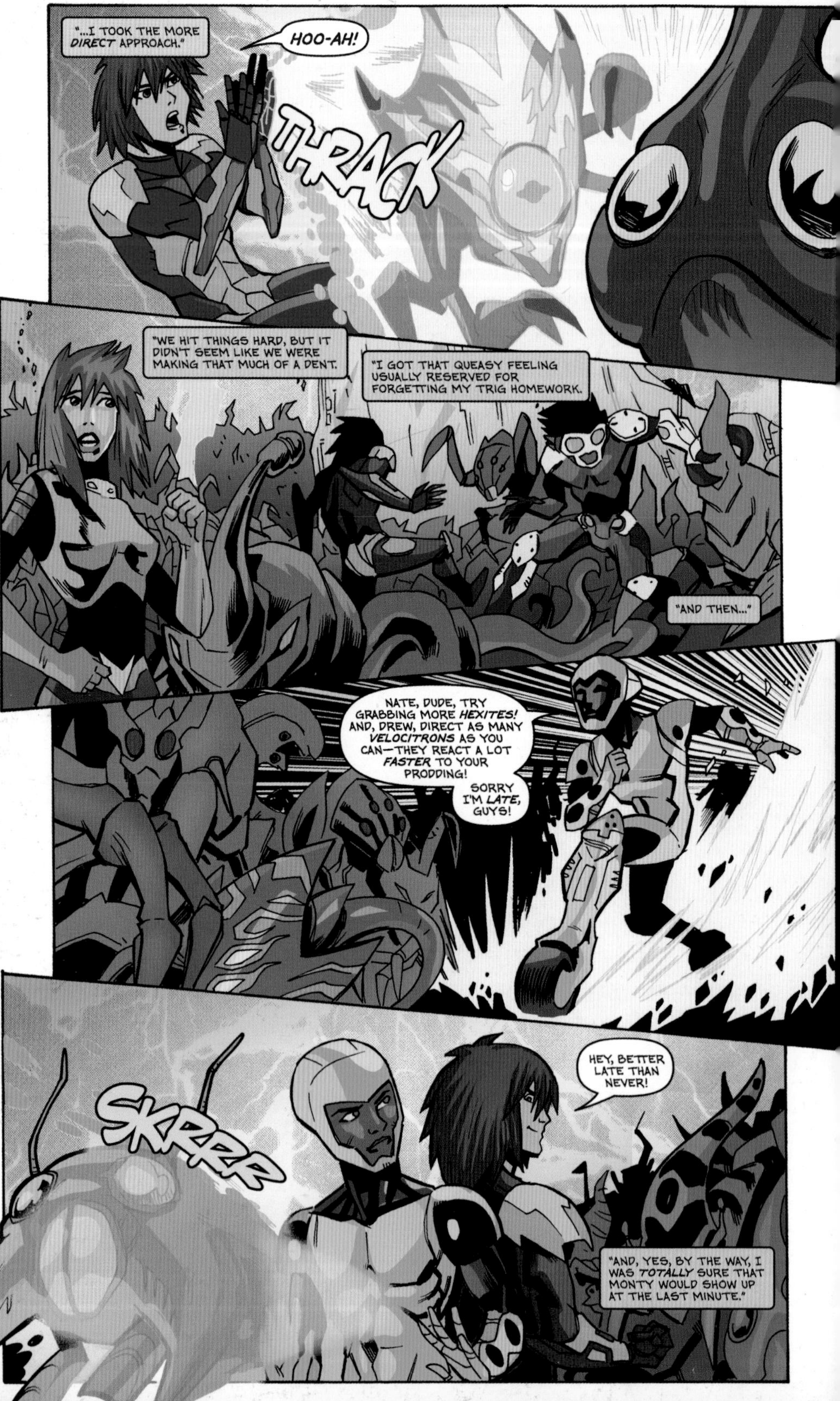

"...I TOOK THE MORE *DIRECT* APPROACH."
HOO-AH!
THRACK
"WE HIT THINGS HARD, BUT IT DIDN'T SEEM LIKE WE WERE MAKING THAT MUCH OF A DENT.
"I GOT THAT QUEASY FEELING USUALLY RESERVED FOR FORGETTING MY TRIG HOMEWORK.
"AND THEN..."
NATE, DUDE, TRY GRABBING MORE *HEXITES!* AND, DREW, DIRECT AS MANY *VELOCITRONS* AS YOU CAN—THEY REACT A LOT *FASTER* TO YOUR PRODDING!
SORRY I'M *LATE,* GUYS!
SKRRR
HEY, BETTER LATE THAN NEVER!
"AND, YES, BY THE WAY, I WAS *TOTALLY* SURE THAT MONTY WOULD SHOW UP AT THE LAST MINUTE."

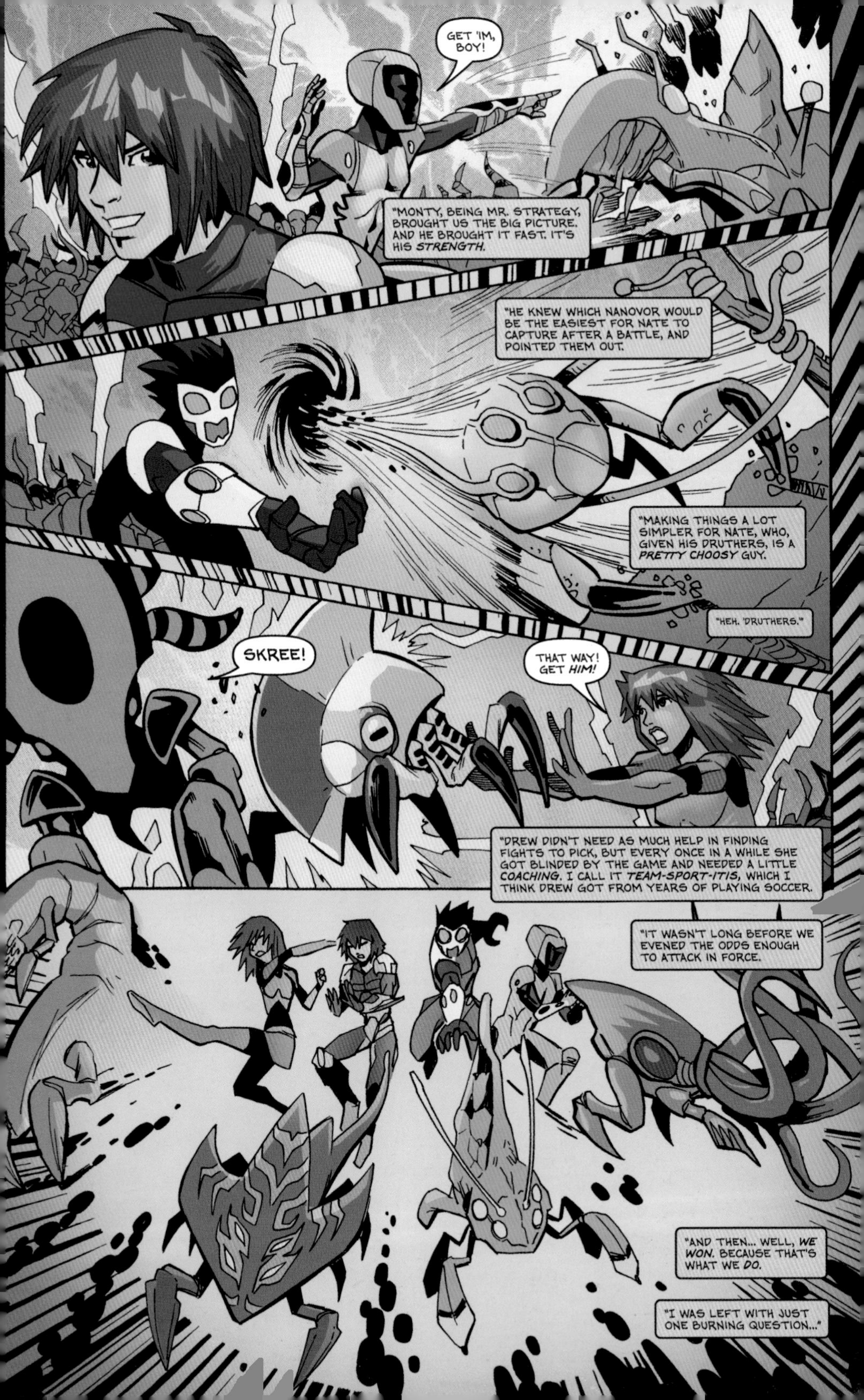
GET 'IM, BOY!
"MONTY, BEING MR. STRATEGY, BROUGHT US THE BIG PICTURE. AND HE BROUGHT IT FAST. IT'S HIS STRENGTH.
"HE KNEW WHICH NANOVOR WOULD BE THE EASIEST FOR NATE TO CAPTURE AFTER A BATTLE, AND POINTED THEM OUT.
"MAKING THINGS A LOT SIMPLER FOR NATE, WHO, GIVEN HIS DRUTHERS, IS A PRETTY CHOOSY GUY.
"HEH. 'DRUTHERS."
SKREE!
THAT WAY! GET HIM!
"DREW DIDN'T NEED AS MUCH HELP IN FINDING FIGHTS TO PICK, BUT EVERY ONCE IN A WHILE SHE GOT BLINDED BY THE GAME AND NEEDED A LITTLE COACHING. I CALL IT TEAM-SPORT-ITIS, WHICH I THINK DREW GOT FROM YEARS OF PLAYING SOCCER.
"IT WASN'T LONG BEFORE WE EVENED THE ODDS ENOUGH TO ATTACK IN FORCE.
"AND THEN... WELL, WE WON. BECAUSE THAT'S WHAT WE DO.
"I WAS LEFT WITH JUST ONE BURNING QUESTION..."

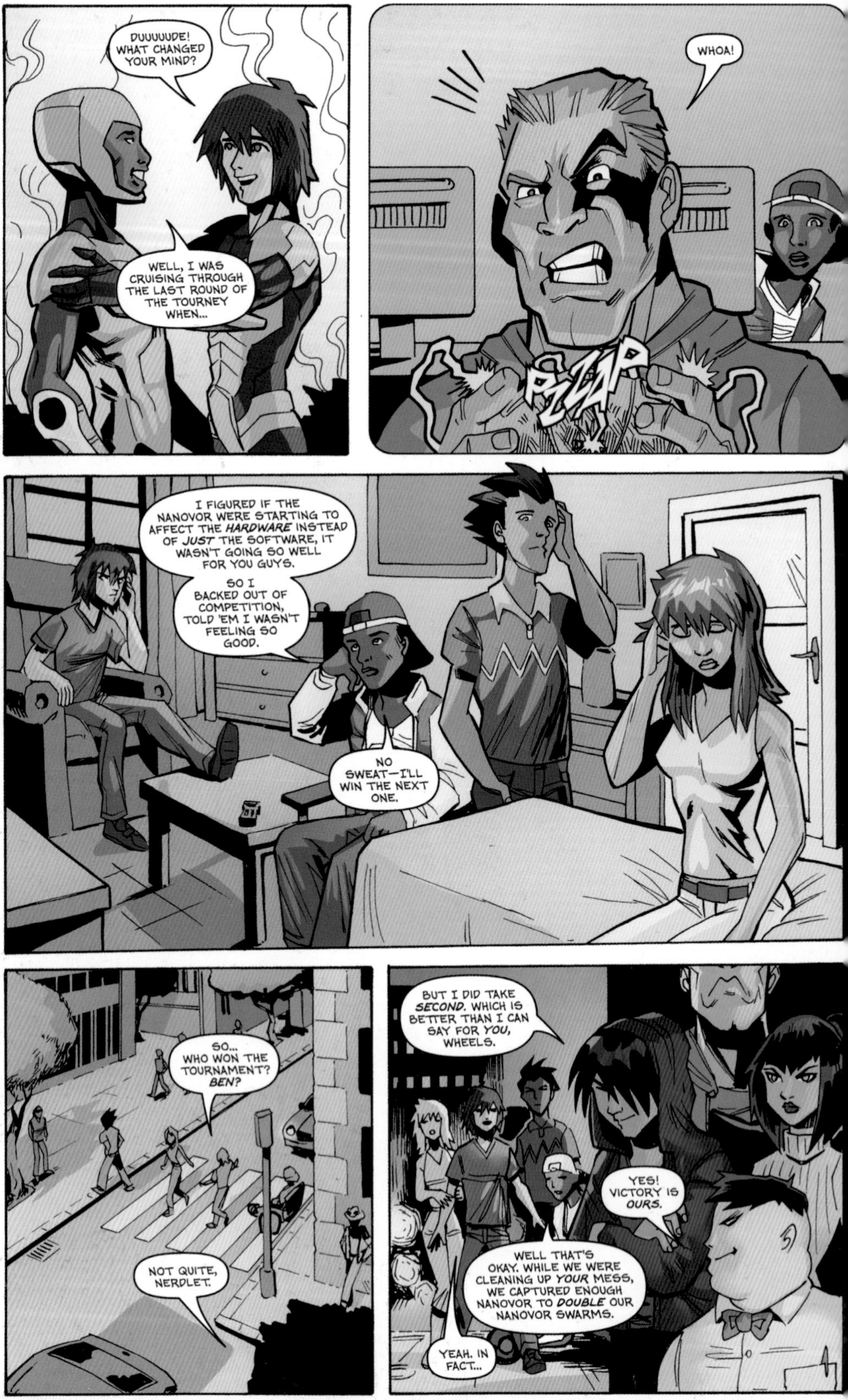
DUUUUUDE! WHAT CHANGED YOUR MIND?
WELL, I WAS CRUISING THROUGH THE LAST ROUND OF THE TOURNEY WHEN...
WHOA!
PZZAP
I FIGURED IF THE NANOVOR WERE STARTING TO AFFECT THE HARDWARE INSTEAD OF JUST THE SOFTWARE, IT WASN'T GOING SO WELL FOR YOU GUYS.
SO I BACKED OUT OF COMPETITION, TOLD 'EM I WASN'T FEELING SO GOOD.
NO SWEAT—I'LL WIN THE NEXT ONE.
SO... WHO WON THE TOURNAMENT? BEN?
NOT QUITE, NERDLET.
BUT I DID TAKE SECOND. WHICH IS BETTER THAN I CAN SAY FOR YOU, WHEELS.
YES! VICTORY IS OURS.
WELL THAT'S OKAY. WHILE WE WERE CLEANING UP YOUR MESS, WE CAPTURED ENOUGH NANOVOR TO DOUBLE OUR NANOVOR SWARMS.
YEAH. IN FACT...

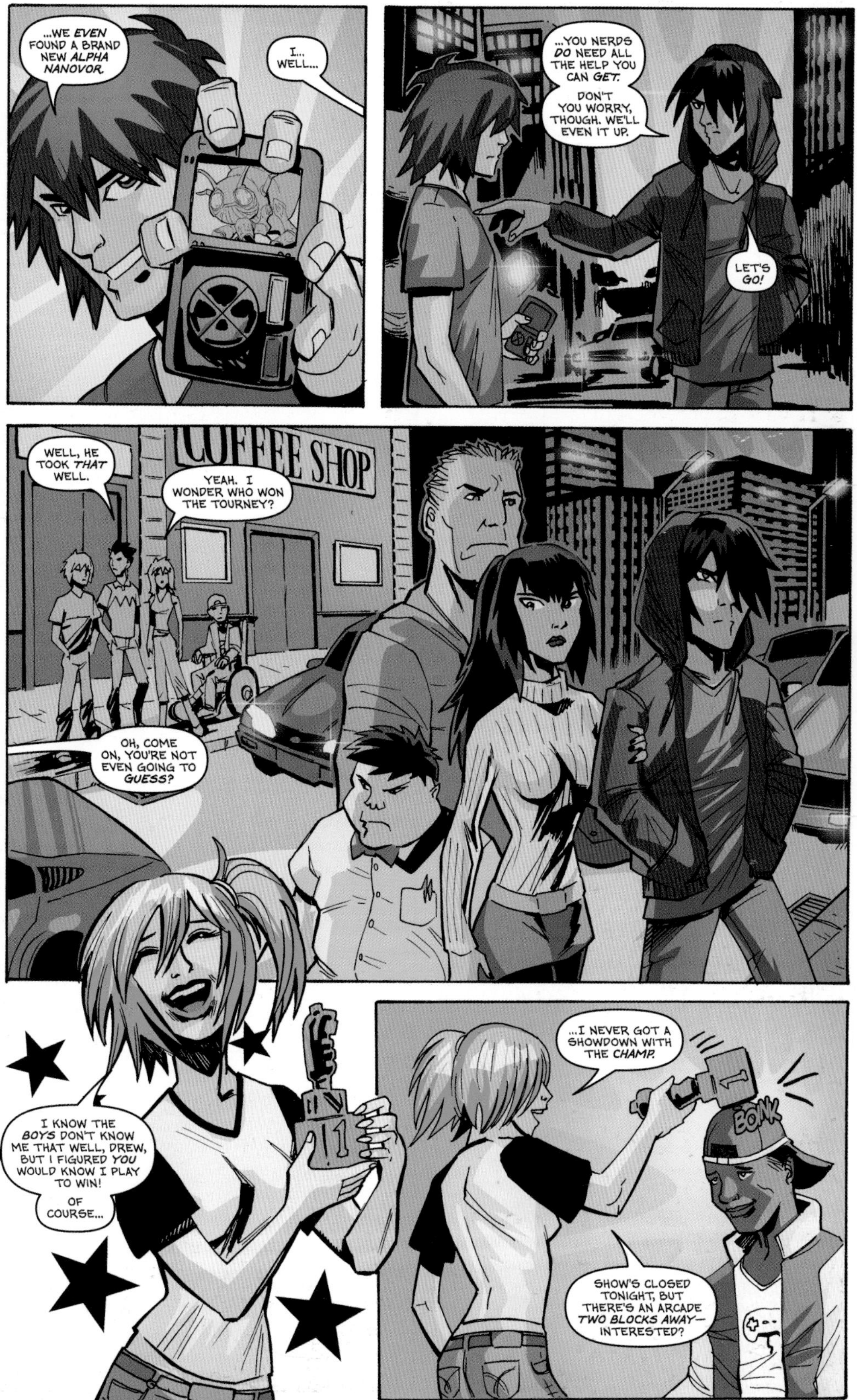

...WE EVEN FOUND A BRAND NEW ALPHA NANOVOR.
I... WELL...
...YOU NERDS DO NEED ALL THE HELP YOU CAN GET.
DON'T YOU WORRY, THOUGH. WE'LL EVEN IT UP.
LET'S GO!
COFFEE SHOP
WELL, HE TOOK THAT WELL.
YEAH. I WONDER WHO WON THE TOURNEY?
OH, COME ON, YOU'RE NOT EVEN GOING TO GUESS?
I KNOW THE BOYS DON'T KNOW ME THAT WELL, DREW, BUT I FIGURED YOU WOULD KNOW I PLAY TO WIN!
OF COURSE...
...I NEVER GOT A SHOWDOWN WITH THE CHAMP.
BONK
SHOW'S CLOSED TONIGHT, BUT THERE'S AN ARCADE TWO BLOCKS AWAY— INTERESTED?

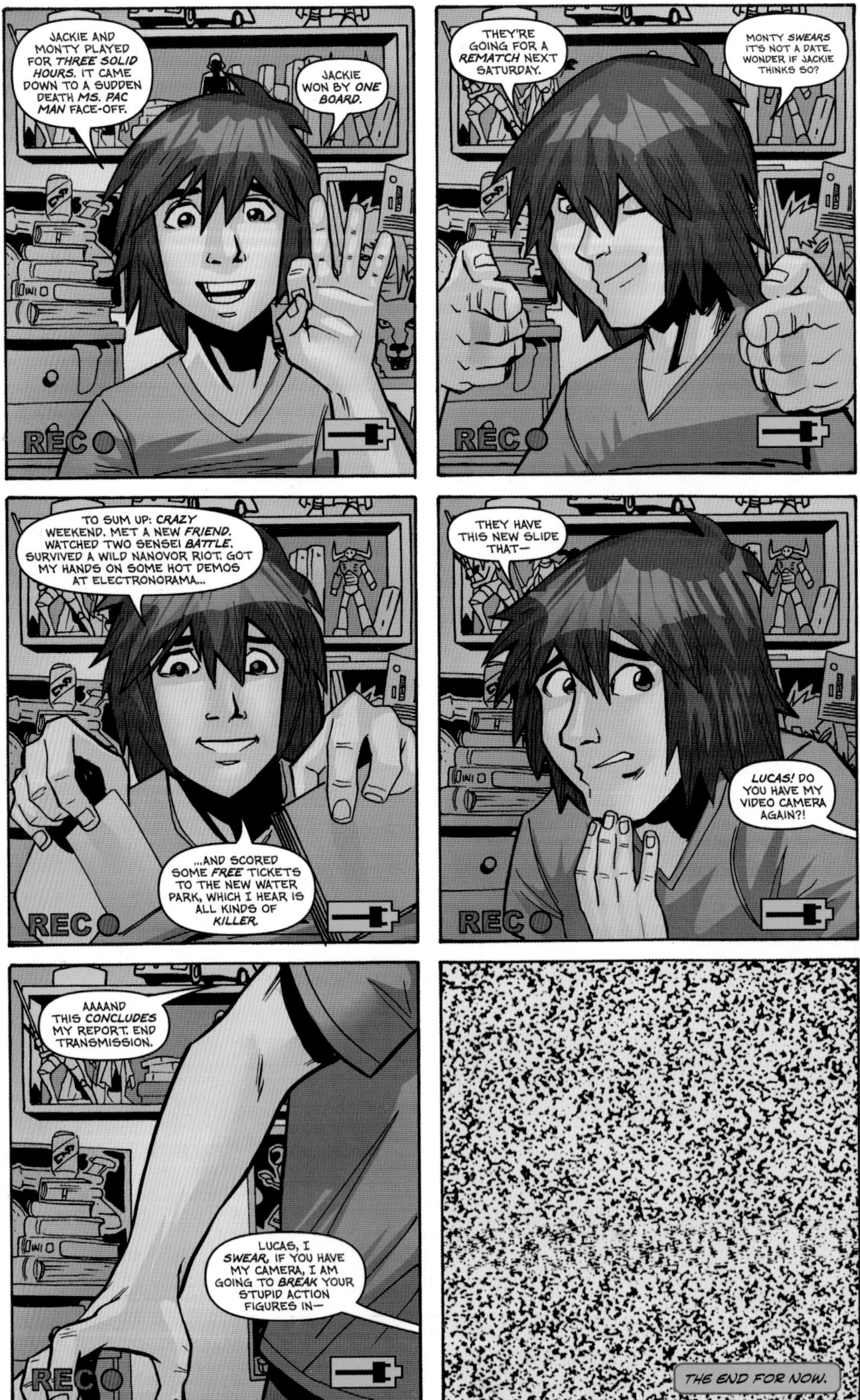
JACKIE AND MONTY PLAYED FOR THREE SOLID HOURS. IT CAME DOWN TO A SUDDEN DEATH MS. PAC MAN FACE-OFF.
JACKIE WON BY ONE BOARD.
REC
THEY'RE GOING FOR A REMATCH NEXT SATURDAY.
MONTY SWEARS IT'S NOT A DATE. WONDER IF JACKIE THINKS SO?
REC
TO SUM UP: CRAZY WEEKEND. MET A NEW FRIEND. WATCHED TWO SENSEI BATTLE. SURVIVED A WILD NANOVOR RIOT. GOT MY HANDS ON SOME HOT DEMOS AT ELECTRONORAMA...
...AND SCORED SOME FREE TICKETS TO THE NEW WATER PARK, WHICH I HEAR IS ALL KINDS OF KILLER.
REC
THEY HAVE THIS NEW SLIDE THAT—
LUCAS! DO YOU HAVE MY VIDEO CAMERA AGAIN?!
REC
AAAAND THIS CONCLUDES MY REPORT. END TRANSMISSION.
LUCAS, I SWEAR, IF YOU HAVE MY CAMERA, I AM GOING TO BREAK YOUR STUPID ACTION FIGURES IN—
REC
THE END FOR NOW.

ART GALLERY

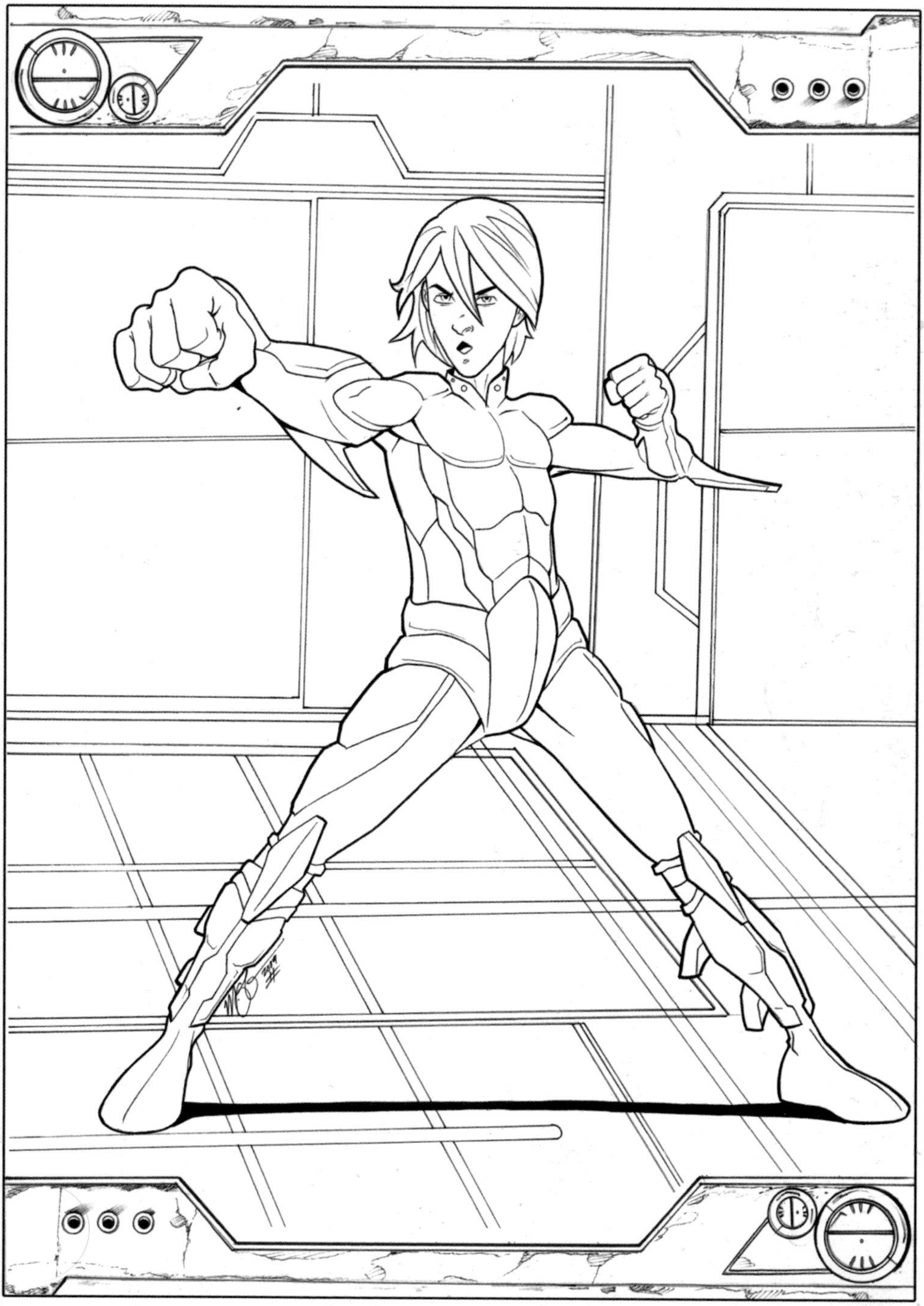

concept art by Martheus Wade

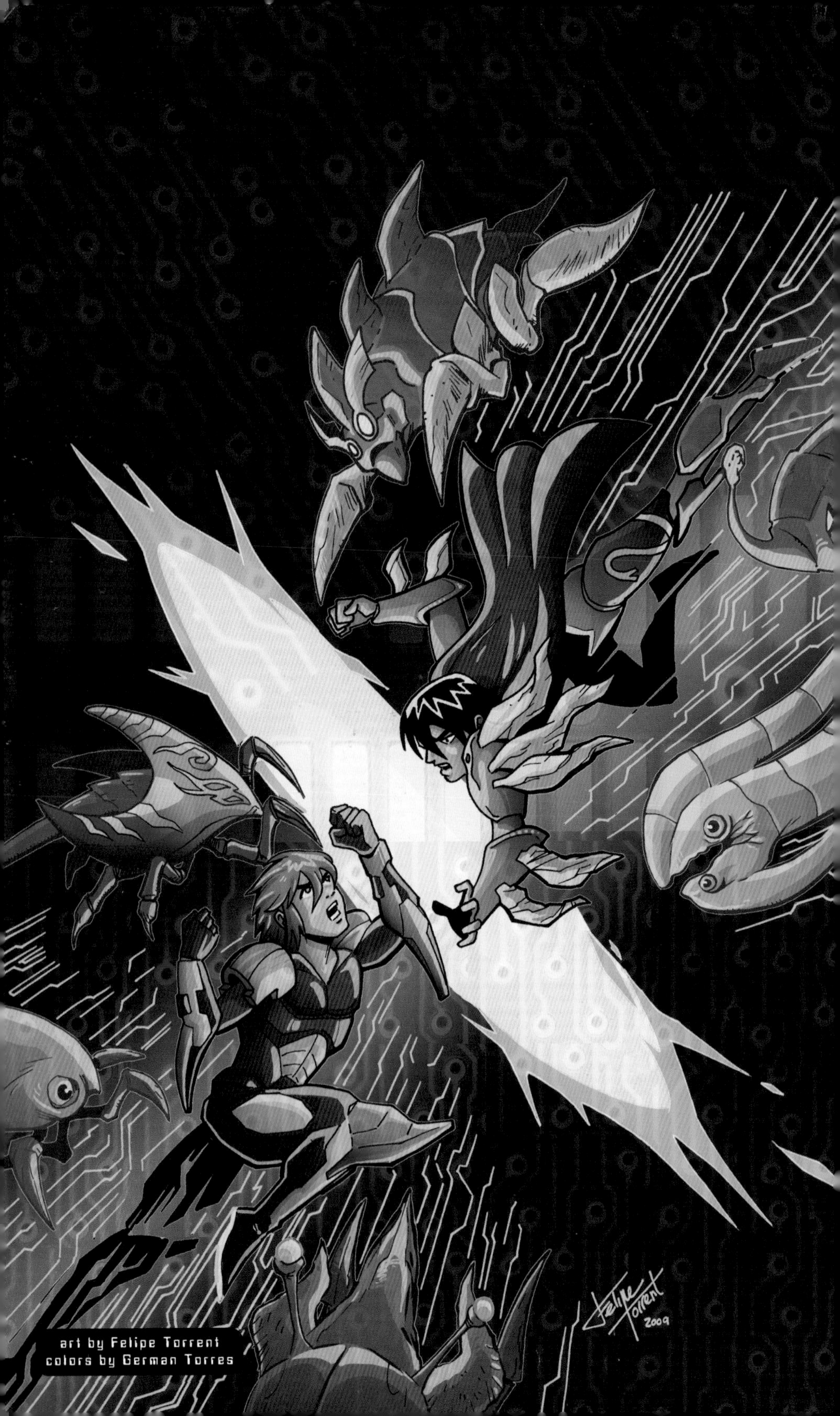
Felipe Torrent 2009
art by Felipe Torrent
colors by German Torres

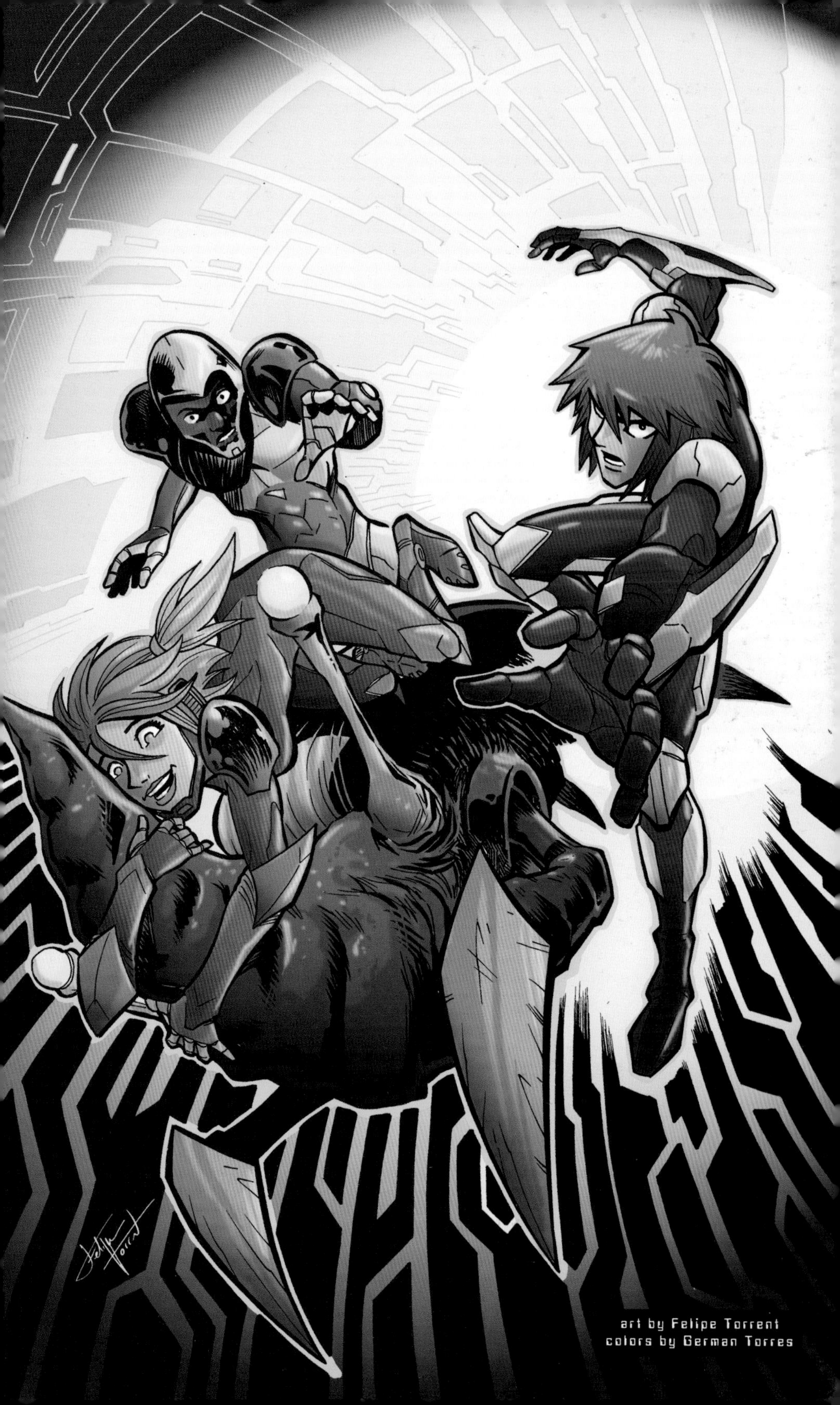
art by Felipe Torrent
colors by German Torres

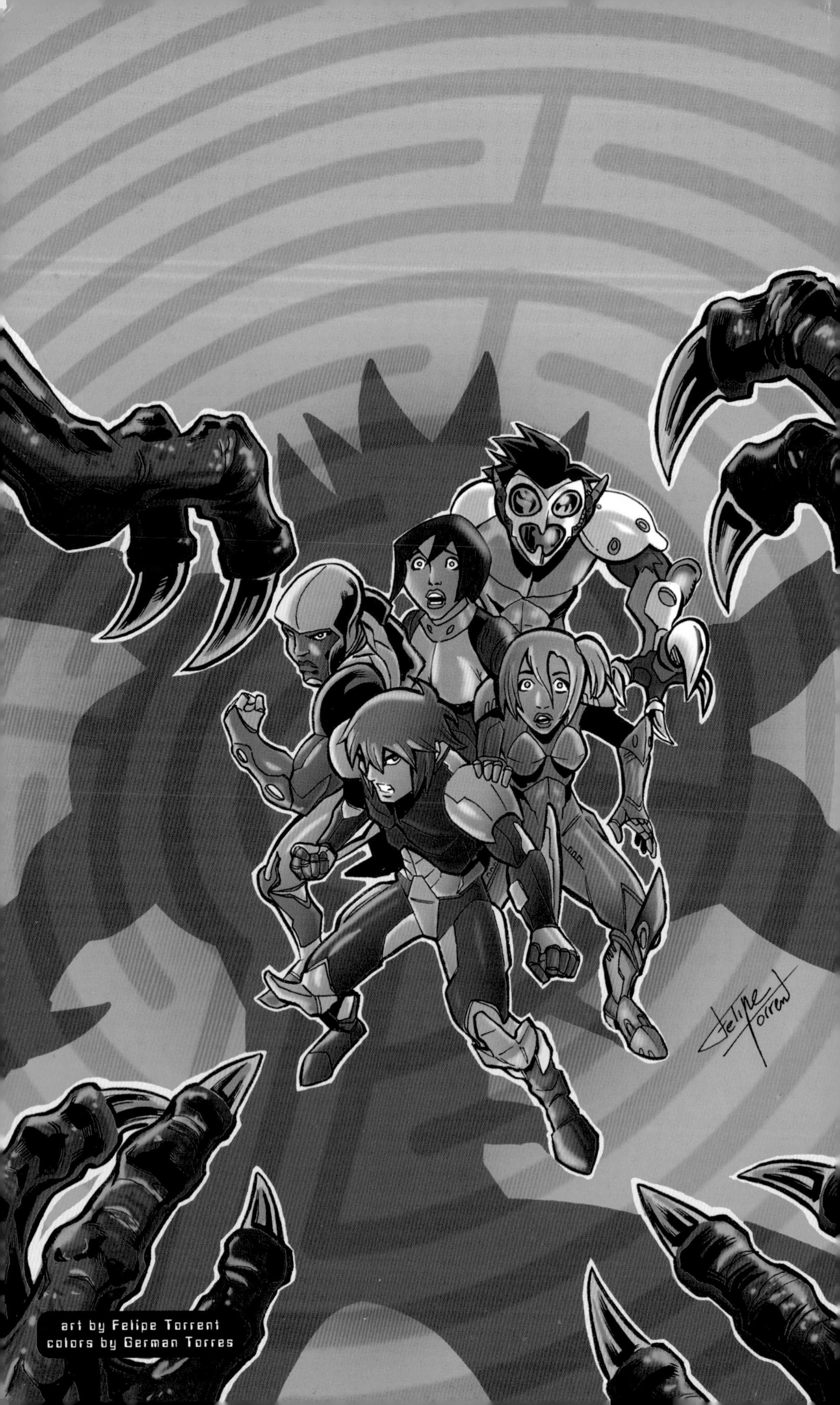
art by Felipe Torrent
colors by German Torres

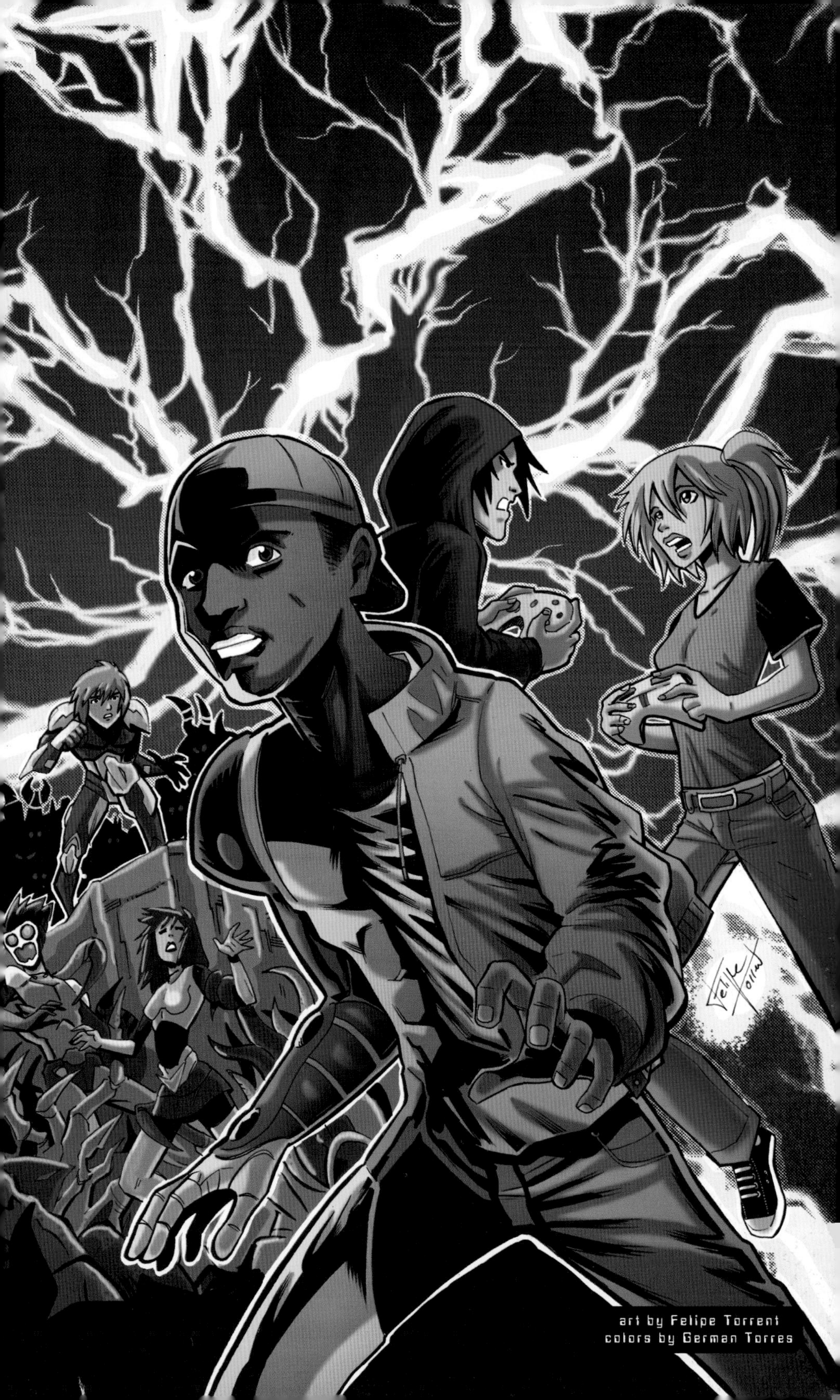

art by Felipe Torrent
colors by German Torres

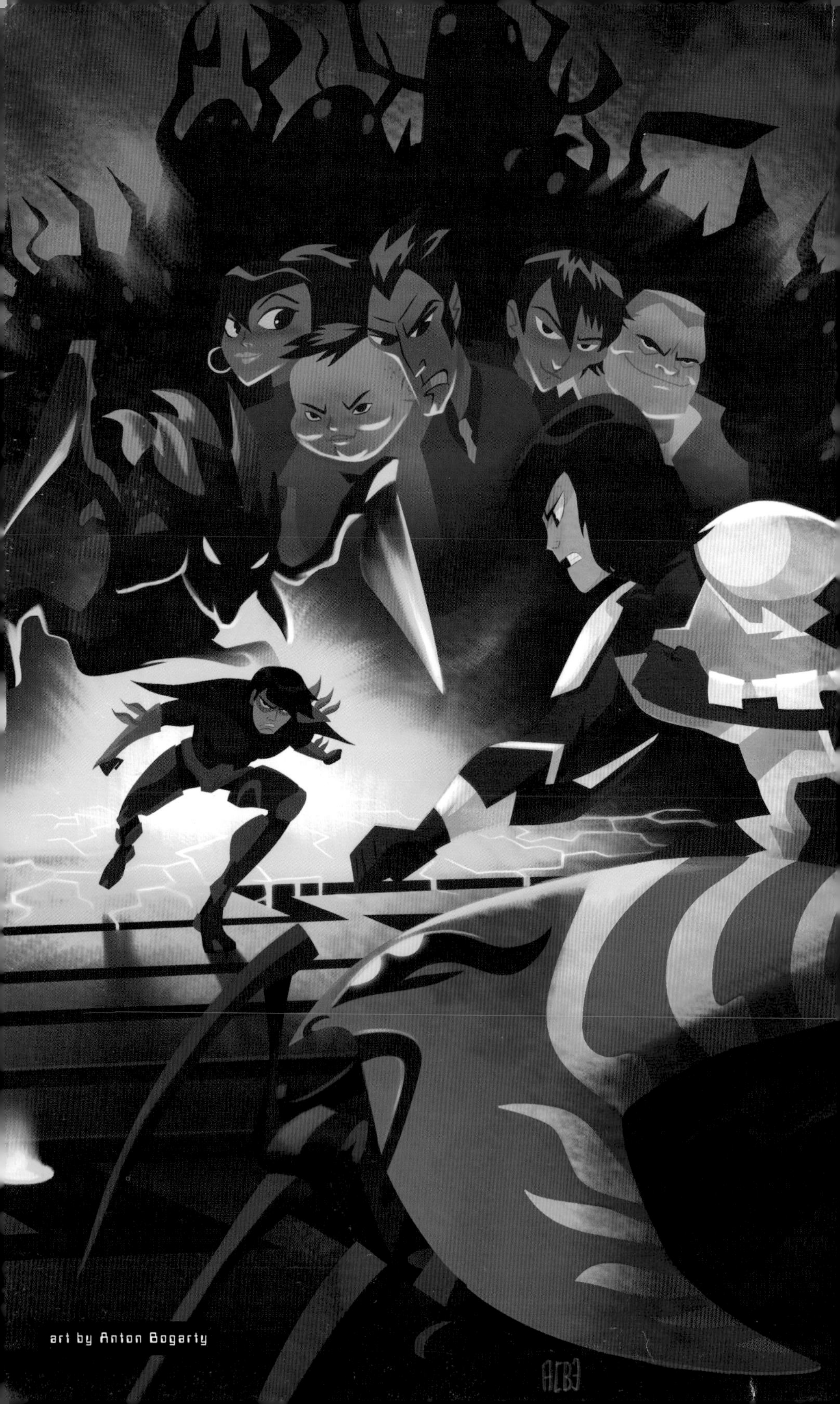

art by Anton Bogarty

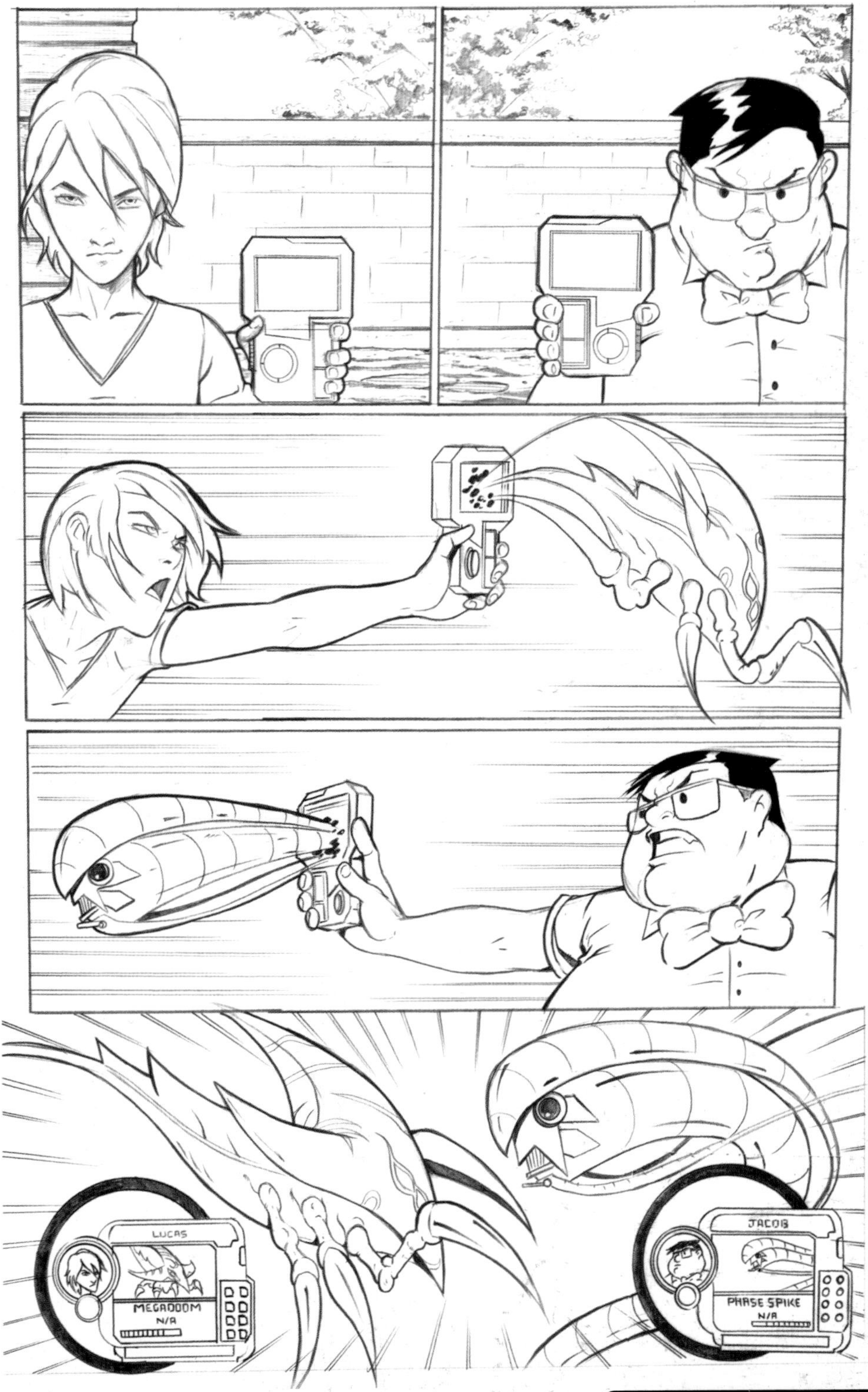
LUCAS
MEGADOOM
N/A
JACOB
PHASE SPIKE
N/A

concept art by Martheus Wade

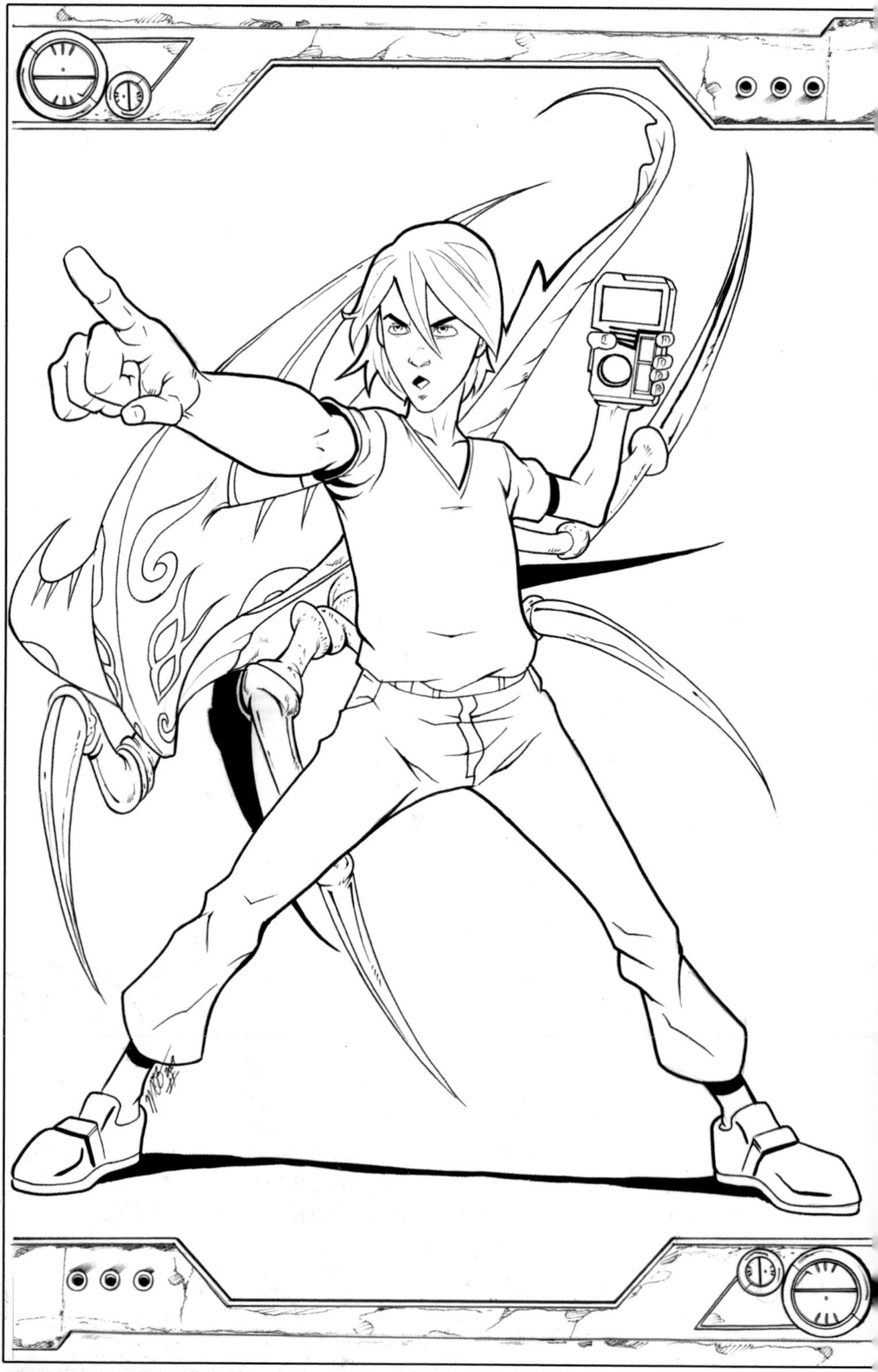

concept art by Martheus Wade

get digital.

The coolest comics from IDW—the leader in digital comic book publishing—for your iPhone or iPod Touch. Individual titles available from iVerse, Warner Bros, UCLICK, Genus Corp, and of course directly through our exclusive IDW application. Search "IDW" on iTunes for a complete list.

© 2010 IDW Publishing, a division of Idea and Design Works, LLC (IDW). All Rights Reserved by IDW and its respective Licensors. Apple, the Apple logo, iPod, and iTunes are trademarks of Apple Inc., registered in the U.S. and other countries. iPhone is a trademark of Apple Inc. iTunes is for legal or rightholder-authorized copying only. Don't steal music. Warner Bros TM & © 2010 Warner Bros Ent. All Rights Reserved. The iVerse "i" Logo is TM and copyright iVerse Media, LLC 2010 . All rights reserved. Karnikaze!™ copyright 2010 , Genus Corp. UCLICK copyright © 2010 UCLICK, LLC. All Rights Reserved.

Nanovor © 2010 Smith & Tinker. STAR TREK © 2010 Paramount Pictures Corporation. © 2010 CBS Studios Inc. STAR TREK and related marks and logos are trademarks of CBS Studios Inc. TERMINATOR SALVATION TM & © 2010 T Asset Acquisition Company, LLC. TRANSFORMERS, and all related characters are trademarks of Hasbro and are used with permission. © 2010 Hasbro. All Rights Reserved. © 2010 DreamWorks LLC and Paramount Pictures Corporation. * and/or TM & © 2010 Hasbro, Pawtucket, RI 02862 USA. All Rights Reserved. G.I. JOE, and all related characters are trademarks of Hasbro and are used with permission. © 2010 Hasbro. All Rights Reserved. GHOSTBUSTERS TM & © 2010 Columbia Pictures Industries, Inc. All rights reserved. CSI: CRIME SCENE INVESTIGATION ™ CBS © 2000-2010 CBS Broadcasting Inc. and Entertainment AB Funding LLC. All Rights Reserved. ASTRO BOY © 2010 Imagi Crystal Limited. Original Manga © Tezuka Productions Co., Ltd. *Tezuka Productions Co., Ltd. THE THIEF OF ALWAYS © 1992 by Clive Barker. Adaptation © 2010 Idea and Design Works, LLC.

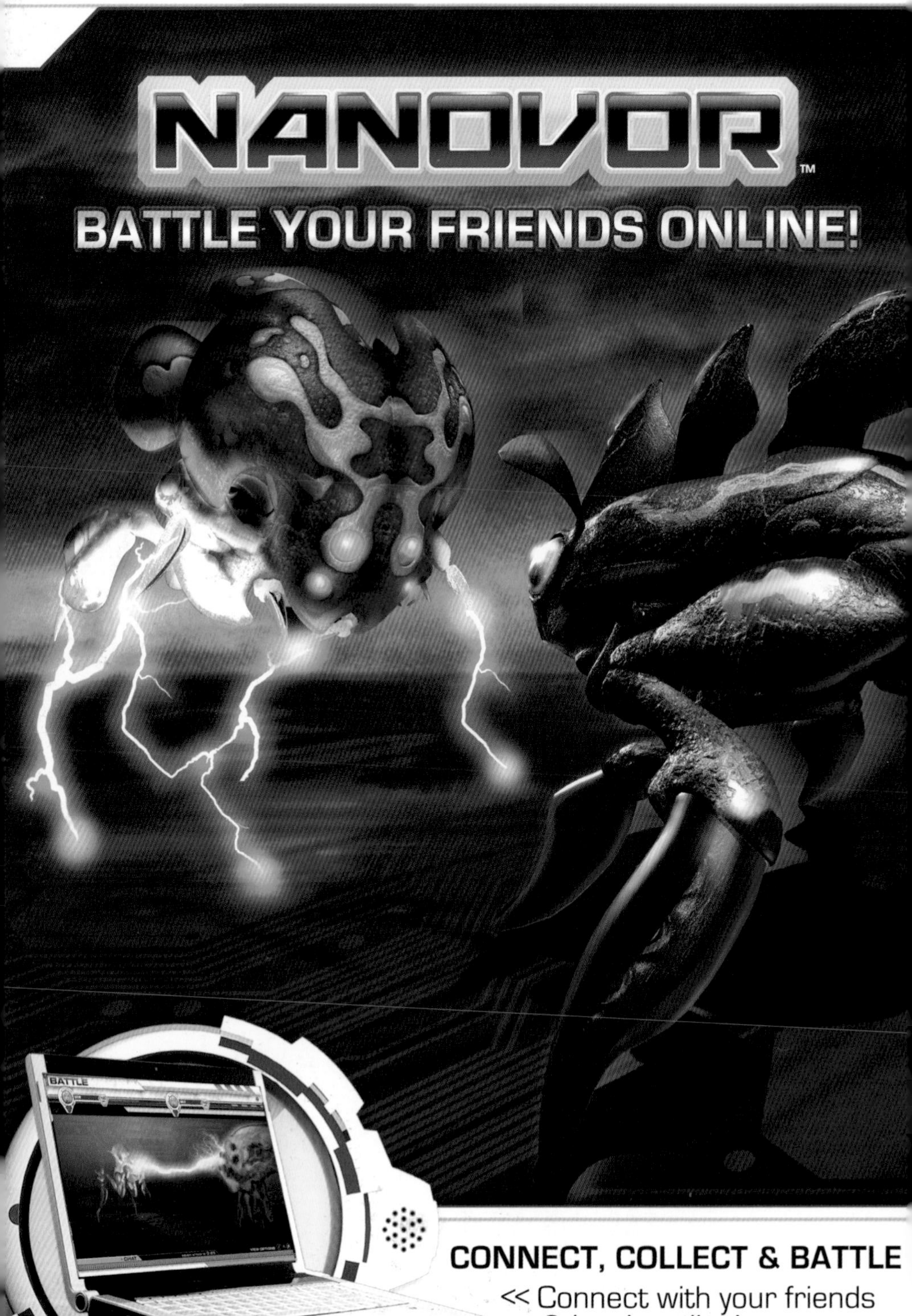
NANOVOR™
BATTLE YOUR FRIENDS ONLINE!
BATTLE
CONNECT, COLLECT & BATTLE
<< Connect with your friends
& battle online!

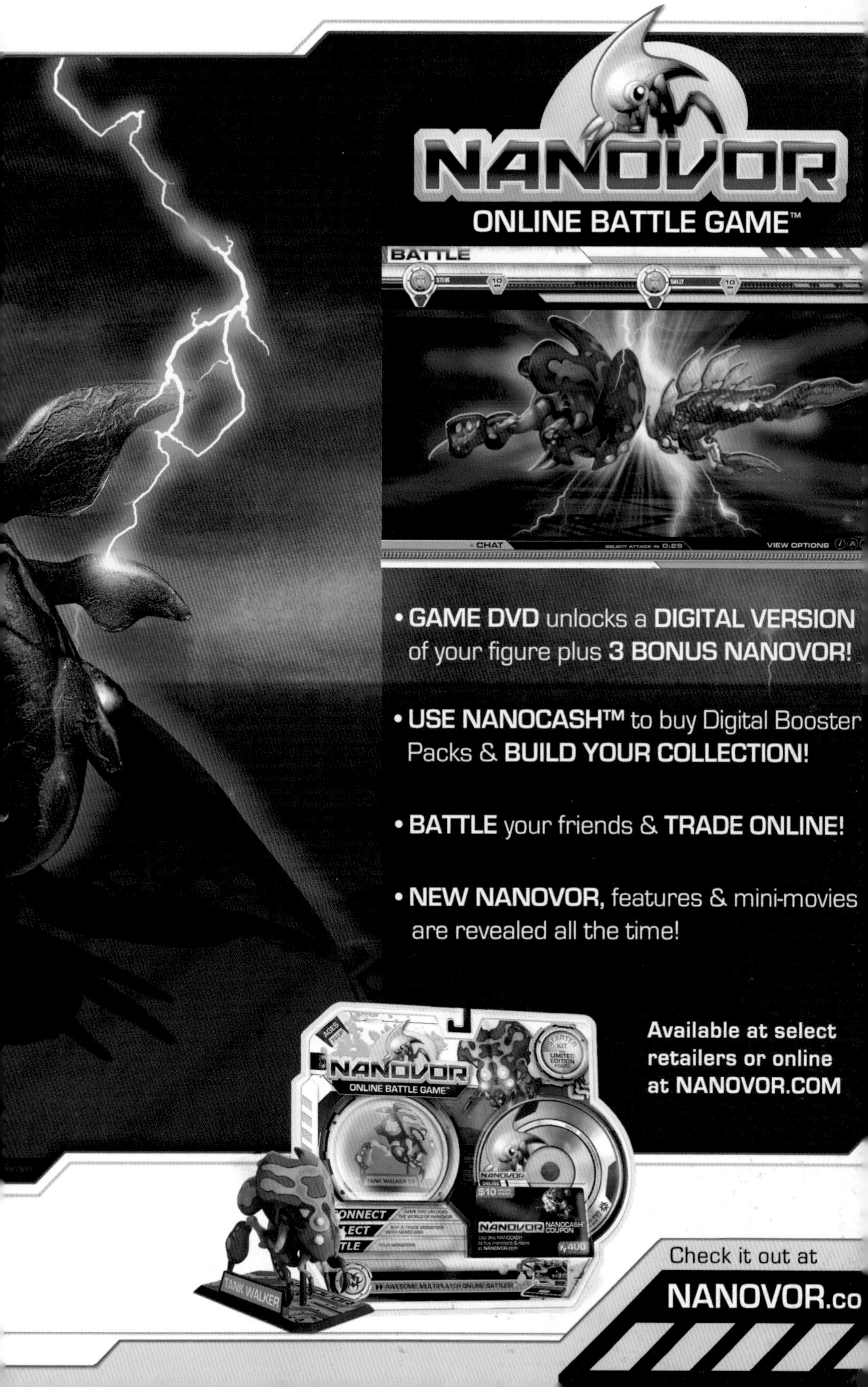
NANOVOR
ONLINE BATTLE GAME™
BATTLE
STEVE
SALLY
CHAT
VIEW OPTIONS
• GAME DVD unlocks a DIGITAL VERSION of your figure plus 3 BONUS NANOVOR!
• USE NANOCASH™ to buy Digital Booster Packs & BUILD YOUR COLLECTION!
• BATTLE your friends & TRADE ONLINE!
• NEW NANOVOR, features & mini-movies are revealed all the time!
Available at select retailers or online at NANOVOR.COM
NANOVOR
ONLINE BATTLE GAME™
TANK WALKER
Check it out at
NANOVOR.co

CONTINUE THE ADVENTURE & WATCH THE
NANOVOR ANIMATED EPISODES
AT NANOVOR.COM

NANOVOR ™

WATCH THE NANOVOR EPISODES
SHARE VIDEOS WITH YOUR FRIENDS

CHECK IT ALL OUT AT
NANOVOR.COM

© 2009 Smith & Tinker, Inc. All rights rese

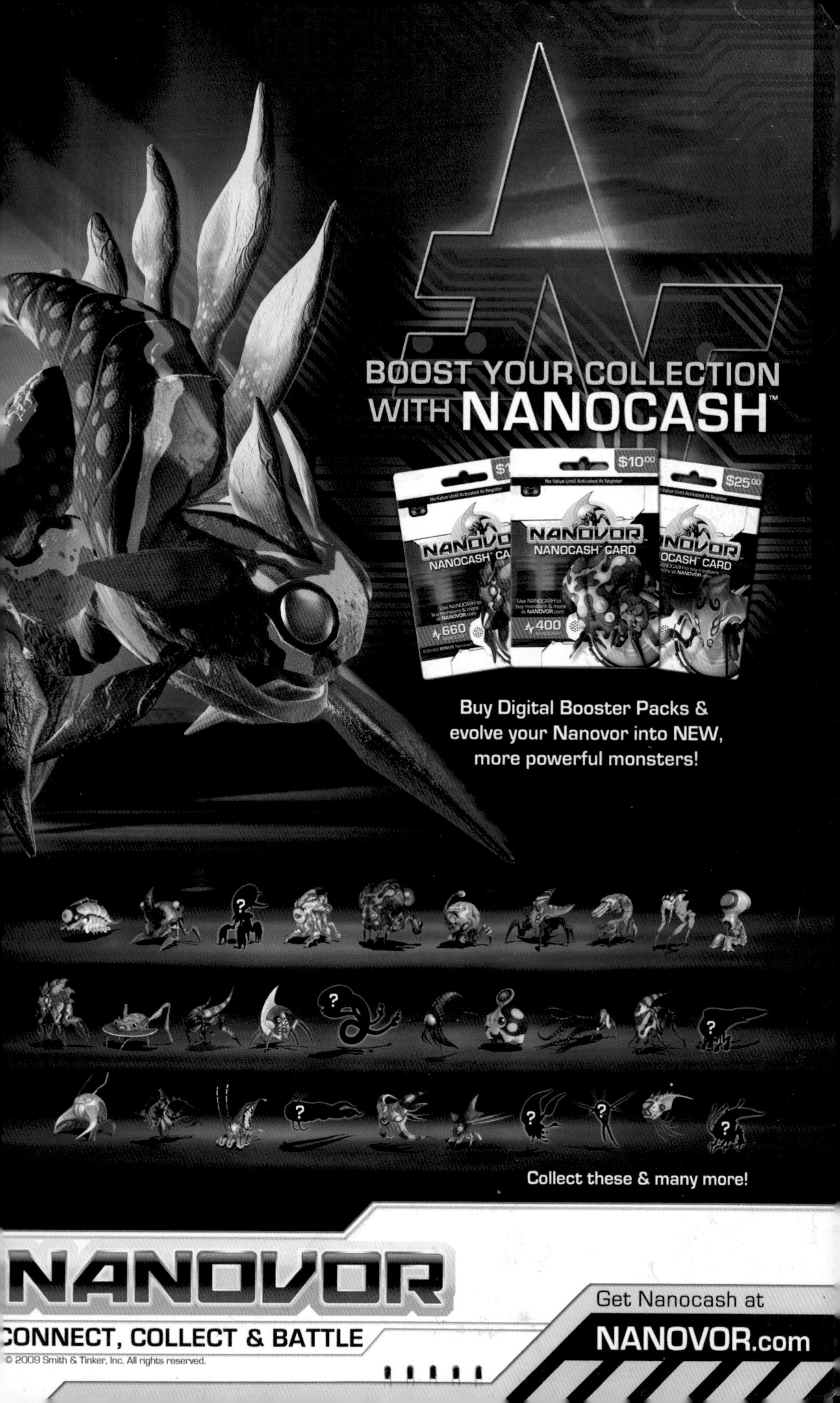
BOOST YOUR COLLECTION
WITH NANOCASH™
$10.00
$25.00
NANOVOR
NANOCASH™ CARD
Buy Digital Booster Packs &
evolve your Nanovor into NEW,
more powerful monsters!
Collect these & many more!
NANOVOR
CONNECT, COLLECT & BATTLE
© 2009 Smith & Tinker, Inc. All rights reserved.
Get Nanocash at
NANOVOR.com

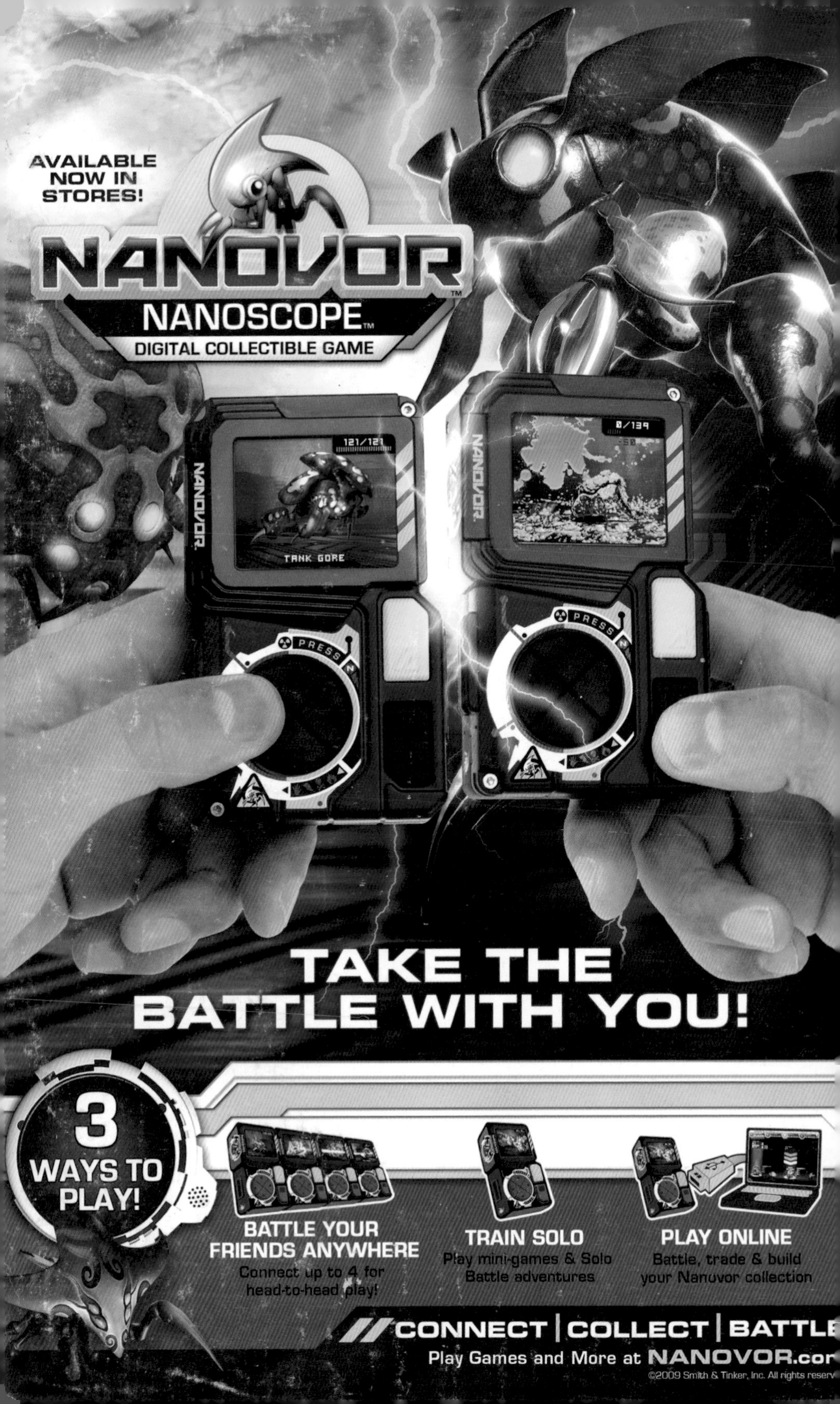
AVAILABLE NOW IN STORES!
NANOVOR
NANOSCOPE
DIGITAL COLLECTIBLE GAME
121/121
TANK GORE
PRESS
TAKE THE BATTLE WITH YOU!
3 WAYS TO PLAY!
BATTLE YOUR FRIENDS ANYWHERE
Connect up to 4 for head-to-head play!
TRAIN SOLO
Play mini-games & Solo Battle adventures
PLAY ONLINE
Battle, trade & build your Nanovor collection
CONNECT | COLLECT | BATTLE
Play Games and More at NANOVOR.com
©2009 Smith & Tinker, Inc. All rights reserved